LIVING ON AFTER FAILURE

IRVING GOH

LIVING

ON

AFTER

FAILURE

AFFECTIVE STRUCTURES OF MODERN LIFE

DUKE UNIVERSITY PRESS
Durham and London 2025

© 2025 DUKE UNIVERSITY PRESS
All rights reserved
Project Editor: Ihsan Taylor
Designed by Dave Rainey
Typeset in Warnock Pro and National 2 Narrow
by Copperline Book Services

Library of Congress Cataloging-in-Publication Data
Names: Goh, Irving, author.
Title: Living on after failure : affective structures of modern
life / Irving Goh.
Description: Durham : Duke University Press, 2025. |
Includes bibliographical references and index.
Identifiers: LCCN 2024055539 (print)
LCCN 2024055540 (ebook)
ISBN 9781478032243 (paperback)
ISBN 9781478028994 (hardcover)
ISBN 9781478061205 (ebook)
Subjects: LCSH: Failure (Psychology) | Fear of failure—
Philosophy. | Ontology.
Classification: LCC BF575.F14 G64 2025 (print) |
LCC BF575.F14 (ebook)
LC record available at https://lccn.loc.gov/2024055539
LC ebook record available at https://lccn.loc.gov/2024055540

Cover art: Lesley Oldaker, *Vortex I*, 2022. Oil on canvas.
Courtesy of the artist.

*To those who have failed
and continue to fail,
and who blame no one and nothing else except themselves,
living or otherwise*

CONTENTS

ix   ACKNOWLEDGMENTS

1   **Introduction**
The Affective Structure of Failure

39   1   **Flopping to Sleep**
The Failures of Ottessa Moshfegh's *My Year of Rest and Relaxation*

63   2   **Drifting in a World of Failures**
From Roland Barthes's Neutral to Rachel Cusk's *Outline* Trilogy

85   3   **Exscribing a Dark Care of the Self of Failed Existence**
Eve Sedgwick's *A Dialogue on Love* and Édouard Levé's *Suicide*

106   4   **The Melodrama of Failure's Shared Unshareability, Suicidal Ideation Included**
Yiyun Li's *Dear Friend, Where Reasons End*, and *Must I Go*

129   **Conclusion**
Postscripting in Kate Zambreno and Afterthoughts on Form and Method

145   NOTES
195   BIBLIOGRAPHY
205   INDEX

ACKNOWLEDGMENTS

I would not have imagined that failure could find companionship. Yet many friends and colleagues have been there to provide help and support for this work. I am always grateful to Priyanka Deshmukh, who always stand by my works. But special thanks go to Yanbing Er, who taught me that there can be so many other wondrous new things to learn, even when one seems at the limits of one's mind; she's the reason this work exists and why there has been "living on." I also thank Renyi Hong for his reading suggestion for the chapter on work; Miguel Escoba Varela for reminding me of the work done on the topic in the field of performance studies; Rachel Tay, who always pointed out to me the works on failure that were appearing; and Adam Stern for leading me to Walter Benjamin's "compass of success." I am also grateful to Philip Armstrong, Jack Halberstam, Samuel Weber, Lee Edelman, and Paul North, with whom I had insightful discussions on the topic. This book would not have been possible, too, without the constant support of Courtney Berger at Duke University Press: I still remember her enthusiasm for the project as I told her about it when we first met in Durham, North Carolina, in 2018, which definitely encouraged me to complete it. Immense gratitude goes out to Ihsan Taylor, too, for the amazingly meticulous editing work done during the final stages of the book's production. My most sincere thanks also go out to my two readers, themselves eminent scholars of "failure studies": Costica Bradatan and Gavin Jones.

Parts of this work were presented at various venues over the years, and I remain thoroughly grateful to the participants at the Poetics of Exscription Workshop in Toronto, in particular Victor Li, Ginette Michaud, Cory Stockwell, and John Paul Ricco; Françoise Meltzer, Salikoko Mufwene, Haun Saussy, John Wilkinson, and the wonderful students and postdocs from comp lit and English at the University of Chicago; Jonathan Culler, Cynthia Chase,

Timothy Murray, Renate Ferro, Cathy Caruth, Timothy Campbell, Patricia Keller, Paul Fleming, Sue Besemer, and the amazing students at Cornell University; Daniel Heller-Roazen, Erin Huang (when she was there), Thomas Hare, and Yiyun Li at Princeton University; Anjuli Gunaratne at the University of Hong Kong; Elissa Marder, Geoffrey Bennington, Jill Robbins, David Marriott, Andrew Mitchell, Lynette Park, Deborah White, the late José Quiroga, Andrew Kaplan, Isabelle Meyer-Ensass, Apala Bhowmick, and all the other delightful students at Emory; Ranjana Khanna, Robyn Wiegman, Carlos Rojas, Stefani Engelstein, Rey Chow, Anne-Gaëlle Saliot, Asta, Corina Stan, Nitin Luthra, Eun-hae Kim, Yeonwoo Koo, and everyone present at the Duke Franklin Humanities Institute, as well as Jaeyeon Yoo, Madeleine Collier, and Luna Beller-Tadiar; Claire Colebrook, Jeffrey T. Nealon, John Ochoa, Shuang Shen, Janet Lyon, Adam DeCaulp, Nathaniel Schermerhorn, David García, Rebecca Cheong, and Eunice Toh at Penn State; Max Cavitch, Andrea Goulet, David Eng, Rita Copeland, Gerald Prince, Corine Labridy, Carla Locatelli, Paule Carbonel, Austin Svedjan, Hugo Bujon at UPenn; Eun Kyung Min, Dong Shin Yi, Hong Jung Kim, and the generously hospitable comp lit and English students at Seoul National University; Alex Taek-Gwang Lee, Yeonhee Kim, and the bright and highly engaged students at Kyung Hee University.

This work also benefited from a Franke Visiting Faculty Fellowship at the Whitney Humanities Center at Yale in the fall of 2018, and I thank especially Maurice Samuels for his support for my candidacy. I remain grateful to Richard Franke, Gary Tomlinson, and Mark Bauer. My Franke Visiting Faculty Lecture then was organized by the French Department, and I thank the department, Alice Kaplan, Pierre Saint-Amand, Agnes Bolton, Doyle Calhoun and other students then, as well as everyone present at the talk.

A National Humanities Center (NHC) fellowship in 2022–23 ensured that I would be able to complete this work in a timely manner, so I am especially thankful for it. A special shoutout to the amazing librarians there are definitely in order: Joe Mililo, Riley Francis, and Brooke Andrade. I cannot thank enough my "special committee": Amy Louise Wood, Tricia Williams, Julie-Françoise Tolliver, and Patrick Greaney. I also owe thanks to my amazing friends and colleagues when I was there: Héctor Pérez-Brignoli, Kiu-Wai Chu, Emmanuel David, Cedric Tolliver, Molly Todd, Nancy Tomes, Jason Miller, Chin Jou, Erdağ Goknar, Wamuwi Mbao, Elena Machado Sáez, Matthew Booker, and Robert Newman. I definitely do not forget my basketball buddy Mike Williams, who taught me how to "fail well" at basketball (he will get what I am saying here). I was awarded the NHC fellowship while with the National University of Singapore (NUS). For faculty applicants there, we had to go through an additional internal selection. I am very grateful to then-Provost Ho Teck Hua, Vice Provost Tulika Mitra, Brenda Yeoh, Rajeev Patke, and the other anonymous reviewer for supporting my application. An NUS President's Assistant Professorship Start-Up Grant also enabled me to make the travels to give most of the above talks. I certainly do not forget my students in the Rethinking Failure graduate seminar that ran twice at NUS.

Last, but definitely not least, I express my deepest gratitude to Dionne Ang and Cheng Ee Lu. This work was written while facing numerous personal failures. Indeed, some have walked away from my life. But Dionne's and Cheng Ee's enduring friendship since I knew them never faltered once. I can say the same for Heather Brink-Roby's friendship, even though we have known each other only for a short time. Ever the nicest and kindest person, she knew not to judge; never probing, she understood well that there are always untold or untellable stories behind every story. This book is for you all, as well as those who have always stood by me—you know who you are.

INTRODUCTION

THE AFFECTIVE STRUCTURE OF FAILURE

This book is about failure. More specifically, it is about living on in the wake of failure, living with the mark of failure henceforth etched indelibly at the heart of existence; it is about articulating forms of living on where existence trails after failure. This will thus not be that typical book where one learns from failure or where one learns to overcome failure. It is not concerned with conjuring an optimistic or positive horizon out of experiences of failure. It will not provide consolation by imagining a life pedagogy from failure for the recuperation or reparation of either the individual or the collective. Instead, this book does not leave the negativity of failure: it examines living on in terms of existing *with* the full force of failure. Not seeking a way out of failure, it is about getting stuck with failure, following where failure leads existence and thought. As such, this book is a coming to terms with the ineluctability of failure and existence, the inextricability of existence from failure. In this regard, it serves, at best, as an ontological reckoning, reminding us of the fact of existence's entanglement with failure, which we tend, or prefer, to forget. Otherwise, to the disappointment or even chagrin of some readers, this book offers little, if anything, for political action or thought in any conventional sense, but I will explain why in due course. Meanwhile, as I would like to put it in this introduction, this book takes into account how failure structures our existence, how it constitutes our existential structure. Indeed, if we care to acknowledge, failure is always there inflecting our lives, refracting our sense of existence: it either cuts across our existential condition with an irrepressible force, relentlessly reminding us that it is perhaps *the* incontrovertible sense of existence, or it subtends our lives, undercutting and troubling our existence with an equally disturbing force. Failure is thus a structure no less affective than existence in all its troubled or troubling registers. In the words of the philosopher Costica Bradatan, "Failure is a profoundly disturbing experience—as disturbing as life itself."[1] To recognize failure as an *affective structure* of existence is to give voice to what we have always feared to acknowledge: that we can never escape the sense of failure, that the sense of failure always stays with us.[2] More critically, it is to give voice to those who have dared accept this irreducible sense of failure in existence, those who cannot, or even do not want to, dissociate themselves from it, those who refuse the ideology of success and its attendant rhetoric of grit and resilience, those who have no wish to carry on. It is to give elucidation and legitimation to their complex and troubled sense of existing with failure, despite—if not precisely because of—the fact that these modes of being run counter to what we commonly or "normally" consider to be productive, meaningful existence, veering pessimistically toward the nihilistic even. This book does not silence them to the margins or lacunae of what it means to exist.

There are several motivations for this book. More immediate and explicit is the constant swarming of failures into contemporary life since the beginning of our present century: 9/11 and the catastrophic collateral damage to civilian lives in the subsequent "war on terror," the 2008 Great Recession, Fukushima in 2011, the 2016 Brexit vote and the US presidential election, police shootings of Black Americans and the continued impunity of police brutality, ineffective gun control policies, the hate crime of 2016 at the gay club Pulse, the 2018 Pittsburgh synagogue massacre, the 2021 anti-Asian Atlanta shootings, #metoo, the global mismanagement of the COVID-19 pandemic, and too many others to name in this ever-growing list.[3] In relation to this list, this book can be said to be very much a response to its time, a response to an implicit imperative made by its time to register contemporary failures. Yet this book is concerned with quite different failures from those listed macro failures. It focuses on failures on a smaller scale instead, which are nevertheless equally important and even urgent for us to attend to. But if this book is not dealing with macro failures, it is also because any beginning of a proper redress for those (geo)political, economic, sociocultural, and institutional failures would seriously require a collective response, something to which a monograph such as this present work—that is, a project undertaken by an individual—can never assume to approximate itself.[4]

The second motivation is the burgeoning of what might be called "failure studies," whose literature now spans the disciplines of philosophy, sociology, economics, the physical sciences, technological sciences, literary studies, queer theory, critical race studies, the digital humanities, performance studies, and more.[5] The works in this literature recognize failure as a contemporary human condition and rightfully claim that we can no longer defer its understanding, critique, and even appreciation. However, as will be seen, most of them can be hasty in giving failure a positive spin, which also entails giving failure an optimistic horizon, leaving us with barely a rigorous thinking of failure, one without any true engagement with the affective structure of failure. It is for failure studies not to be a superficial engagement with failure that this book insists on a more veritable thinking of failure: one that faces failure straight on, one that is more truthful or honest with respect to not only what failure reveals to thought but also what thought feels before, if not amid, failure. As I will argue in this introduction, this would be a thinking of failure that stays with failure and all its negative affects *without trying to get out of them*; this would be nothing short of thinking at, or as, an impasse, yet this would perhaps also be thinking *failure as failure*, finally.

This leads us to the third motivation, which is the emergence or publication of certain works of contemporary literature that include Édouard Levé's *Autoportrait* and *Suicide*; Rachel Cusk's *Aftermath* and her *Outline* trilogy; Ottessa Moshfegh's *My Year of Rest and Relaxation*; Yiyun Li's *Dear Friend, Where Reasons End*, and *Must I Go*; and Kate Zambreno's *Appendix Project*, *Drifts*, and *To Write as if Already Dead*.[6] These texts are arguably representative of our present zeitgeist as they register the contemporary sense of overwhelming failure, but they point indeed to personal failures or the personal sense of failure rather than macro failures such as those listed earlier. They thus deal with relationship failures (in Cusk), the failure to will oneself to do anything (in Moshfegh), career-related failures (in Zambreno), and the existential failure to want to live (in Levé and Li), and they illustrate how such failures can effectuate lasting emotional, psychological, and physiological transformations in the individual, rendering them no longer the same, forever changing their relations with others and the world. These texts also show how individuals subsequently recalibrate (or not) both their sense of existence or what it means for them to exist and their means of living on after failure. One could say that genres, in Lauren Berlant's sense—that is, both discursive and nondiscursive gestures, or nascent forms of expressions, that endeavor to respond to, or cope with, surrounding phenomena—are flailing here.[7] Following Berlant's line of argument, genres sustain living on for the moment, and elucidating them can be critical for recognizing and respecting modes of being that are trying to survive certain pressures of contemporary life. And yet, the genres—especially the nondiscursive gestures—in these literary works, while seeking to manage the entanglement of failure and existence, may not be successful after all. Or else they might not even want to succeed at that. Thus, they *might* render—albeit in thoughtless, purposeless, will-less, or disinterested ways—some form of minimal living on after failure possible; they can make existence—that is, existence that coexists with failure—at least bearable for the moment. But they also leave individuals with the hopeless condition where they, alone in their respective solitary selves, continue to grapple with the veracity of failure as an incontrovertible sense of existence. They are always left irreducibly and unbearably with their failures, their sense of failure, on their own.

The texts suggest, therefore, that failures at the personal level can oftentimes be felt more intensively and enduringly than larger-scale failures at the social, economic, political, and even historical levels, and that attending to them can be critical too. They underscore how personal failures cannot be ignored or bracketed when thinking about contemporary failure, and this is something we will heed here.[8] More significantly for this book, they are narratives through which individuals reckon with how the sense of failure constitutes an irrefutable or unsurpassable sense of existence that no recuperative or reparative rhetoric or philosophy, no progress narrative, and no talk therapy can sublimate (indeed, the narrator in Moshfegh's *My Year of Rest and Relaxation*, Cusk in *Aftermath*, Levé in *Autoportrait* and *Suicide*, Sedgwick in *A Dialogue on Love*, and Li in *Dear Friend* either express doubt or suspicion about psychoanalysis and/or psychotherapy or they profess an ineffectiveness of these practices with regard to their sense of failure). As said above, the genres in these narratives do not seek to overcome failure, to leave failure behind and get on with life, as if failure is then but a distant or insignificant memory of a mishap. This is how the texts, more than failure studies, can be instructive for a staying *and* coming to terms with the relentless nature of the affective structure of failure that negatively undercuts contemporary existence. It is precisely because of their deeper and more sustained engagement with failure, their willingness to stay longer with the affective structure of failure, their expositions on the difficulty of extricating existence from failure or the near impossibility of surviving the ineluctable entanglement of existence with failure, that these works of contemporary literature will be the focus of this book.[9] In turn, it is in view of a better approach to these texts, one that faces straight on the problematics of failure in them and/or failure in general, rather than anxiously or paranoidly seeking to overcome, dispel, or repress them, that this book, again, argues for the tarrying with failure and all its negative affects, for the inhabiting of the impasse that failure as an affective structure of existence is. With this, we can perhaps better approximate ourselves to a thinking of failure that will correspond to forms of living on in the aftermath of failure in these texts as well as others that deal with the contemporary sense of personal failure. The stakes, though, are not only hermeneutical. As suggested earlier, the elucidating of such a thinking of *failure as failure*, of failure's affective structure, can help us better understand the inextinguishable sense of failure in real, contemporary existence as well, helping us understand those who cannot shake off the sense of failure in them, those who have a particular attachment to their failures, those who no longer want to carry on in the wake of failure. It is, in short, to accord them a discursive and affective space that grants them the freedom to articulate and languish in their sense of failure, instead of telling them to snap out of it and reappropriating or reinterpellating them into ideologies of success and their norms of grit and resilience. If there is one failure that we should avoid, perhaps it is that which makes them feel that there is no legitimate space to attend to their sense of existential and ontological failure except in a suicide note.

Twenty-First-Century Epic Fail

The primary task of this introduction is the explication of a thinking of *failure as failure*, of failure's affective structure, of the thorough impasse that such a thinking of failure is. Put simply, it is to outline how we can arrive at such a thinking, how such a thinking looks like, and what entails from it. Before proceeding, a slight return to the backdrop of contemporary failure is in order, so as to identify a trait of failure that will be important for us and to draw out a linguistic mode of articulating contemporary failure that seemingly prefigures the general prose style of our selected literary works. From there, we will be able to mark the stylistic difference with regard to writing about failure in this present century in comparison to the preceding one. We will also be able to discern why there is the preoccupation with, if not sympathy and/or empathy for, personal failures, rather than macro failures, in contemporary writings. All this will precisely lead us to the important consideration of the affective dimension of failure, as well as unravel for us how we still do not have a thinking of failure in a strict sense.

Let us, then, recall our earlier list of twenty-first-century failures. If one indeed grants them the status of failure, we might be tempted to call our present century the century of failures.[10] Quite immediately, though, there will be others who will oppose this claim and counterpropose the preceding century as *the* century of failures. The twentieth century, after all, was witness to two World Wars, the Holocaust, the Vietnam War, the Great Depression, the Watergate scandal under the Nixon administration, the Chernobyl nuclear accident, the AIDS epidemic, the 1918 influenza pandemic, the phenomenon of "failed states," the Columbine school shooting, etcetera. This is not to mention that the most quotable or cited words on failure have come from one of that century's great modernists: indeed, Samuel Beckett's phrase of "fail again. Fail better" resounds till this day, as if there can be no other, *better* way to capture the sense of failure.[11] And yet, as if in response to this, we have had in the early part of the twenty-first century the millennial-speak "epic fail." What the phrase or even "speech act" does is to pronounce almost immediately the failure of anyone, anything, anywhere, anytime. With "epic fail," not only are political, juridical, or social institutions failing but a dress, or a cupcake, can also be a "fail." "Epic fail" clearly is no longer "trending" today but looking back at it at present can give us enough critical distance to assess its values and shortcomings for a thinking of contemporary failure. I will come back very soon to this. For now, let it be said that "epic fail" has perhaps captured the zeitgeist of sensing—and needing to call out—failure everywhere, on every scale, in almost every domain of contemporary life; it registers or encapsulates the sense that no other century like the present had failures so prevalent and pervasive in practically every aspect of life. In addition to "epic fail," perhaps we should also not forget to mention the establishment of the Museum of Failure in Sweden in 2017, which arguably stands as a concrete artifact attesting to the sense of failure overwhelming us today, so much so that we need a physical space to archive our failures for all to see.[12]

To be clear, this book is not interested in determining the present century as the century of failure par excellence; its purpose is not to compare this and the preceding century in order to see which comes out tops in terms of having greater or more failures. This is not the conversation I am interested in entering in this book. Each epoch, after all, will understandably consider some of its failures to be incomparable to others in history, if not for all time. Hence, rather than staging a competition between centuries to determine which of them has failed better, it is more just, reasonable, and perhaps helpful to say that failure is accumulative. In other words, each age adds its failures to the one(s) after. From the perspective of the latter, then, it can seem that failure is but mounting and piling in its time, that the sense of failure is weighing especially upon it, since it has to remember the failures of the previous century or centuries as well, as if the failures of its own time are already not enough to bear or account for. The compounding effect of failure notwithstanding, perhaps what we need to acknowledge is that every epoch has its failures or that failure is for all times (even though, as I will restate later, we hardly give it time, we do not accord it its own temporality). The sense of failure being with us all this time or throughout time becomes more salient if we recall the failure since the beginning of time of Adam and Eve to heed the commandment to not eat from the Tree of Knowledge, which led not only to their expulsion from the Garden of Eden but also the impossibility of mankind to ever reclaim residency there. Against the backdrop of this "original" failure, one could say—and this would only reiterate failure's accumulative nature and/or effect—that mankind's subsequent failures are but *postscripts* to this first failure. Postscripts and failure share several characteristics: like failures that pile on one another, one can always add a postscript to another, a post-postscript to an existing postscript, ad infinitum; failure is also oftentimes acknowledged after the fact—that is, the consciousness of failure might come only after the act that constitutes that very failure is already completed, and this again renders it like a postscript in the sense of an addendum to the main text, not unlike an afterthought. It will be important to think postscripts alongside failure, therefore, and I will do so in the conclusion of this book. For now, let me simply posit, in light of failure's postscripts, that the thinking of failure is constant across time; failure preoccupies the thought of each epoch, regardless of it manifesting as an explicit subject in the epoch's philosophy, literature, and the arts or as an implicit backdrop to the discourses of the epoch.

It remains critically important, nevertheless, to underscore how failure is thought about and/or articulated differently in each epoch. This is not only to recognize that, despite failure being a constant phenomenon across time and space, each failure can be different from the next. This is also to allow us to illuminate how differently we treat, respond to, and cope with failure according to each epoch; it might even enable us to offer a different way of thinking about failure *within* an epoch—which is indeed a principal endeavor of this book, a chance presented to us by the deluge of failures that have been overwhelming contemporary life so far to think about failure in a way that stays with it rather than seeking to surpass it. This is why it can still be insightful to emphasize the difference between our century and the one before, specifically with regard to the representation—that is, the inscription, of failure. This difference is perhaps already evident in the free citation by anyone of "epic fail"—admittedly quite the frivolous amalgamation of the two terms *epic* and *fail*[13]—in contrast to the exclusive attribution of the phrase "fail again. Fail better"—thoughtfully crafted in spare modernist style—to Beckett. Furthermore, what "epic fail" has done is to wrest the title of "failure" away from exclusively monumental events oftentimes on a global scale, as was typically done in the twentieth century, and to recognize that ordinary, everyday happenstances are worthy of the title too. What "epic fail" has taught us, then, is that we should not be attuned only to major, geopolitical failures but also to minor, supposedly mundane, or even banal ones. Indeed, there is no reason to marginalize or deny ordinary, everyday failures; there is no good reason either for us to hierarchize failures or prioritize which ones to consider. It is not as if we have learned well from past major failures. If anything, we have only *not failed* to repeat them, and one recalls Fukushima here, where the lessons of Chernobyl seem to have gone unheeded, proving Beckett right about failing again only to head "worstward." As "epic fail" has arguably led the way, then, perhaps it is time to give as much attention to every failure, to all sorts of failure, but especially those that we tend to overlook or disregard: those that seem so ordinary or pedestrian, those that seem so minor or insignificant, those that are personal and hence seem less "eventful" than those of larger, historical, or planetary dimensions.[14]

"Epic fail" also belongs to common, everyday, or even banal language, and this highlights another critical difference in the articulation of failure between our present century and the preceding one. Just as failure in the twentieth century was typically invoked in relation to major events, the writing of failure at that time was also seemingly the domain of major writers, including Beckett himself. Indeed, Beckett never failed to make failure the mark of artistic genius, and he and other (largely male) modernist writers or artists would wear this badge fiercely and proudly as if it were their prerogative to write or think about the grand failures of their times in their highly stylized manner.[15] This explains the seriousness they bring to the treatment of failure, despite or in spite of the dark humor that can be found in their works, in contrast to the frivolous laughter that accompanies the pronouncements of "epic fail," which generally signals an insouciance with regard to whether the failure in question will be addressed or not.[16] In general, then, twentieth-century failure may be considered a "grand narrative" writ large by the "great" modernist writers/artists. With "epic fail," though, the genre of writing or speaking about failure is no longer the privilege of "great" writers/artists; as part of common speech, "epic fail" has given everyone—or rather, has reclaimed for everyone—the right to proclaim the failure of just about anything. Put another way, "epic fail" has democratized both the way we consider what constitutes failure and the way we write or talk about failure. I would like to think that the vernacular and democratizing spirit of "epic fail" is somewhat reflected in the works that interest us in this book, across which we find a notable majority of female voices: voices of female writers at various stages of their writing careers, of various standings in literary circles and institutions today. I have already mentioned the ordinary failures with which these texts are preoccupied. These failures are also correspondingly recounted largely in prosaic language, oftentimes bereft of stylistic (dis)ingenuity, which not only grants these texts the capacity to expound with raw or brutal honesty on the affective structure of failure but also allows them to stand apart from the heavily stylized twentieth-century modernist writings of failure. (Nevertheless, ordinary or personal language in these texts can also fail in managing the ineluctability of existence and failure. When this happens, one is left with bodily responses that react clumsily, awkwardly, uneasily, ineptly, failingly, and this is where we will need to turn our attention to more corporeal genres in Berlant's sense.)

But to go back to "epic fail": despite its democratizing force with regard to what counts as failure and who gets to proclaim failure, it nonetheless has its problems. We have earlier briefly highlighted its flippant, if not uncritical, nature. Indeed, when uttered so often without much thought, the enunciation "epic fail" can reduce everything to failure, and this reduction threatens to erase the very notion of failure, since if everything is failure, then nothing is effectively a failure. (Or, as the literary scholar Gavin Jones puts it, "To say that failure is everywhere condemns it to being nowhere."[17]) This reduction flattens out not just the differences of each failure but also the different *experiences* of each failure, even though we might be speaking of a similar failure. For example, my experience (as a scholar of the humanities who trucks mainly with books most of the time) of failing to replace a lightbulb and my affective responses to this failure (minimal, if not none to speak of) can be very different from another's—say, an engineer who furthermore prides himself in handiwork. Affects surrounding failure are important; therefore, not only do they articulate the critical difference between one failure and another, or between one's experience of failure and another's, they also help us recognize how every failure is registered differently in every one of us, hence teaching us how every failure counts, how every failure in fact matters. This is why it will be insufficient for us to think failure solely in terms of structure, not especially the cold, antihumanist, or anhuman structure according to French theory of the late 1960s and early 1970s.[18] This will be inadequate to a thinking of failure that dwells in failure and that exposes itself to all that comes with or after failure. Taking into account (negative) affects of failure will be necessary, too, and this is why we need a thinking of failure that reckons with failure's affective structure.

Toward an Affective Structure of Failure

Now, any engagement with affects cannot elide the personal.[19] And the personal cannot be bracketed from any thinking of failure. The personal, after all, has his or her unique relation to failure. This explains how even though failure might be pronounced or established by a collective, it cannot have an enduring force in, or effect on, the individual if it did not resonate strongly with (something within) the individual. Put another way, even though failure can be produced by political, economic, sociocultural, and institutional shortcomings, there remain undoubtedly affects of failure that speak very much, if not more insistently, to the individual.[20] These are affects by which the individual still feels largely and irreducibly affected. Or else they are affects that reawaken and thereby amplify a prior affect of failure within the individual, one that precedes and goes beyond political, economic, and social determinations. By affect here, I follow scholars such as Teresa Brennan, Sara Ahmed, and Jonathan Flatley to think it generally in terms of something that is in the air, something atmospheric, which generates from the confluence of personal and external forces and which can leave one with a great unease, a lingering sense of undefinable dread if not a debilitating effect not unlike a "suspended agency" that results from an "ugly feeling," according to Sianne Ngai.[21] To all this, I would add that we can also think of affect in terms of pressure, the effects of which become palpable through either a change in an atmospheric system or an interaction between two such systems. Thinking failure as such an affect would perhaps help us understand how the sense of failure exerts some form of real bodily and psychical force from either within or without the individual. But I stress here the cases where the collective might try all it might to dispel any notion of failure but the individual insists nevertheless on his or her failure, thus rendering all external attempts to negate it simply futile. In these cases, the pressure from the sense of failure within is too insistent or overwhelming to enable one to be receptive of outside forces. If we keep this in mind, it would not be difficult to think how failure can largely be a personal affair. In this regard, we could even say that it is at the level of the personal that failure finds its true force, where failure is sustained and gathers its intensity, and that the personal is perhaps where a thinking and understanding of failure true to failure should locate or immerse itself.

I would like to argue here that the personal sense of failure can be articulated in terms of what Raymond Williams has called a "structure of feeling." Certainly, "structures of feeling" pertain to the social, although this social has to be understood *not* as an established or institutionalized grouping, *not* as a gathering with its dominant or normalized and normative comportments: the social here does not refer to "social forms" that are "recognizable" or "explicit," embodied by "institutions" or "formations and traditions," and projected in "dominant systems of belief and education" or "influential systems of explanation and argument."[22] In other words, the social, for Williams, is not a formed community or collective that considers the thoughts, feelings, and experiences to shape its social consciousness to be done, that takes its construction to be something of the past and no longer ongoing. The beginnings of "structures of feeling" are not to be found there; in fact, they might even be suppressed by the social, (mis)understood as "formed wholes" or "fixed," not granted legitimation or recognition.[23] In Williams's words, "structures of feeling" are "experiences to which the fixed forms do not speak at all, which indeed they do not recognize."[24] (Putting this in relation to our thinking of failure, there is no doubt that contemporary cultures of success or our success-oriented societies would find what we are considering a "structure of feeling"—that is, one that tarries with failure—hardly acceptable.) "Structures of feeling" thus find their outlets in "social experiences in solution, as distinct from other social semantic formations that have been precipitated and are more evidently and more immediately available" or, in short, in "emergent formations."[25] Put another way, they unravel in certain pockets of society, among minor groups or groups that have yet to find their grouping; it is there where thoughts and/or sentiments that are refused currency in the larger social context can find some minimum expression or be shared at least to a minimal extent. This does not preclude "emergent formations" from counting (on) individuals who are disparate and isolated from one another as they can be, which is to say, individuals who, again, have not yet found their social grouping. This is why Williams would further argue that "structures of feeling" are markedly registered in the works of individual literary writers of a particular period who might not necessarily be in conversation with one another but work "in relatively isolated ways."[26] Williams's examples are "the new semantic figures of Dickens, of Emily Brontë, and others" wherein one finds "exposure and isolation as a *general* condition, and poverty, debt, or illegitimacy as its connecting instances," as opposed to "early Victorian ideology" that "specified the exposure caused by poverty or by debt or by illegitimacy as social failure or deviation."[27] In our case, it is in the selected works of Moshfegh, Cusk, Levé, Li, and Zambreno that we are locating a contemporary "structure of feeling" in terms of a staying with the personal sense of failure more as a general condition than a "social failure or deviation."

It is with Williams's reference to individual literary writers that we lean into the personal dimension of a "structure of feeling." A faithful reading of Williams, again, would counsel meticulous use of the term *personal*. According to Williams, the traditional positing of the personal against the social is a false distinction, whereby the social is regarded, once again, as already complete and fixed, and the personal as something that lies as if outside the social, a "this, here, now, alive, active, 'subjective'" entity that is seemingly antithetical to the constitution of the social.[28] For Williams, both the social and the personal are always in a germinal relation with each other: the personal feeds the social and vice versa.[29] Thus, even though the first articulation of a "structure of feeling" may be identified in the domain of the personal, it can in fact find its resonance in another individual or other individuals, and this will become irrefutable once these individuals begin to communicate with one another. This social dimension of a "structure of feeling" is affirmed, as Williams points out, when the linguistic idiom or style particular to a "structure of feeling" finds itself shared among other individuals, without there being any conscious collective effort for such a sharing—and we need only recall for our purposes the prevalence of the phrase "epic fail" or the commonality of the prosaic prose style of our contemporary literary works engaged with personal failures.[30] But to return to the *personal* in its traditional usage: what remains useful for us as well as for Williams is its indication of a "living presence" or "the specificity of present being" or what might be regarded as "private, idiosyncratic, and even isolating."[31] The extant dimension of a "structure of feeling" at the level of the personal, or what might seem so "alive" of it, however, can also paradoxically be anguishing, defeating, or even deathly, such as what I am underscoring in this present work the refusal to extricate oneself from the despairing and debilitating sense of personal failure. It can thus generate a "tension" that is "an unease, a stress, a displacement, a latency" for fixed, social forms, which typically predicate themselves on the hopeful, optimistic, and the productive.[32] It is critical, therefore, to elucidate the unfolding of a "structure of feeling" in all its manifestations as thought, bodily experience, and affective dimensions at the personal level, no matter how pessimistic or depressing they are, before this "structure of feeling" gets smoothened out or resolved by the larger social forms, before it becomes "formalized, classified, and in many cases built into institutions and formations," by which time, according to Williams, "a new structure of feeling will usually already have begun to form, in the true social present."[33] This is indeed the reason for our focusing on the personal in our understanding of failure as a "structure of feeling," in order to register that sense of personal failure, which can be mundane or even banal but is nevertheless difficult for, and even constitutive of, everyday existence for some individuals, before it is being glossed over or sublimated into something else at the larger social level.

For us, then, failure as a "structure of feeling" is an affect traversing the world (in our absence), to which some of us (in our presence in the world) are then more attuned. Some of us indeed allow ourselves to be affected by this affect. Or, as Ahmed would say, this affect of failure "sticks" to some of us.[34] There are indeed some of us who sense this affect of failure more than others: we, the (un)lucky ones in this elective affinity with failure; we, born always untimely, with stars always misaligned; we, predisposed—as psychologists like to say—to this affect, to this affinity. Again, some might insist that this select group is particularly sensitive to failure due to prior or existing sociocultural conditionings that perpetuate the ideology of success or determine success as a norm. However, if we keep in mind how affects work—that is, how they precede and exceed both institutionalized or normalized ways of feelings and personal emotions—then we might also understand how failure can be something that lies outside of sociocultural logics too. In this regard, we could also say that failure circulates or operates like a more general, neutral, or even impersonal *sense*. Sense may indeed mean common sense, intelligible sense, or even nonsense. In other words, failure can be, as common sense, something commonly agreed upon to be so; as intelligible sense, the undesired outcome despite following steps programmed to avoid precisely this negative result, or else the consequence of not following strictly those steps; and as nonsense, something that defies all reasoning, going against both common and intelligible senses. But I would say that it can also be more and less than these senses, something less identifiable or categorizable than these senses, or else exceeding these categories. This sense—which is, again, general, neutral, or impersonal—pervades existence undeniably or irresistibly but which, like affect, is felt more acutely, more intensely, more lastingly, by a select few, the few who are more willing to recognize it than the rest of us are willing, or else dare, to do so. In any case, this sense, this "structure of feeling," can never be ignored or dispelled completely. With what Williams calls its "palpable pressures" exerting on us, the "structure of feeling" of failure is all too real and visceral, constituting parts of our existence with its undeniable "tensions, shifts, and uncertainties."[35] "Structures of feeling" do not remain silent, in other words. They need to be articulated; they seek their articulation. Thus, even though a "structure of feeling" might not resonate with a more general sentiment or historical consciousness, it is nevertheless irrepressible in the sense that it will find "qualifications, reservations, indications elsewhere."[36] According to Williams, it is in language that a "structure of feeling" will find its murmurings, albeit "at the very edge of [an epoch's] semantic availability," with its "specific feelings, specific rhythms," and this is also how it sees to its nascent forms or formation in works of literature.[37] For us, to reiterate, the contemporary "structure of feeling" in terms of a dwelling with personal failure finds expression in (the style of) the literary texts that we will be discussing in this present work, with the prosaicism or even banality of "epic fail" arguably contributing as an ambient soundscape to this affective structure.

The Problem of Failure

Before going further, there is undoubtedly a lingering question that begs to be answered: What is failure? The following definition might help us with a provisional response: "Failure doesn't come from falling down. Failure comes from not getting up." This is a common enough definition that can be found printed on T-shirts. But it is a negative definition of failure. In other words, the definition is there *not* for us to heed it, *not* for us to embrace failure. Rather, it is meant for us to do otherwise. It is a rallying call for us to get up, to rise from the fallen or prone state; we are to climb out of the hole of despair, to move on, scale greater heights. The definition is thus meant for us to be motivated to overcome failure, surpass it, negate it, leave it behind us. But this is precisely how we have stopped thinking about failure in any strict sense. Or, as Bradatan has said, "As a rule, we fail to take failure seriously."[38] As we are urged, or as we urge ourselves, to quickly emerge from failure's psycho- and topological depressions, we renounce failure, disavowing it, repressing it, refusing to face it straight on. We shun failure. We do not give it due attention, denying its temporality, resisting its duration. Here, it will be instructive to follow Jones in thinking that "failure is... not, like error, a single instant, but an ongoing experience, or rather a set of foundational and all-encompassing human experience."[39] Otherwise, we fail failure in terms of not taking failure for what it is. All this is how, despite centuries or even millennials of failures, we still do not have any rigorous thinking of failure—one that takes into account its entire conceptual and affective dimension. Put another way, this is how failure, while being a problem to existence, also comes to have its problem—that is, how failure is yet to be thought of *as failure*.

The all-too-human tendency to gloss over failure, or the endeavor to turn failure into something else—into its very opposite even, which is success—can be found in most works of failure studies too. Many of them take failure to be but a (necessary) step to success, a critical lesson that will only lead to better things in the future, if not make one a better person. So, for example, the biologist Stuart Firestein will identify failure as a building block for scientific discoveries or breakthroughs.[40] Or else, Bradatan, the philosopher whom we have been citing so far, while wanting as I do to take on failure with a "eyes-wide-open approach," also cannot resist imputing to the thinking of failure the positive, moral lesson of humility for humanity.[41] For him, the understanding of failure must be a way to "narrate our way into humility," which is not simply a bildungsroman of sorts, allowing us to "come to terms with our imperfection, precariousness, and mortality, which are all epiphanies of failure" or "to realize who we are" but also a writing that leads us *out of* failure, a "cathartic" narrative through which "failure can work wonders of self-realization, healing, and enlightenment."[42] Success is no doubt in his horizon, as he says too: "Having taken failure as a guide, you stand a good chance to succeed."[43] Otherwise, the queer theorist Jack Halberstam, even though desiring, as is also my commitment, to explore the "darker territories of failure associated with futility, sterility, emptiness, loss, negative affect in general, and modes of unbecoming," would quickly attribute to failure the political potentiality to counter systemic inequity, racism, and gender or sexual discrimination.[44] According to Halberstam, "Failure [is] a way of refusing to acquiesce to dominant logics of power and discipline and as a form of critique. As a practice, failure recognizes that alternatives are embedded already in the dominant and that power is never total or consistent; indeed failure can exploit the unpredictability of ideology and its indeterminate qualities."⁴⁵ And the composition scholar Allison D. Carr, whose thoughts on failure such as its visceral or limitless dimensions, including her attempt to "reconstruct failure in its own image," while largely resonating with mine, nevertheless supplements the experience of failure with a positivity—that is, "to validate its worthiness as a meaningful part of composition."⁴⁶

Laudable definitely as their engagements with failure are, a veritable staying with failure, as I see it, hardly has any room for imagining a future effective politics, ethics, or pedagogy, however.⁴⁷ Thinking *failure as failure*, as I would argue, is very much without such, if not any, use-value or merit; it is an impasse in the strict sense of the word, a thorough *inoperativity*. We can understand *inoperativity*, from the French *désœuvrement*, in Maurice Blanchot's sense, which signifies that which, from within, undoes every endeavor to give a work some sense of accomplishment, completion, wholeness, or totality. In the wake of Blanchot, Jean-Luc Nancy has also enlisted the term in the context of thinking about community, to indicate how any constitutive, constructive communitarian project is ultimately for nothing since there is, in fact, nothing to be done for it.⁴⁸ Giorgio Agamben also has his own take on inoperativity or *inoperosità* in his native Italian: for him, it returns us to our ontological condition where the horizon of existence is never solely circumscribed by what we can or must do either through our vocation or our personal and/or collective pet projects (aesthetic or otherwise) but also by our (im)potentiality of "*not* making a work."⁴⁹ Agamben's point no doubt resonates with what I have said at the beginning of this introduction that the thinking of *failure as failure* is but an ontological reminder of how our sense of existence can be ineluctable from failure. So, if there is "a questioning of use" to our thinking of failure, then it would only be, to follow Sara Ahmed, "a questioning of being," "a question about how a person lives their life";⁵⁰ that is, again, ways of living that are essentially unproductive or even useless to any political economy, including any political aspiration, and such an ontological reminder clearly deviates from Halberstam's political thinking of failure as that which can be "*productively* linked to racial awareness, anticolonial struggle, gender variance, and different formulations of the temporality of success."⁵¹ Otherwise, we could follow Lee Edelman here to say that this would be failure as "bad education," one that teaches us *nothing*—a nothing that is radically outside of, and inassimilable or "inimical" to, normalized, institutionalized ways of thinking what a meaningful life is or should be, a nothing that is "a disturbance of order."⁵²

There is the question of aesthetics, nevertheless, in which "inoperativity"—in Blanchot's, Nancy's, and Agamben's senses—and Edelman's "bad education" are deeply entrenched. It is undisputable in my turn to literature in this present work, too, and in this respect I share much with Jones's *Failure and the American Writer*, another work of failure studies that I have cited a fair bit as well. Certainly, Jones's focus is on nineteenth-century American literature, but he is also interested in texts or writers who take a "probing look at the *personal* dimensions of failure, at faults more generated than imposed."[53] Other than locating the site of the personal for the study or theorization of failure, we have also seen Jones insisting on the specificity of each failure rather than making the generalizing move to label everything failure and on failure's lasting duration. As we will soon see, too, he furthermore takes failure to be an entity "*in itself*" and not in relation to something else.[54] With regard to literature, Jones undoubtedly aligns himself with Herman Melville, one of his studied authors, in the conviction that it "is the finest medium to express an overwhelming failure that haunts us personally, and an existential failure that defines us as human beings."[55] I echo this conviction, but where I depart from Jones is his apparent submission of failure to a literary function or use (and not bringing it back to the ontological and/or the existential). For Jones, "failure as a literary question" entails a working through of existential failure as formal literary experimentations such as "the shaping of style, genre, character, plot, and narrative voice."[56] Not only would this see to "a special kind of writing [come] into being" but also the determination of failure "as a kind of aesthetic practice and literary identity."[57] Not unlike many scholars of failure studies, then, there is in Jones the reflex to render failure productive, to invoke a positive horizon for it. As he says of his selected authors, "Failure comes to light as a specifically literary condition, the motor of stylistic expression itself.... In the hands of these writers, literary discourse possesses a peculiar power to mean as it fails."[58]

It can further be said that there is something Beckettian in Jones's investment in failure, since almost all his authors are not just known today to be literary geniuses but who also in their time regarded their failures as a "sign of election of artistic distinction," bestowing them with an exceptional ability to translate existential failure into literary forms.[59] In this respect, I find the force and eminence of literature over failure seemingly overstated while ordinary failures of ordinary people, which fall outside the purviews of aesthetic judgment (or religious morality or geopolitical interest, which are the social and historical factors against which the personal sense of artistic failure of some of Jones's authors are determined), get sidelined. Forgotten are failures at the ontological level that can never be translated into formal literary elements; the discomfiting senses of failure that no literary discourse can inscribe except intimated at best by nondiscursive gestures. The difficulty of failure for common existence, at the end of it all, is overshadowed while difficulties at the level of formal experimentation are celebrated or privileged. This is how, for Jones, in his reading of Melville's *Pierre*, "failure would... be flipped into aesthetic power by a new style of self-conscious difficulty and irony."[60] It is through such a transvaluation of failure into some form of literary "power" for literary ends that Jones will also write that "difficulty becomes failure's cure."[61]

Away from the literary vocation and in more general terms, the above "difficulty" can be understood as a demonstration of tenaciousness, of having grit and resilience. In the face of a failure that proves difficult to dispel, grit and resilience are indeed the counsels of common understandings of failure and most works in failure studies: through grit and resilience, we will overcome failure, and we will be on the path to success. Yet we have to be wary or even critical of the calls for such terms, for we have since recognized them to be part of the vocabulary of neoliberal capitalism, fueling the latter's compulsion for us to keep trying, keep working, despite setbacks, and regardless of our minds or bodies being capable of laboring on or not.[62] To demonstrate grit and resilience is to apparently prove our continued productivity, our potentiality to still contribute to the economy, hence our sustained employability. Yet the cruel reality is all too evident: hardly any employer picks up a past failure. Or else, when that happens, one is made to continue laboring with a much compromised remuneration (even more) incommensurate to one's real worth.[63] This is not to mention that under neoliberal capitalism, we have been conditioned to assume individual responsibility for whatever failures that have befallen us, compelled to refrain from highlighting the fault—systemic or otherwise—on the part of social, economic, and political institutions, further discouraged by the almost insurmountable task of holding these institutions accountable. Not only does the neoliberal capitalist order not acknowledge its failures, it also does not accept those on the part of its subjects.[64] Essentially, failure in itself is anathema to this order. The only condition where failure can be admitted is when it goads neoliberal subjects to improve their operativity or try another tack in order to perform better, all only in the service of the political economy. This is precisely how Beckett's phrase "fail again. Fail better" has been able to gain currency in Silicon Valley, through a gross or deliberate misreading to take the phrase to only mean "failure can become big business."[65] Failure as such is clearly not failure per se. (And because failure per se cannot be business, it can only be, as I would say again, personal.) In this case, one imputes to failure a tangential trajectory whereby some other productivity, or more precisely profit, can be extracted from it. As Silicon Valley–speak goes, one must not only fail but also "fail often and fast." Put another way, if failure is allowed to disseminate within the neoliberal capitalist order, we must recognize this failure as but programed and controlled, produced only to see to the order's even longer lasting functioning. As Stefano Harney and Fred Moten put it, "The algorithm of work subjects every labor process on the production line to undoing, disassembly, and incompletion, in order to demand it be completed better, assembled better, done better. It leaves behind not an improved organization but a metric to ensure the organization will never be satisfied. The metric measures everything against its last instance, ensuring that the last instance never comes."[66] Should there be a real failure, they go on, the order "must everywhere convert [this] failure from a perversion to a point on [the assembly] line. It must everywhere reduce failure to a bell curve. It must be everywhere. It must be a total education."[67] Against this, Harney and Moten will insist on still instantiating real failures within the order. They would call for the experimentation, if not improvisation (which is different from, and opposed to, the notion of improvement according to the neoliberal knowledge economy), with a "kink," which would constitute a "block" or "a dread or jam" against the order's general and incessant flow of "the assembly line, the flow line, the high line"[68] To put it in our terms, this "kink" would be nothing short of an impasse, undoing any sense of "resilience and preparedness," failing or letting fail any regulatory and surveillance regime of testing and improvement instituted by exploitative and racist neoliberal capitalism.[69]

The unwitting mobilizing of lexicons that form part of neoliberal capitalist rhetoric notwithstanding, there is also, I repeat, the invocation of a positive or optimistic horizon for failure by failure studies (invoked no less, to be sure, by neoliberal capitalism's appropriation, misrepresentation, and even profiteering of failure). I consider this its recuperative or even reparative move with regard to failure. More critically, however, it reveals that when it comes to failure, we are typically delimited by a binary mode of thinking or what Anne Dalke calls the "success/failure complex."[70] We tend to define failure by its supposed, apparent opposite: success. We make failure and success polemic terms by which one (failure) is to be abandoned for the other (success). What the binary presupposes and entails is that there can be no failure if we do not have something like success, that there can be failure only in relation to something else considered a success. This binary way of thinking is reinforced by the consideration of failure in perspectival terms, where someone or something is rendered a failure for having fallen short of what has been viewed to be success. The notion of failure as a matter of perspective belies the other common definition of failure as the inability to meet certain expectations. Accordingly, anything less than the anticipated outcome, or anything that does not meet the defined targets or objectives set along the way, is considered a failure. Keeping in mind, however, those who are particularly responsive to the sense of failure, one should not assume that the view or horizon of success owes it to others or to a general consensus. Keeping in mind also what has already been said about the affect of failure, the vision of failure (and success) is not necessarily always imposed upon the individual by a larger sociopolitico-economic apparatus, and the individual does not necessarily internalize this vision passively. The perspective of failure might be an insistence coming from within the person who thinks he or she has failed while others do not see that failure. (It is in this regard that one person's failure might even be seen as a success to another and vice versa. I leave aside the reprehensible case of one person's failure being seen as a success *for* another.) No doubt, the insistence of such a perspective might undoubtedly be conditioned by sociocultural institutions or norms. Yet, one must not neglect to consider how the personal perspective remains even though those conditionings have been relaxed via, for example, psychological interventions such as cognitive behavioral therapy or when views toward some of these norms, if not the norms themselves, change. The perception of failure thus owes it to the persons themselves, as they know that there is a sense of unmistakable or irrefutable failure within, despite or in spite of all those conditionings. They see failure only in themselves; there is no failure except themselves. No excuse—racial bias, systemic inequality, sheer dumb luck, etcetera—will be admitted; nobody's fault, no fault of anything, except theirs. Call it the curse of perfection; the perfectionist's curse.[71]

Even in the perfectionist's case, failure seems undeniably trapped within a perspectival framework. Failure, then, is as if all but a matter of perspective: the perspective of those who cannot let go of their failings, of those who can see only failure and nothing else, or even of those who do see success (elsewhere and in others) but choose nonetheless to see failure only in themselves. They would say, as one of the characters in Cusk's novel *Outline* does: "Your failures keep returning to you, while your successes are something you always have to convince yourself of."[72] Perhaps there is no escape from the perspectival trap with regard to failure. Or else, what I am also suggesting is that, at the end of it all, it is perhaps difficult, almost impossible, to think that there can be an originary perception of failure unconditioned by other people and/or things that have been conferred the status of success. But perhaps this is because of failure's irreducible nature: it is as *the* irreducible that it invites various perspectives, yet at the same time is indifferent to them. Nevertheless, the problem of thinking failure in perspectival and/or binary terms, if it is not already evident, is that it only traps the thinking of failure within a relativism, leading us admittedly nowhere in the thinking of failure, leaving us further away from any thinking of failure itself, if not setting up any thinking of failure to fail. To sidestep this relativism, I do propose picking up from our earlier reference to Williams, to think failure especially in terms of structure: a structure of existence, which is to say, failure as an integral part of existence, if not the sense or feeling that is constitutive of the fact of existence. I deviate slightly from Williams at this point, though, and take structure to mean the minimal (dis)organizing force or principle that either perpetuates existence or from which existence can never escape but has to roll with it. I am leaning more toward another French thinker, Gilles Deleuze, in this regard, who has said that structure is something like the perpetual noncoincidence of "an extremely mobile *empty place*" and "an *occupant without a place*,"[73] which is to say, a never-ending nonfulfillment for both a space to find its tenant and a person to find a place of their own.

Deleuze's notion of structure is arguably shot through with a certain sense of failure, and I would add to this depressive feeling to say that thinking failure as a structure of existence or an existential structure is to accept the state of being thrown or having fallen into failure from nowhere, without a higher ground to attain, without any previous elevated terrain to reclaim. It is to think failure as irreducible to nothing, comparable to nothing. Failure as structure of existence is to experience failure in a way that is indifferent, or rather blind, to what others say about failure or success, to how others define them. Or, to borrow the words of the French novelist Catherine Cusset, the "structure of failure" that underlies existence is one that, at the end of the day, cannot be attributed to the fault of others, the hubris of one's egotism or narcissism, the susceptibility to viciousness, the consequence of madness, or the effects of youth.[74] Failure as such, to put it another way, can just be a state of being, an existential ontology, or, rather, an ontological existentiality into which one is not so much thrown but, again, fallen, fallen *as such*, without a determinable cause, without any external push.[75] It is, to borrow the words this time of Roland Barthes, the zero degree of existence.

Failure as structure of existence would also mean that failure is something that touches every one of us. No one is immune to it. This explains why, for many of us, life is oftentimes seen as a project that seeks to rectify some kind of previous or even original failure, to fill the sense of failure with something else, turning our entire existence into a lifelong struggle to overcome that failure. There is, of course, no guarantee that we will ever succeed at this project in our lifetime. In fact, we might just keep failing, which is to say that we keep repeating the structure of existential failure, as Beckett reminds us in "Worstward Ho!" from which the phrase "fail again" is taken. According to Beckett there, we constantly fail, or our lives are irreducibly structured to fail over and over again, no matter how much we try—ad infinitum and ad nauseum—to figure out if our sense of ontological failure precedes the world with all its sociopolitico-economic structures setting us up to fail. As Beckett also intimates, settling this issue—if it were ever possible—would not make us feel better about our failed existence either. Heeding Beckett's lesson, then, we can say that it is erroneous to determine whether failure or success comes first. Success does not precede failure, nor vice versa. Failure and success are firsts. Failure and success are always already there, on their own, each not dependent on the other. Or, to cite Jones again, "Failure is not simply the inverse of success. It has its own story to tell."[76] If we accept all this, we will then begin to free ourselves from delimiting the thinking of failure to a relativist, perspectival affair and/or a binary mode of thinking.

To ensure that there is not another sliding into relativism or binarism, we will also have to refuse, despite the negative definition of failure, wondering if there can be a positive one—one that does not render failure a defective, undesirable, disavowed, disdained term. We might even say that we do not need a new definition of failure after all. The definition "failure comes from not getting up" is already sufficient. In other words, failure, defined in itself, is "not getting up." It is just that, precisely that, and nothing else. Failure is essentially falling down *and* staying down.[77] (And if failing is falling, these two terms are incidentally differentiated but by a change of a letter: the letter *i*, which surely brings us back to the personal dimension of failure.) To think *failure as failure* is to stay with this definition and not be preoccupied with the idea of getting up. And one should not bear down on this state or condition with any judgment, not especially one that gives staying down or "not getting up" a negative value. (Is it not better at times to stay down too? One hears the advice to "stay down" in a fight—sportive or otherwise—in order to not suffer any more injuries, to stop the blows from coming.) This is where a thought of failure should linger or even settle; this is the topological depression with and/or in which thought should rest. Thought should be prepared to sink in this abyss; it should be prepared to dwell in it, wallow in it even. In the face of this depression, thought should not be anxious to lift itself up from there: renounce all *Aufhebung*—that uplifting (but also canceling) move in dialectical thinking—if one wants to truly think about failure, if one wants to arrive at a true thinking of failure. The thinking of failure, in all, perhaps does not concern any dialectics, and this is perhaps how a thinking of failure breaks with the restricted economy predicated on the success/failure binary. This is also to say that there should henceforth neither be any looking forward to something else beyond the fallen state, no thought of any "after" following the state of staying down.[78] In this space and time of interruption that disrupts or suspends all dialectics, progress narratives, and linear (capitalist) chronology, thought will finally look at failure straight on, face it squarely, stare at it with eyes fully opened; thought will tarry with failure, allowing failure to take it wherever failure likes to go in failure's own time and duration, if not in its contretemps—that is, its inopportune phenomenality or inopportunity that defies (*contre*) all chronological or linear time (*temps*), enduring beyond the latter.

Instead of seeing the definition of failure as "not getting up" as a negative one, then, we should embrace it, reclaim it from its abandonment, if we are committed to the thinking of failure. This is not to say, though, that we are turning the definition into a positive one—this would only be to sneak in a progress or success narrative. We avoid this move as long as we keep in mind failure as an affective structure of existence, which is also to say, and we return to a thinking of structure closer to Williams's here, an affect that is a "neutral kernel" that will accommodate whatever feelings or emotions that accompany it, as Ngai would say in borrowing the term from Paolo Virno.[79] In this regard, the sense of failure need not be all doom and gloom; it need not be all depressive, festering only with sadness, dejection, hopelessness, anguish, resignation, regret, etcetera. We certainly feel all these negative affects or "ugly feelings" (to borrow Ngai's term again) especially if failure is taken as a lack—that is, again, failure understood as a falling short of expectations: we fall into the crevice of despairing underachievement as we consider ourselves not having done enough for ourselves, for others, or in comparison to others. But failure can also be constituted by doing too much, doing more than required. Here, failure comes in the form of excess, manifesting itself in the superfluous. And instead of a hole into which one sinks, as in the case of one failing to perform within expectations, one spills over (no doubt into another, different hole) along with the excess that overflows the limits of what is deemed acceptable. Failure here, as excess, is pleroma, if not jouissance.[80] And if jouissance bears the sense of the ecstatic, then failure is indeed not all doom and gloom all the time: there can even be a perverse glee in failure, a joyous death drive, to extend the psychoanalytic rhetoric in relation to failure. To be sure, this jouissance, or death drive, does not have a positive or optimistic dénouement; it knows that nothing is going to turn out well, that there is no happy ending.[81] Here, one could think of the sometimes mocking, sometimes imprudent laughter that accompanies certain pronouncements of "epic fail" and the subsequent shrugs, which can signal some form of resignation with regard to the state of things, knowing that the failures will remain and that nothing can be done about them. With such a jouissance, let us, then, acknowledge and accept that there is no escaping things negative in thinking about failure, in recognizing failure *as* failure. "Any failure is hell," as Yiyun Li would say.[82] Failure *is* negative, but it is not negative in comparison to something considered positive. It is negative in itself, without any further dialectical move.[83]

Negativity, Impasse

In the negation of the call to get up, of a next step forward/upward, of a progress narrative, and of recuperation, reparation, or recovery, one could also call failure as such *negativity*, if we understand negativity, following Berlant and Edelman, as not only "a resistance to or undoing of the stabilizing frameworks of coherence imposed on thought and lived experience" but also that which "reject[s] the impulses to repair social relations that appear to us irreparable."[84] This is the example of those who inhabit the sense or affect of failure and refuse to (re)connect with those in the larger society who reject failure or who buy into the ideology of success; they would be the "inconvenient people" according to Berlant's vocabulary in the posthumously published *On the Inconvenience of Other People*.[85] Failure as negativity is without recuperation or reparation, and staying (down) with failure would be, following Edelman, "enacting a negativity with no other end but its own insistence."[86] As I would put it, such a negativity would be a "depressive position" tout court—that is, a "depressive position" more absolute than Melanie Klein's (or Eve Sedgwick's reading of Klein's) because it will be taken in its very literal sense, and because it is not derived from any prior "paranoid position." In fact, the "paranoid position" here—which sees failure everywhere—is constitutive of, fused with, if not coterminous with, this more absolute "depressive position." Keeping in mind again the personal dimension of failure, it is important to state that the "paranoid position" here of seeing failure everywhere pertains only to oneself and not others. As such, in contradistinction to Sedgwick and/or Klein, there is actually not much, or even no, reparative work demanded of the self to compensate another who would have been symbolically but nevertheless violently rendered a part-object through a typical "paranoid position." In our absolute "depressive position," the self does not seek reparation either. There is no do-over here, no position to rectify or remedy, no (re)calibrating of one's perspective with an optimistic horizon. There is just the acceptance that things are as such: a depressive position through and through, without any will to working toward, without any hope for, a reconstitution of a new whole (whether of oneself or of the other) from the ruins of failure.[87] Here, I would like to borrow Berlant's phrase in her reading of Sedgwick's *A Dialogue on Love*—even though I am aware that Berlant refuses a thoroughly absolute depressive position—and call this "unconditional negativity."[88] Or we can recall Blanchot's and Nancy's term *désœuvrement*, which underscores the "inoperative" (nothing works, indeed, in failure) or the "unworked" (everything falls apart, no less, in failure), and lets be the existential condition whereby nothing can be done, nothing is to be done. If not, Agamben's reiteration of the term as *inoperosità* might be closer to what we are getting at, since it not only names the "potential not to act" but also the "*potential for darkness*," whereby existence not only "undergoes and suffers its own non-Being" but also welcomes it.[89] In any case, any endeavor to turn failure into some pedagogy—aesthetic, moral, philosophical, existential, etcetera—or motivation for productivity is simply the fantasmatic work of the imaginary.[90]

In all, then, failure is simply and precisely the impasse. It is all about being stuck. There is no way out; no exit.[91] No passage through; sheer intransitivity.[92] The reckoning with this impasse is essentially a personal, solitary experience (and this is what the literary texts that interest us will reaffirm too). This also accounts for how, even though failure can be a very common occurrence for all, the experience of failure and its accompanying affects, if one indeed acknowledges the impasse that traverses them all, can be very unique to each person. It is because of this impasse that one's experience or perception of failure, and one's feelings about failure, can never be completely communicated to another, can never be fully understood by another. There will always be a trace of failure that will remain to haunt only the individual, one that speaks only to the individual. Once again, then, even though failure is a common enough phenomenon for all, there is no commonality in the experience of it among those who undergo it. This is failure's *shared unshareability*, as I would put it, and which I will say more in one of the chapters of this book.[93] Or else this is failure as structure that is more *infra* than Berlant's "infrastructuralism," especially if we hold *infra* to its literal meaning to pertain to what lies deep within (the individual), which can certainly surface at a later time to cause displacements (in the individual) in yet different ways. Berlant's "infrastructuralism," meanwhile, with its debt to Marshall Sahlins, concerns connecting with other measures practiced by others in order to make the present bearable and to build better responses or coping mechanisms to a phenomenon should it come up again in the future.[94] The idea of failure's shared unshareability clearly pushes back against this communitarian contour or horizon of Berlant's "infrastructuralism." But to come back to failure as impasse: if thought is to truly commit to thinking about failure, then thought must be prepared to precisely get stuck in this impasse. Thinking about failure will be the experience of not only thought at an impasse but also thought as impasse. And again, thought must not seek to get out of this impasse. In this regard, I veer closer to Derrida's idea and thinking of the impasse than Berlant's especially in *Cruel Optimism*. For Berlant, one can still find some sort of footing in the impasse, the possibility of productively making sense of the situation, of possibly gaining some enlightenment out of it. According to Berlant, "The impasse is a stretch of time in which one moves around with a sense that the world is at once intensely present and enigmatic, such that the activity of living demands both a wandering absorptive awareness and a hypervigilance that collects material that might help to clarify things, maintain one's sea legs."[95] In this impasse, one is preoccupied with preparing oneself for what is to come; one remains on guard, looking forward to what arrives from the horizon, hopeful even. For Berlant, then, this horizon can be an optimistic future, recognizing that "for many . . . , living in an impasse would be an aspiration."[96]

For Derrida, though, the experience of the impasse—or what he would prefer to call by its other name of "aporia"—leaves one with less certainty, less confidence in one's way. It is essentially about "not knowing where to go,"[97] which is to say again, getting stuck, seeing obstacles (mental and/or physical) on all sides, a pure lostness or errancy, with no illuminating light to make sense of things.[98] Thought finds itself in a state of helplessness and/or hopelessness here—nothing much to be done. Derrida goes on to say, and I quote him at length:

> It had to be a matter of the nonpassage, or rather from the experience of the nonpassage, the experience of what happens and is fascinating in the nonpassage, paralyzing us in this separation in a way that is not necessarily negative.... It should be a matter of what, in sum, appears to block our way or to separate us in the very place where *it should no longer be possible to constitute a problem,* a project, or a projection.... There, in sum, in this place of aporia, *there is no longer any problem.* Not that, alas or fortunately, the solutions have been given, but because one could no longer even find a problem what would constitute itself and that one would keep in front of oneself, as a presentable object or project, as a protective representative or a prosthetic substitute, as some kind of border still to cross or behind which to protect oneself.[99]

Thinking failure in light of Derrida's impasse, then, is where thought approaches paralysis. And just as what we have said earlier about failure being indifferent to binary structures, this impasse or paralysis should not be seen in negative and/or positive terms either. Perhaps the best or only way to put it is to call it negativity again, and here it will involve negating failure as a problem to be solved, negating failure as a project to be accomplished by overcoming it. Thinking failure would be to immerse in this negativity, which would also mean that failure is no longer seen as something placed before us from which we should always avoid. It is always too late for that anyway. Here, if there is any movement, it would be, according to Derrida, "to move not against or out of the impasse but, in another way, *according to* another thinking of the aporia, one perhaps more enduring," which is to say, tarrying only with the impasse of failure, as long as failure lasts.[100]

And let there be (no) disappointments: moving according to failure or enduring with failure as such is also where thought fumbles, flops. The thinking of failure implicates a fumbling or flopped thought. It goes nowhere. It produces nothing. It does not advance thought or thinking itself. Quite to the contrary, in fact: it sends thought into catatonia. It is where thought really breaks down, where it finds itself amid a true "inoperativity." It collapses, runs aground, falls apart. It lets itself lapse. It is thought slumped, dejected, rejected. It has nothing much, nothing new, nothing impactful to say. It is thought stuck in the rut, exposed in its utmost vulnerability. It is thought thoroughly weakened, a real weak thought (without dialectics).[101] It can only drift aimlessly, finding itself degenerating into a state of torpor, falling into a sleepless sleep that seeks not so much a recuperation but perchance to cease existing. To cite Berlant again, genres are flailing here no less, as thought tries to grapple with failure, as it stands in the face of failure, as it tarries with failure. With genres flailing, there will also be, as Berlant tells us too, drama. We would no doubt be witnessing a histrionics of thought here, if not the "drama of negativity" in Berlant's terms, arising from a sense of "out-of-syncness"—which I would say is not too foreign to the sense of displacement cutting through the structure of failure if we follow, as we did earlier, Deleuze's understanding of structure as the noncoincidence of a place without tenant and an occupant without a place—whereby dramatics is "a way to maintain an affective mess for which most people do not have the skill or trust in the world's, or other people's, patience."[102] With all the drama, I would even say that this is perhaps thought's "epic fail" moment: thought with a sense of failure so common, so unexceptional, even embarrassing, like any other "epic fail," for all to see. But to state it one more time: while the occurrence of failure might be common to all, there is always something of its experience or the sense of which that remains unshareable. In this regard, the drama here is closer to the melodramatic, where melodrama, to follow Li again, is unlike tragedy and comedy that desire an audience in "sharing themselves to elicit tears and laughter"; melodrama, on the contrary, "meets no one's expectations but its internal need to feel," letting one be awash with what "alienates and discomfits" oneself, including, as Li underscores, suicidal ideation.[103]

In this melodrama, then, thought does not allow for itself any respite. It goes along with the sinking feeling, the sense of imminent drowning, inhabiting the discomfort, unrest, agitation, unease, restlessness (*inquiétude*), shame even. And even though all these are undoubtedly unbearable, such a thinking of failure perhaps not only cannot but also does not want to let go of failure. It sticks with, or to, this impasse without any aspiration, and one might say that this attachment to failure is a crueler optimism than Berlant's "cruel optimism," since there is no illusion or delusion of a "good life" promised by the object of attachment, no keeping faith with any "good life" despite or rather in spite of one's knowing that that promise will never be fulfilled.[104] It is a crueler optimism also because, to recall the dark side of melodrama, it holds on to existence *not* because it is hopeful of existence but is only waiting for the time when it can exit existence, when this exit opens up. And this exit will be granted not because it finally finds the resolve to let the ideation pass into an act, for this would only mean getting out of an impasse, but only because it has slid or fallen inadvertently into it, without ever knowing it. This crueler optimism is but an all-out pessimism, not unlike what Eugene Thacker has called "infinite resignation," in choosing the impasse.¹⁰⁵ I add here that this is where our present work distinctly deviates from Halberstam's project once again. So, even though this present work shares with Halberstam the appreciation and the commitment to elucidate (without judgment) failure's "awkwardness, clumsiness, disorientation, bewilderment, ignorance, disappointment, disenchantment, silence, disloyalty, and immobility," we will *not* be optimistic enough to "revel in and cleave to all of our own inevitable fantastic failures," not to mention that we consider our failures here to be not at all fantastic but common or banal.¹⁰⁶

What remains for a true thinking of failure is to learn to respect the very impasse that constitutes the affective structure of failure. Put simply, it is all about learning to accept failure, to let it sink in fully (in us). Then we will begin to truly listen to all the cries of thought in its tarrying with failure, in its endurance of failure: the sobs of disappointment, the cries of help (without actually wanting any real help), the declarations to quit, the depressive discourses, the words of despair, the sighs of pessimism, the moans and whines of regrets, and the silent resignation to give up everything, including existence.¹⁰⁷ Every cry deserves to be heard, all of thought's no less. And as Werner Hamacher has taught us, language has that capacity to register and transmit both pains and the cries of pains.¹⁰⁸ Contemporary literary writings, as suggested and as will be shown, are already doing this. For the language of thought—under the names of philosophy, theory, "autotheory," critique, "postcritique," etcetera—to not lag too far behind in responding to the "structures of feeling" of our times, it must let resound all those cries of pains from the anguish of failure, from the sickness of depression while experiencing failure, from the weariness in enduring failure or being beaten down by failure, from the fatigue in trying to overcome failure, from burning out in enduring or in endeavoring to surpass failure. To reiterate, this is thought laid bare, exposed in probably its most intimate vulnerability. Yet this would be, to borrow Heidegger's term, the unconcealment of thought in its honest or truthful response to the undeniable affects of failure (and to be sure, again, there will be no illumination in this unconcealment but the exposure to the dark abyss that is the irreducible structure of failure in existence).¹⁰⁹ And to extend the Heideggerian vocabulary here, we could say that failure asks of us an attunement (*Gestimmtsein*) to it, an attunement to an ineluctable aspect of existence, one from which we have however always tried to extricate ourselves. Failure does not call for its *fine*-tuning, which will only modulate it into something else, its opposite, at worst. We definitely should not tune *out* (of) failure either. In our attunement, we should be *in* tune with it, once again with all its affects, pains, cries, genres, dramas, and melodramas, and this is where we are exposed to the fuller dimension of the mood (*Stimmung*) of being. And while Heidegger reminds us that being is not all existence but also involves the exiting from existence, or, as Halberstam so deftly puts it, "To live is to fail, to bungle, to disappoint, and ultimately to die."[110] I would like to highlight that there is no less a mood to this exit, albeit a darker mood than Halberstam would want it.

To be sure one final time, all this is not about coming to terms with failure in the sense of recognizing it only in order to rid or relieve oneself of it, to get over it, to be free of it. In a sense, one never gets over it, or one can never come to terms with it, because one can never really be at ease with it even though one now stays with it, tarries with it. There is always a lingering dread.[111] This is not talk therapy or talking cure for thought, as if one would be on the road to some form of recovery thereafter. If thought should rest with failure here, this rest is no convalescence; there is no "better" to aspire to. Neither is this a session in psychoanalysis nor an exercise in symptomatic reading, as if to uncover some unconscious element, which once unraveled will trouble us no more.[112] Perhaps there is only, at best, "descriptive reading" that draws out the relations between thought and failure.[113] At the end of it all, one might also wonder what the point is with such a thinking of failure. I have said earlier in this introduction that a thinking of *failure as failure* is necessary if we want to avoid any superficial understanding of the topic at hand in any form of failure studies. I have also suggested that it could provide us with a heuristics into the aforementioned works of contemporary literature, appreciating the genres that are flailing there to be those with respect with failure and not distort them by rendering them to serve other ends. I have also claimed that such a thinking of failure, which also attends to all the affects that failure could bring, can be critical in terms of according a discursive and affective space to those whose sense of existence is ineluctably tied to failure, where they can have the freedom to articulate and languish in their sense of failure. To repeat what had been said earlier: if there is one failure that we should avoid, it is perhaps that which makes them feel to have no legitimate space to express their sense of failure except in a suicide note. In whichever case above, we are no doubt endeavoring to answer the questions that are typically posed to the act of thinking: What are the stakes of such a thinking? To what ends would such a thinking serve? Yet perhaps these are the wrong questions with regard to the thinking of failure because they imply the refusal, once again, to let failure be: they betray the anxiety to turn failure into something else again, the will to make thinking failure a productive activity and/or with a positive outcome. These questions constitute, then, another letdown, if not a failure, in the thinking of failure, the failure of thought to follow through with failure. Perhaps we do not need to feel so apologetic, therefore, and just say that there is no point to the thinking of failure. It is wasted time, implicating wasted lives, but only so in the perspective of the progress narrative of neoliberal capitalism, and not so for any honest elucidation of the sense of existence that does not bracket the ontological and existential structure of failure. Or else this is failure "study"—"study" in the singular as Harney and Moten would want it, which is to say, an incomplete or incompletable thinking with "no end and no connection to improvement, never mind efficiency," and which does not constitute any point on, or to, the flow of the knowledge economy's principles or dictates of instrumentality, achievement, excellence, and accreditation, but always an "(in)permanently unformed, insistently informal, underperforming commitment" to failed existence.[114]

Drifting With/in Failure's Shared Unshareability: The Chapters

Throughout this book, then, we will not be seeking any effective or productive use of failure. We will simply keep in mind failure as the affective structure of existence, staying with its negativity, irreparability, inconsolability, and intransitivity. We will be looking at selected works of Moshfegh, Cusk, Levé, Li, and Zambreno that largely keep to failure's impasse rather than try to get out of it, involving at times wasted lives, no less. This is not to mention the largely "autofictional" dimension of most of these texts, which stresses the urgency for us to attend to the personal sense of failure. And we will look at genres there—especially nonclassical ones—that tend *not* to contest or push back against failure; genres that seek, instead, to incorporate, embody, or assume the sense of failure. Some of these gestures can be unwilled, flailing without intention: mere bodily responses or reflexes that are dragging along the rest of one's self—call it mind, spirit, or soul—that equally has no interest in escaping the negativity of failure. To reiterate, these genres might, on the one hand, help one cope with existence after the reckoning with a sense of failure that never goes away. On the other hand, they do *not* help make life better.[115] Like the impasse discussed previously, these genres, in short, bear no "cruel optimism." Ultimately, they are but the minimal gestures that remain for the individual in their living on after failure, as the individual inhabits the negative affects of failure, tarrying with the sense of failure. They keep the individual drifting along a stranded existence that follows wherever failure takes it. Let it be said here that there is no hoping or expecting that this drifting will arrive at any safe, stable, comforting ground. It is a drifting by which one knows one can sink anytime. Sinking might even be the more apt movement that corresponds to failure's falling and staying down. Yet, given that many of the principal characters or narrators in our literary texts do not sink, we will keep to the image of drifting, albeit, to be sure again, *not* a drifting whereby one stays above failure but a drifting in which one is very much immersed or awash with failure.

The genres that we will be examining across the chapters are: (1) flopping, (2) drifting itself, (3) a dark care of the self, (4) melodrama, and (5) *postscripting*. In a way, one could read the movement of chapters as the stages of reckoning with failure, of what one feels or does as the sense of failure irremediably sinks in. Put another way, it could be read as that which charts the sense of descent or degeneration in the wake of failure, as one finds one's existence henceforth hopelessly entangled with the sense of failure. In this regard, and perhaps true to the thinking of failure called for in this book, the chapters laid out as such are meant to resist any ascending narrative arc, to refuse suggesting any narrative of progress. Again, if anything, the narrative flow, if there is one, at best echoes the notion of falling that we have claimed to be "proper" to failure. (The citational marks are there because there is nothing proper to failure; failure is without propriety, property, properness.) To be sure, though, we will not to be merely listing or describing the stages of falling. In explicating the genres in question, the chapters also demonstrate how this exposes the fact that some genres of failure can be granted full or fuller expression only on conditions of class and race, or else that they are driven by practices predicated on assumptions of unequal gender privilege or dynamics.[116] This is especially the case of the first two chapters. In the following chapter, then, we will look at the genre of flopping in Moshfegh's *My Year of Rest and Relaxation*. Flopping implicates falling, the movement, to repeat, that corresponds to failure. Flopping also involves staying down, which, as seen, too, constitutes the very experience of (staying with) failure. The narrator in Moshfegh's text is determined to do just that, to stay down, and perchance to sleep, to take a break from the world, to allow herself to wallow in her sense of failure. For all this, she is willing to lay waste to everything around her: her well-being, her career, her relation with her best (and only) friend. She languishes in a mode of existing that gives in to breakdowns, or to use the terms invoked earlier, to *désœuvrement* or *inoperativity* or *unworking*. As she acknowledges, such breaks, however, are afforded to her only because of her white upper-middle-class privileged position while the Egyptian migrants must work the graveyard shifts at the bodega that she visits in her drugged-out/somnambulistic state; while the Asian "artist" Ping Xi who, in order to gain recognition and success in the art world, must produce ridiculously provocative pieces while repressing the sad affects surrounding the seemingly broken relationship between him and his mother. Staying with the genre of flopping thus allows us to further pursue the questions about race and class in relation to failure: Who is allowed to fail? Who gets to wallow in failure, to ride out the entire sense of failure? Who can afford the breaks in all senses—the physical and mental breakdowns, the break from work, the break from the world—that failure brings with it? Perhaps without surprise, we will see that the access to the sense of failure, to the freedom to flop and languish, is not equal to all, even though, as said before, failure can be common to everyone. As the chapter will recognize, too, this is not only because of failures in places or cultures of work such as their systemic racial inequity but also of a personal failure to think about work otherwise.

The chapter after turns to Cusk's *Outline* trilogy, which consists of the novels *Outline*, *Transit*, and *Kudos*. The genre that interests us here is precisely that of drifting, which the narrator does in all three novels, but particularly so in the first, and that is why we will be focusing on *Outline* more than the other two novels of the trilogy. In general, drifting can be said to be the mode of being in the wake of failure, arguably after falling or flopping; it is existing in a state of lostness as one finds oneself in a world that is no longer the same, as one sees the world differently. Regardless of this drifting arriving at an intended destination or not, which in turn depends on whether the drifting in question has an aim or not, drifting here is, to reiterate, where existence is paradoxically buoyed, kept afloat while being awash by the negative affects of failure. In Cusk's novels, drifting is very much aimless, without a real point of arrival in mind or view.[117] It comes to the narrator in the aftermath of her divorce, unmooring her from what she had believed to be meaningful or purposeful existence. In drifting, she inhabits the negative affects of this relationship or familial failure, occupying space after space wherein each space is already imprinted with the lingering dread of finding oneself still living on when everything seems meaningless. Through her drifting, she comes to further recognize her unbelonging in the world; her almost timeless peregrination only affirming her sense of failed existence as being out-of-sync with the rest of the ordinary world, where nothing changes, where the drudgery of everyday work—be it renovation works for a house, a hairdresser's work, or the work of narcissistic peripatetic writers—goes on as usual. At the same time, her drifting also exposes a world that is thoroughly egotistical, which is to say, a world always anxious to proclaim its successes only to conceal its inherent sense of insecurity, denying its own failures, and barely lending any sympathetic ear to the stories of failure of others. Her drifting is not exactly smooth sailing, therefore, and this drifting will be seen as complicated, if not delimited, by unequal gender power dynamics, specifically the overbearing sense of male privilege, which also drifts or drones incessantly on their own failures and successes, without a care for others. To better understand and critique such conflicting drifts, we will, in this chapter, turn to Barthes's notion of the Neutral, which has *dérive* or drift as one of its qualities, and which might even be a way to free us from a thinking of failure predicated on a positive/negative binary.

A sinking feeling becomes palpable in the next chapter. Now, if the world, as in Cusk's novels, shows no care for failed existence that is unable or refuses to extricate itself from failure and its negative affects, or if the world in general does not know how to care for failed existence that darkly desires an exit from existence, then the individual is left very much to their own devices. In a way, Michel Foucault can be said to be quite sensitive to such a precarious existence in his writings on a "care of the self," when he writes about "the plunging view" (*la vue plongeante*) that opens up at the moment when one weighs the choice of either suicide or living on in the face of existential crises. Foucault counsels looking up and away from the abyss of pessimistic negativity, turning instead to a more optimistic and positive "care of the self" that attends to one's bodily pleasures unrestricted by (heteronormative) sexual codes. Yet, as we will see in this chapter through Levé's *Suicide* (and *Autoportrait*) alongside Eve Sedgwick's *A Dialogue on Love*, one oftentimes fails (to attain) that uplifting view: one languishes at the edge of abyssal negativity; one plunges into it. As I will explicate, this is the *other* "plunging view" that belongs to Ovid's Narcissus, one that is no less a "care of the self," albeit a darker one, no doubt, which attends to the self that seeks to follow the sense of existential failure to its very end. Dark or otherwise, a "care of the self" calls for a genre too. Here, genre takes on a more traditional or conventional sense since it deals with, according to Foucault, writing, specifically one that records everyday ordinary activities, thoughts—and Foucault admits thoughts of dying here—feelings and desires, all without any claim to larger pedagogical or political ends. In this chapter, we will consider such a writing in terms of what Nancy has called "exscription." According to Nancy, exscription is a mode of writing that is reticulated with existence;

it marks the traces of the body as the body moves out of its ipseity and into the world in its everyday existing, in its everyday interaction with the world. In tandem with existence as such, we will see how exscription in Sedgwick and Levé also registers the sense of an irreparably failed existence, supplementing any record of life with the desperation to exit existence.

A dark care of the self, with or without deliberate exscription, leaves one nevertheless with a great unease. This is where the genre of melodrama begins to brew. As mentioned before, this melodrama, according to Li, is not melodrama as we know it: this melodrama refuses spectacle, drawing the melodramatic into his or her interiority where he or she dwells in the discomfit of the sense of failure. This is melodrama exercised with reserved, if not reluctant, sentimentality. It does not give in to the fantasy of a "good life"; it does not aspire to reach it; it is not even frustrated by the fact that such aspirations always end in disappointment. This is also where we reckon with what we have earlier called failure's shared unshareability, which is, to reiterate, the recognition that no matter how much of the experience of failure is shared with others through conversations or writing, something of failure will always be reserved only for ourselves, never communicated or communicable to others. In the subsequent chapter, then, which reads across Li's *Dear Friend, from My Life I Write to You, Where Reasons End*, and *Must I Go*, we will look at how those who are particularly attuned and attached to the sense of failure would want to keep failure's shared unshareability to themselves. They even take it to be their private sanctuary or bubble. They thus resist the sublimation of failure into some form of collective reparation, which is the typical move made in failure studies and/or affect theory as they impute to failure a communitarian trajectory and horizon. Trouble arises, however, when another, especially someone close or a loved one, lays claim to failure's shared unshareability, too, if not first. This is when the genre of melodrama becomes a response that attempts to come to terms with how this shared unshareability was not recognized earlier; it can even be the attempt to wrest failure's shared unshareability back for oneself. Troubled or even frustrating as this melodrama is, it only affirms failure's shared unshareability, and this is important in helping us recognize, accept, and respect the desire of those who prefer to keep the sense of failure to themselves, their wanting to dwell or wallow in it, their refusal of any communitarian project that would turn failure into a reparative object or collective pedagogy. It brings us to the acknowledgment of how inescapable the sense of personal failure is, how there can be no relief to it, how failure, at the end of it all, is just so personal.

The chapter on melodrama in Li also brings us back to the notion of genre in the classical sense. This is because we will see how the melodrama of failure's shared unshareability plays out across the novel in its conventional register (*Must I Go*), the novel in its contemporary "autofiction" mode (*Where Reasons End*), and a hybrid text that mixes dimensions of memoirs, talks, and the essay form (*Dear Friend*). No doubt, we are, through this book, working with genres in both its more contemporary sense of discursive and nondiscursive (hence bodily) gestures and its classical or formalistic sense. In so doing, we want to suggest that, with regard to failure, we cannot do without one and the other. In other words, it might be the case that the classical genre can never be adequate in registering and making sense of personal failure, requiring the supplemental gestural or corporeal genre; at the same time, though, the latter in itself is not sufficient either, needing in turn more conventional representational genres as coping mechanisms. This oscillation between the nonclassical and classical senses of genre can indeed be said to chart our trajectory in this book, as we move from discussions of Moshfegh's and Cusk's texts to those of Li's. Picking up from the chapter on Li, the conclusion will consider how failure does not escape writing. To follow Nancy's rhetoric again, failure exscribes itself, furthermore beyond the determination or mediation, filtering, or control of consciousness. In this regard, and in consideration of the different modes of writing that Li mobilizes, the composition of failure is barely composed; it is without composure. Failure can never settle with one form of writing; it is always anxiously abandoning one form for another. As if in its embarrassment, it can never find (formal) closure. We will put all this in terms of a genre of *postscripting*, which will refer not only to writings that come after the sense of failure but also posthumous writings, even though their author is not yet dead—which is to say, scribblings that struggle with the absurd fact of living on with, or after, failure, when one feels already dead. As the conclusion suggests, no one *postscripts* as well as Kate Zambreno through her works that include *Appendix Project*, *Screen Test*, and *To Write as if Already Dead*.

To return to the general trajectory of this book, it can be said otherwise too that the chapters follow closely the movement of a "structure of feeling," if we recall how the latter can find its murmurings from within the individual before it gets communicated to the outside world. The difference here is that failure does not get recognized or acknowledged by the world to be its historical consciousness; the world very much denies the sense of failure as its zeitgeist. It remains generally indifferent to an individual's sense of failure and pushes failure back to the domain of the personal. At the end of it all, there is no time and space in the world for failures—especially if they concern failure *as* failure, failure without reparation, recuperation, and restitution—no matter what Silicon Valley, motivational talks or books, T-shirts, and even failure studies say. The chapters thus confirm, once again, the personal dimension of failure, or how the sense of failure is essentially or ultimately a personal affair. They all point to the fact that only individually do we feel the full force, impact, or weight of our sense of failure; only individually do we inhabit the moods of negative affects that swarm or linger during the course, and in the remainder, of our failed existence, without any consolation.

1

FLOPPING TO SLEEP

THE FAILURES OF OTTESSA MOSHFEGH'S
MY YEAR OF REST AND RELAXATION

Let us recall from the introduction our definition of failure: failure is all about falling down *and* staying down. As said, too, this fall does not necessarily require an external push; it does not need a force—be it physical or psychological—from the outside. The force can come from within, for which there can even be no clear reason. Put otherwise, the force contributing to such a falling, which is also to say *failing*, can only be overdetermined (and this also brings us back to our thinking of the sense of failure as an affect, which shares this overdetermined nature).[1] But to stay a little more with falling through an internal force, which is arguably more complex than one resulting from an external push, we could say that this occurs when there comes the sense of failure that overwhelms existence, that becomes indistinguishable from existence, and that renders carrying on with everyday existence or life henceforth unbearable. This is when the sense of existence begins to break, break down, break apart. And failure is indeed when nothing works, when everything falls apart, when everything that should come together to make something happen, or to make things hold or stick, or to even make sense, comes undone, is torn asunder. (In addition to things breaking, or breaking down or apart, we also speak about the failure of a relationship in terms of breaking up, and this is the sense of failure that we will see in Cusk in the next chapter.) Things no longer add up. Things are not going well; they are not flowing as they should.² Things are not working; nothing is working out. As Bradatan says, "Failure is whatever we experience as a disconnection, disruption, or discomfort in the course of our patterned interaction with the world and others, when something ceases to be, or work, or happen as expected."³ Or we could also reinvoke the term from French thought previously mentioned in the introduction and add that failure is when an "unworking" befalls people or things, when everything becomes "unworked" or "inoperative," and there is nothing to be done: this is failure as *désœuvrement*.

To be precise, we are certainly not talking about break as an "evental" rupture as Alain Badiou would want it, which arrives with a forcing [*forçage*] that instantiates and founds the Subject faithful to the event, fully committed to actualizing every aspect of the event, while sovereignly disregarding any difference that deviates from the latter.⁴ Any break, or breakdown, or breaking apart associated with failure here corresponds more to what I would call the *reject*—that is, the passive nonsovereign figure, abandoned to its despair and hopelessness.⁵ Or else, any sense of rupture here resonates with Claire Marin. Marin not only associates rupture with failure but also, like us, "will resist . . . the temptation of optimism" in thinking that "a new life" or "a blank page" will unfold from rupture and/or failure.⁶ Instead, rupture, as she sees it, is more an obstacle to "sleep, eating, sleeping, [and] living"; it sees to "the disappearance of the subject, its effacement" or "its evaporation," the loss of "its thickness [*densité*]," rupture being only "vivid sensations" of "lightning bolts of suffering [*douleurs*] without respite."⁷ According to her, too, we need to reckon with such enduring pessimistic, debilitating qualities of rupture. To bring it back to our thinking of a break, I would say that, at the breakpoint, one flops. The body that is awash with the sense of failure, with the sense of failed existence, languishes, falls to the ground, and lies prone; it lies flat there, deflated, with no will, power, or ability to rise again and continue doing whatever it always or typically does; at times, it even has no wish whatsoever to live on. The spirit is broken; the muscles do not cooperate either to lift the body up or to keep it moving. It is just difficult, if not impossible, to get up. Or to borrow Anne Helen Petersen's phrase, one simply "can't even."⁸ This is where one finds oneself swamped in a sticky flood of negative affects, caught in a mix of melancholia, despair, hopelessness, mental and physical catatonia, shame, etcetera. Yet, as proposed in the introduction, this is actually where one begins to dwell with or in failure, where one is immersed in a tarrying with failure and all its negative affects. In other words, flopping is very much the genre, the bodily gesture, that announces the imminence or occurrence of total failure, which in common parlance is signified by nothing but flop.[9]

To be sure, there is barely a good feeling here. Hardly anyone would deign to stay with such a time and space of failure. More often than not, one would rather get out of it. Or else, as underscored in the introduction as well, ideologies of success that govern the social, which in the contemporary context are accompanied not only by the rhetoric of grit and resilience but also the demands for constant high levels of productivity, operativity, efficiency, and efficacy, will make experiencing or living out failure according to our definition—as falling and staying down—rather difficult. No doubt, the idea of "self-care" and/or "mental well-being" now informs the architecture or infrastructure of contemporary society, but it is quickly becoming clear to see that this is only the next global exploit of the neoliberal capitalist economy. Thus, one may be allowed to not feel up to something, to have a bad day or two, to languish a little, but social institutions and workplaces will require that one seeks help for oneself as immediately as possible—without, however, necessarily providing the individual the adequate means to do so—in order that they can quickly return to their "normal" productive or high-performing self. Otherwise, it becomes the individual's fault for falling and staying down.[10] As Jonathan Malesic has observed, "In an individualistic culture where work is a moral duty, it's up to you to ensure you're in good working order."[11] We thus see once again failure barely given due attention, barely allowed to run its course or to fully unfold in its own time or duration as well as in its complete affective dimension. This is also to say that genuine care—which takes time and requires specific attention due to each different individual—from social and work structures is seriously wanting with regard to whether the individual is able to afford those "self-care" or "mindfulness" regimes, not to mention the right or appropriate ones rather than the superficial, cosmetic packages peddled by the exploitative market.[12] There is undoubtedly a pervasive and prevalent inequity regarding who gets to fall, stay down, get proper help, rest, recuperate, rejuvenate, regroup. This inequity also includes the question of *when* one can do all that. There is no telling when a personal sense of failure hits and overwhelms the individual. In fact, there is never a good time for failure; failure is always untimely. As said in the introduction, failure is the contretemps of existence, which can indeed inconvenience both oneself and others, including the institutions within which one functions as a dutiful citizen contributing to the general political economy. And there is no guarantee, despite the self-congratulatory (or rather, defensive) claims of being mindful of individuals' "well-being," that corporations and institutions will allow their employees to wallow in their sense of failure whenever it arrives. There are many individuals who are simply not accorded such time, in addition to not being able to afford such a time to fall and stay down. And suppose one is fortunate enough to be granted, or permitted, to take some time off to languish, it will not be too long before one is chidingly reminded, as Beckett had seemingly been prescient to say in the final lines of *The Unnamable*, that one must carry on, even if one cannot.

What the above suggests is that the sense of failure can find itself entangled with work culture, and the call for a tarrying with the former thus cannot exclude a critique of the latter.[13] We will indeed pursue this thread that knots failure and work culture together in this chapter, and we will expose the difficulty of allowing genres of failure, specifically that of flopping, to flail in the face of such a culture. Now, it can be said that contemporary culture or society, in general, adopts a punitive stance toward falling and staying down, which is to say, toward flopping. This is rather evident in the domain of professional sports such as basketball.[14] In 2012, the National Basketball Association officially declared flopping a deliberate act of pretense by a player to gain an advantage. In the case of flopping here, the player would, with limbs exaggeratedly flailing, fall to the ground, making referees and spectators believe that he or she had been excessively fouled by a player or players from the other team. The purpose of such a flopping would be to create a turnover situation whereby the opposing team would lose possession of the ball, if not concede free-throw opportunities to the flopped player. The NBA has now recognized such ruses, and in addition to condemning flopping to be lacking in sportsmanship, it has also began imposing fines on players who enact such practices. The rule so far has been that the second time the player is called (out) for flopping, the player would be fined $5,000. They would then be fined $10,000 for the third and $15,000 for the fourth. On the fifth occasion, the fine would be $30,000. The financial cost of such an act is, of course, relative to each player's income, and one could imagine more highly paid players having no qualms in repeatedly flopping. Nevertheless, one could also perhaps consider flopping here to be some form of "unproductive expenditure," which, according to Georges Bataille, involves an extravagant dispensing with one's possessions, without any care or calculation if one might receive any returns from such an expenditure,[15] or if one might even be able to sustain oneself in the wake of such a laying waste to everything one owns. The flop becomes an "unproductive expenditure" when, caught by the referee, it earns the flopping player and his or her team no effective advantage except a bad name. "Unproductive expenditure" or not, such calculated, dishonest, and disdainful flops certainly warrant criticism or even condemnation.

I would like to consider, however, flops that are actually void of such ruses, that is to say, those that are more genuine where the player, no matter if they are in a position of winning or otherwise, loses their will to go on, where their muscles give in or give way, where one finds themselves somehow gassed out (without having actually expended much physical energy), or more accurately deflated, losing all of their grit and tenacity, and sinks to the ground, giving up, and losing the game. I would say that this is the more veritable "unproductive expenditure" since there is no strategic gain whatsoever here. There is nothing left to play. The game is simply thrown away, forfeited by the flopped player. In this scenario, there is no doubt that the player feels the world both within and without crumbling or crashing down. There remains only an overwhelming sense of failure that floods over the player, making it almost impossible to pick themselves up from the ground. This flop does not have to happen mid-game; it can even occur before the game begins. In this regard, one could think of the four-time Olympic gold medal gymnast Simone Biles withdrawing from the 2021 Tokyo Olympics, although already having qualified for the finals and expected to win gold again for at least three of the four events; or the tennis player Naomi Osaka, a four-time Grand Slam singles champion, suddenly pulling out of the 2021 French Open during a media event.[16] I would like to think that this more genuine flopping occurs not only in sports but also in life. It can hit one at the onset of depression or burnout, almost similar to the cases of Biles and Osaka where mental health issues and past traumatic events have been cited as causes for their pulling out. Or it can befall existence without much reason either, arriving at some unanticipated instance, without, again, any determinable or identifiable cause.

In any case, flopping, to repeat, is oftentimes met with suppression or repression by social structures. Yet this is also why it is critically urgent that we give expression to it, especially if we recognize it to be a genre trying to tell us something about failing, about the sense of failure, or as a gesture or bodily response signaling us to something about the confluence of internal and external forces accounting for the affective structure of failure. As I would put it, flopping is a crying out on the part of a form of existence. This cry would not be so different from that of Mrs. Rooney in Beckett's *All That Fall*: "How can I go on, I cannot. Oh let me just flop down flat on the road like a big fat jelly out of a bowl and never move again!"[17] But *form* is perhaps not the right term here, since existence in this instance embodies rather a sense of its own deforming, deformation, or dissolution. We will return to the question of form, so let us just say here that it is precisely because this form of existing is failing or extinguishing that attending to this crying out is even more necessary, deserving of our recognition and not its delegitimization. We will argue in this chapter that flopping tells us how one recalibrates *or not* one's existence; it makes us take into account why and how existence has come to be so, which is to say, it can also expose the failings that are happening around it, making us reckon with them. We will explicate this genre alongside a reading of Ottessa Moshfegh's *My Year of Rest and Relaxation*.

The backdrop to the narrative is the 9/11 attacks of the Twin Towers in New York City, which we have intimated in the introduction to be one of the major "eventful" failures that marked the beginning of the twenty-first century, arguably a response to problematic American foreign policies and a result of internal security lapses. The (hyper)mediatization of the attacks has also predicated itself on the dissemination of the *"falling* man" image, which finds its re-presentation at the end of Moshfegh's novel. But 9/11 is only hinted at in the beginning and finds its brief exposition at the end of the narrative. It is not the story. *My Year of Rest and Relaxation* is not a 9/11 novel. What the novel does, then, is to point to less than "eventful" failures: failures not on a major (geo)political scale. Certainly, 9/11 is a national tragedy, and the political failures that presupposed and followed it need to be understood and addressed, but the novel reminds us that there are also other crises that should not be neglected, even though these crises or failures might pertain to the personal and seem so ordinary, pedestrian, or even banal. Put another way, the novel points to another form of falling, one that is not so horrifically tragic but nevertheless a falling over which one has little or no control, a falling that also critically exposes all the fault lines surrounding it, highlighting how precarious things stand around it, how they might be crumbling and falling too.[18]

Failure Befalls Everyone

If Moshfegh's *My Year of Rest and Relaxation* is to stand as a critical text for the understanding of failure, it is because it underscores how the sense of failure can befall anyone. In other words, it affirms the claim of failure as an affective structure of existence—that is, one that touches everyone, leaving none unscathed by it. Failure hits all of us, no matter our class, race, or gender. Thus, we have in Moshfegh's novel a narrator and main protagonist who is very conscious and unabashed about her white, privileged, upper-middle class status. She has everything going for her: good looks, the opportunity to have attended Columbia University without needing to accrue student debt, an apartment in New York City's Upper East Side that has been fully paid for, inherited wealth, rent to collect from her dead parents' house, returns from investments, etcetera. She "wasn't worried about money," as she says at the outset, which also means that she does not really need to work.[19] And when she does, for example, during her stint as a "gallery girl" at the art gallery Ducat, it is definitely not out of necessity. She did it to convince herself that "employment would add value to [her] life" but quickly realized that such a thinking is only the false ideology of neoliberal capitalism, since it was almost always "unnecessary labor" that she was performing, not to mention the other quick realization that she was mere "fashion candy" or "hip decor" for the gallery space.[20] For almost a year, then, she skives, messes up, sleeps on the job without a care whatsoever. Meanwhile, she can still afford all the designer fashion, which only generates envy in her best and only friend Reva. Her jealousy notwithstanding, Reva adores the narrator. The narrator, however, condescends to Reva's trying too hard to fit into the trendy New York City crowd albeit with imitation fashion; she discounts the adult Reva to be an extension of the high-school Reva—that is, "a reject" and "an outcast, a fuckup."[21] Put simply, she sees Reva's life as nothing more than a failed existence.[22] And yet, we find this unnamed narrator overwhelmed nevertheless with a sense of existential failure, which we actually do not find in Reva. Something about existing is just not working for her. In her words, existence for her is only "pretending to live a life."[23] Otherwise, existence is living out a sense of dread, an existence "plagued with misery, anxiety, a wish to escape the prison of [her] mind and body" and with "miserable" sleep patterns that make her feel worse than being an insomniac.[24] Life is clearly breaking down for her: she senses herself "crumbl[ing] into [an] ineffectual slob," if not flopping, to put it in this chapter's terms. This is not to mention the many times when she "feel[s] dead."[25] And if we keep in mind that existence is always coexistence, as Nancy would remind us, the dread of her "solipsistic terror" would drive her to seek detachment from others, desperate for "something that'll put a damper on [her] need for company," hence looking toward the undoing of what in Berlant's understanding would be the communitarian infrastructure that, despite the "inconvenience of other people," would sustain life and make living in the present, no matter how dreadful, bearable.[26] There is nothing she wants to do except to fall into a real deep sleep, which she believes can be the cure for that dread. And as long as she cannot achieve such a sleep, there is only "the failed, stupid life" that the narrator—whom shall we also call *unnamable*?—has to live or bear with.[27]

To make matters worse, she cannot explain (away) that dread. She doubts it is her occasional obsession with her ex-boyfriend Trevor, with whom she had only "many failed romantic reunions" but who has since left her definitively for someone else.[28] She suspects it might have something to do with her fraught relation with her now-dead mother,[29] as if there is some unfinished work of mourning on her part, some remaining working through to be accomplished of either "the pain of having lost [her] parents" or the denied love and intimacy by her mother.[30] At this point, with respect to her semi-obsessive desire for Trevor and the memories of her mother's cold and distant treatment that haunt her present, the narrative no doubt invites a psychoanalytic reading.[31] But my sense is that the narrative at the same time demands more than the latter, since there are moments when the narrator would recognize that the lingering dread in her sense of existence is reducible neither to her sexual obsession nor the drama of her family history. In fact, as she would declare early on, she "can't point to any one event" that is constitutive of her dread and "that resulted in [her] decision to go into hibernation."[32] Or else, at Reva's mother's funeral, she would think of her parents but "felt nothing"; she goes on to say, "I could *think* of feelings, emotions, but I couldn't bring them up in me."[33] This is also not to forget that the narrator games her psychotherapy sessions. When asked by her "irresponsible and weird"[34] therapist Dr. Tuttle to keep a "night vision log" of her dreams to keep track of the efficacy of the medication, the narrator compromises the exercise as she gradually "copied the dreams over in crazier-looking handwriting..., adding terrifying details"[35] only in order to get Dr. Tuttle to prescribe her even more sedative drugs.[36] Given this, one could suspect that the narrative might just be setting a trap for psychoanalytic readings too, sending such readings on a wild goose chase. In any case, heeding the earlier point about the impossibility to definitively pin the cause of dread to a singular event, I would say that the narrative brings us back to a thinking of affects, which, to repeat, can only be overdetermined. This would suggest, then, that attending to her affective state and the genre that is flailing in response to that might provide us with a more nuanced reading, and this is what I will try to do in the following.

Let us go back to her sense of lingering dread. Paradoxically, she has difficulty translating this into a corresponding emotion. The best she can describe it is "whatever it was I was feeling."[37] Or else, that dread oftentimes leaves her unfeeling, if not generally with a flat affect, as Dr. Tuttle would call it. Otherwise, we could also say that she is largely disaffected (though I am using this term in a sense very much other than Xine Yao would want it—we will come back to this). She "feel[s] nothing" most of the time, acknowledging herself to come across as a "cold bitch" or an "ice queen," for which Trevor would find her "frigid."[38] Or else, slightly better than "whatever," she feels irritation, which counts as one in the taxonomy of what Sianne Ngai calls "ugly feelings." According to the narrator: "Irritation was what I knew best—a heaviness on my chest, a vibration in my neck like my head was revving up before it would rocket off my body."[39] This irritation, when projected outward to the world, is what accounts for her aversion for companionship, her desire to destroy all communitarian infrastructures. When singularly and more cruelly directed toward Reva, it can degenerate into yet another of Ngai's "ugly feelings": disgust. As if the narrator were not already harsh in having no sympathy or empathy for Reva's grief—she feels "no sorrow" at the funeral of Reva's mother—she would say, seeing Reva cry at the thought of her mother, "I was intensely bored of Reva already," and then, "I was . . . sitting there full of disgust."[40] To follow more strictly Ngai's terminology, the narrator's treatment of Reva aligns rather with what Ngai understands as contempt, whose object is "too weak or insignificant to pose any sort of danger" or "perceived as inferior in a manner that allows it to be dismissed or ignored";[41] it is less than disgust in Ngai's understanding because disgust would involve the expulsion or even annihilation of its object, which the narrator never really does to Reva, no matter how tempted she is to do so oftentimes. But let us stay with irritation. According to Ngai, irritation is "the index of a more general affective opacity," or else "a mood, distinct from emotion in that it lacks an explicit occasion or object."[42] Irritation thus affirms our suspicion that the narrator's sense of existential failure can only be overdetermined, that we can never point to a single or definite source. Irritation, according to Ngai furthermore, can also be the discomfiting brushing-up of what lies "under one's skin" against external forces.[43] Considered in this light, we can also understand, in Berlant's terms this time, how, for the narrator, people in general are just as inconvenient as she is inconvenient to herself.

Flopping to Sleep

With no way to locate whither her sense of failure, the narrator is stuck with irritation. And as her irritation oscillates between disaffectedness and disgust, she is left with the sense of dread of having fallen into "whatever existential wormhole."[44] As mentioned earlier, the narrator believes that for her irritation to go away, for her sense of dread to dissipate, the solution is to fall into a real deep sleep, the "good strong American sleep," as she calls it.[45] As I would read it, this is the beginning of flopping: the desire to let the body fall to wherever the body can be in a state of repose—on the bed, the couch, or even the ground—to let the body lapse into inaction except to rest; to let the body just languish without needing to will it to do anything, without having it, in fact, to respond to anything.[46] Flopping is the genre that is flailing in order to cope with her sense of failure, if not to respond to the latter by precisely seeing to the shutting down of the body, to render it inoperative or unworking, to grant herself "solitude and purposelessness," which is also nothing more than being "the bum that [she] *felt* [she] was and should have been."[47] In other words, flopping does not recalibrate ways of living to make life better; it is not seeking to make one's life more productive or fulfilling. It does not seek to do more in life but *less*, including giving up on any infrastructural building with others, which could make life more bearable or develop collective reparative pedagogies in response to a negative phenomenon, such as the sense of existential failure found in the narrator.

Before going on, I do note here that the *Oxford English Dictionary* lists one of the meanings of *flop* to be sleeping.[48] However, I do want to insist on a very subtle distinction between flopping and sleeping in Moshfegh's novel: there is flopping, then there is sleeping. The narrator flops to sleep. In my view, her sense of irritation that discomfits her in the world or through which she finds the world inconvenient, and her sense of purposelessness, of not knowing what to do but to mess up the job that she was doing, to then give it up and not do anything else, constitute the flailing genre that is flopping. Consequently, and in contradistinction to flopping, sleep is what the narrator seeks to quell that flailing genre. As I would put it, too, the narrator attempts to give *form* to the genre of flopping through sleeping. Hence begins the narrator's quest for such a sleep, which is none other than the eponymous project of a year's rest and relaxation. Yet, as the narrator discovers along the way, the giving of such a form to this genre of flopping is not as easy as it seems. Thus, even though at the beginning she may be "sleeping upwards of twelve hours" (23), this becomes insufficient as she feels the need for medical supplements from Dr. Tuttle so that she could go even further to "sleep all day."[49] And when she sleeps on her job, which she willfully and gleefully does, one is never sure if these sleeps offer her any real ease, or if they are truly "peaceful," since she would describe in rather negative terms not only her sleep state as "blank emptiness, an infinite space of nothingness" (39) but also her sleep space—the supply closet—as an "infinite abyss."[50] Yet *emptiness, nothingness,* and *abyss* are but terms that one would typically associate with a depressive feeling, or else a sense of negativity, which, as we have taken care to state in the introduction, is irreducible to any binary logic that bears the positive as its polemical opposite, hence without any comparison to anything considered to be positive.

It remains questionable, therefore, after being fired from her job and "hitting the pills hard and sleeping all day and all night with two- or three- hour breaks in between," if "something," or anything at all, "was getting sorted out."[51] This suspicion is confirmed when, a few months later, she realizes that a "carefree tranquility of sleep" has been, or can only be, quite the delusion. While she thought that "sleeping full time" after leaving her job was freeing her from the attachments to the world or life in general, she will shockingly learn that her online communications actually exponentially increased during her "medicated blackouts," including the unconscious and quite the unproductive expenditures on lingerie, designer jeans, "a dozen unopened boxes of Chinese takeout," and items from the bodega that she visits during her drugged-out somnambulic states.[52] Sleeping then becomes distressing, becoming quite the burden to the narrator. She would say, as if heralding Jonathan Crary's fear of the surveillance of, and hence intrusion upon, the private domain of one's sleep by the capitalist machinery that never sleeps, "My stress levels rose. I couldn't trust myself. I felt as though I had to sleep with one eye open."[53] With material desires still working, this clearly cannot be sleep, especially if we keep in mind Lacan's reminder of Freud's observation that "the only fundamental desire in sleep is the desire to sleep."[54] It is no surprise, then, that the narrator's endeavors to sleep begin to fail. Flail to flop again, therefore. Yet, more drugs, watching pornography on the TV, and watching reruns of films (especially those featuring Whoopi Goldberg) barely help. When the VCR broke, she would declare, "Nothing was working."[55] Flopping then takes a darker turn, as she entertains the thought of death as a way toward sleep. Riffing on a Hamletian motif, she would wonder: "What if the only way to sleep is death?"[56] Or, in a more desperate register, she would say, "I might jump out the window ... if I couldn't sleep."[57] To die: perchance to sleep.

At this point, let us recall our earlier suggestion that sleep might be the form that the narrator is seeking to give to the genre of flopping. Given how sleep essentially fails the narrator up to this point, we might say that sleep as a form is bound to fail. This is because as long as the genre of flopping is still flailing, it can never settle into a form, if we understand form as something rather fixed or stable. Put another way, genres as genres—that is, as flailing—resist assuming a form. The moment they settle on a form, they are no longer flailing (explicitly, at least). Here, one could also venture to say that form is perhaps more the prerogative of aesthetics. It is the aesthetic mind that knows how to give shape to a novel, a poem, a painting, a sculpture, a film, etcetera; it judges and decides which forms these genres (in the classical sense) should take.[58] Perhaps this is why (the form of) sleep becomes more successful under the curation of the supposed artist Ping Xi. Yet, perhaps because Ping Xi is not a true artist—the narrator sees (through) him as "an opportunist and a stylist, a producer of entertainment more than an artist," or in short, "an art-world hack"[59]—that a pharmaceutical supplement is still necessary, which now comes in the form of Infermiterol, once again prescribed by Dr. Tuttle, and which the latter promises to be more potent than all the previous drugs given. It is thus through this curated "Infermiterol blackout" (from which she will regain consciousness every three days) over several months that she will finally seemingly flop, finding herself "falling," just falling (as failing does or is), where, as she says: "There was no need for reassurance or directionality because I was nowhere, doing nothing. I was nothing."[60]

The Failures of Flopping and Sleeping in the World of Endless Work

But to what extent does the narrator stay true to flopping as a genre of failure? Does she give herself fully to this genre? Does she follow its flailing to its ends, which, as suggested, might not actually be sleep? To be sure, even though the narrator finally assumes the space, duration, and mode of existence that is of nothingness, of being without a place (perhaps in a way not too foreign to Deleuze's occupant in search of a place of their own, as mentioned in the introduction), we should state that there is actually no wish on the narrator's part to stay in the impasse of failure, to stay with the negative affects that accompany the sense of failure. Right from the start, she seeks recuperative, if not reparative, ends through her project of falling into deep sleep. She is hopeful that she will emerge "a whole new person," that her past will never haunt her again and thence "start over without regrets, bolstered by the bliss and serenity that [she] would have accumulated in [her] year of rest and relaxation," or else "become immune to painful memories."[61] She is furthermore optimistic that it is not just herself who will be positively transformed upon waking from her sleep/hibernation project but also "everything—the whole world—would be new again."[62]

In a way, her initial visions of herself and the world after her project do bear positive tinges. As she says, "My sleep had worked. I was soft and calm and felt things. This was good. This was my life now."[63] She no longer feels stuck with either dread or any lingering emotions about her fraught relation with her parents. She "could move on" now and sell her parents' house, which she previously felt unable to because the house was "proof that [she] had not always been completely alone in the world."[64] And when she collapses—undoubtedly because of some form of muscle atrophy developed while confined to her "sleeping prison"[65]—just outside her building the first day after her sleep/hibernation project, she experiences the doorman and other people rushing to help her, something which, upon reflection later at the garden, would lead her to say: "There was kindness. Pain is not the only touchstone for growth."[66] Looking at the flora in the garden, she would also say, "Things were alive. Life buzzed between each shade of green."[67] One would no doubt be tempted to say that she now occupies the reparative "depressive position," according to Melanie Klein, where there is the attempt to reconnect with the surrounding world, against which, in a prior "paranoid position," one would push back and hence symbolically tear apart. This new desire to reconcile with the surrounding world, to rebuild past broken relations, to be hopeful and optimistic about the future, and to approach the world and the future with love rather than paranoid suspicion, will manifest in the narrator's refurnishing of her apartment with products from the Goodwill store, such as used furniture that bear the traces of others in the world. And instead of always trying to get rid of Reva, she now "didn't want her to leave";[68] she would even say to Reva, as never before, and with effusive italics that Reva would use for the narrator, "I *love* you."[69]

And yet, with 9/11 as the backdrop, with it imminently looming over the narrative, the novel sets us up to paranoidly expect no real surprises: it leads us to anticipate that the positive or optimistic horizon will be curtailed, that her recuperation or reparation would be short-circuited, that things will fail. Indeed, the tragedy of 9/11 strikes, and it does so swiftly and briskly in the novel—in just under one page in a short paragraph. As the historical event, 9/11 would only usher in a world of worse political depression, since global counterterrorism measures—undertaken under the rubric of the "war on terror" and framed by intensified surveillance technologies and biometric captures of people's lives—far from deterring global terrorism, have instead seen to cities such as Bali, Munich, London, Manchester, Paris, and Nice becoming testaments to the tragic cost of civilian lives under such policies. Worse for the narrator, she will lose Reva to 9/11, as Reva was working in one of the Twin Towers when one of the planes hit. Yet, even before the tragedy of 9/11 in the novel, there are already hints of a world that has not changed, that the world is still failing in significant ways. We go back to one of the first moments when the narrator emerges from the sleep/hibernation project. It concerns her visit to the Met. Like any other visitor to the museum, she is prohibited from touching any of the artworks there. Yet, despite warnings from security personnel, she leans in—it is unsure if it was an involuntary movement that might again be a lingering effect of muscle atrophy or an attempt by the narrator to test social and/or institutional limits—to one of the paintings and touches it. Nothing much happens to her, though. She is not handed any disciplinary measure but is simply left free to go. Nevertheless, I suspect that underlying the narrative is an implicit indictment of systemic racism: the text seems to be hinting that it is white privilege that enables the narrator to walk free with impunity after such an act. White privilege (which comes with the ability or even entitlement to elicit sympathy) is also probably the reason why, when the narrator collapses at her apartment entrance, people and the doorman rushed to help.

To be sure, the narrator herself is not without racist tendencies. Her disdain for the Egyptian migrants at the bodega is rather palpable, and she regards Ping Xi through a racist lens as well.[70] Essentially, she puts a wall between herself and racial others, refusing any real connection with them.[71] Thus, without really knowing Ping Xi, she would say, "Ping Xi disgusted me—I didn't respect him or his art, I didn't want to know him, I didn't want him to know me."[72] Or else, in her relation with racial others, which is again more of contempt—which, to recall Ngai's argument, does not deign the other to be a living force that could significantly affect oneself—than disgust— which anxiously and paranoidly sees the other to be a potential threat and hence an entity to be obliterated—the relation is predicated on nothing more than racial capitalism. She needs the Egyptian migrants to keep the bodega open so that she can get her "working class coffee" anytime of the day or night during her somnambulic states.[73] She also needs Ping Xi so that her sleep/hibernation project can materialize. Even then, she would still insist on a superior opacity on her side. Therefore, even though she and Ping Xi have now entered into an aesthetic contract, she would still derogatorily say of Ping Xi, he "couldn't understand me. He wasn't supposed to."[74] This is not to mention her strict condition for Ping Xi to not leave any trace of his presence in her apartment during the execution of the project, which reiterates the sovereign distance that she insists on between herself and racial others.

Of course, Ping Xi capitalizes no less on the narrator's state of existential failure, her flopping to sleep. It is all part of his general plan to "shock people" with his controversial aesthetic practices, to get people "to love and despise him for it," all of which renders him "successful."[75] But the final "artwork" nevertheless involves some form of racial compromise. It consists of a series of videos of the narrator in her "Infermiterol blackout" states, though still seemingly able "to narrate some personal stories."[76] Ping Xi dubs her voice over, however, with his mother's voice messages in Cantonese. No doubt, there is a devoicing of the Caucasian female subject, but there is also the disembodiment of the Asian female mother figure. Given also that Ping Xi does not provide any translation in closed captions of his mother's voice messages, this voice and its accompanying messages are undoubtedly going to be left taken largely as meaningless, nonsense, noise, or cacophony by the generally white artworld market to which Ping Xi panders, which is either mostly monolingual or more familiar with European (Romance) languages.

Racially problematic certainly too is the narrator's dependence on video footages of Whoopi Goldberg to help her sleep. As she flops and tries to sleep, it is indeed to playbacks of films featuring the Black actress that the narrator turns. For the narrator, watching Whoopi Goldberg seems to reaffirm her sense of the world as a farce: her appearances only mark or expose how it is essentially a failed world that we all inhabit. As the narrator says of the actress, "Wherever she went, everything around her become a parody of itself, gauche and ridiculous."[77] It is probably as such that the narrator calls her "my hero," since the latter is able to unveil the essential absurdity of the world.[78] Otherwise, it is because there are times when the reruns do help her fall asleep. So, when she has problems sleeping, she will make the following invocation: "Whoopi, can you help?"[79] The problem here, as I see it, is the narrator's reduction of the racial other to a repetitive image, repeatable under the narrator's control through the VCR remote. There is furthermore the bracketing, not unlike the distancing she establishes between herself and Ping Xi or the Egyptian migrants, of any regard for the full corporeal dimension of the actress' real life outside or beyond not just those repeated and largely decontextualized images but also the roles that the actress is playing in them. Here, we do not forget Walter Benjamin's thesis of how a reproduced and reproducible image essentially brings about the erasure of the "aura" of the object(s) in the image, which is the object's "authenticity" or unique immersion in the "here and now" of a specific time and place; its connections with its milieu there and then; its situatedness among the affects that are traversing between itself and that milieu, some of which might demand (unreproducible) improvisations on the object's part; its material mutability across time; the marks of ownership or proprietorship behind the production of the scene in which the object finds itself. As Benjamin notes too of the relation between the spectator and the reproducible film image, it is one where the former stands "without experiencing any personal contact with the actor. The audience's empathy with the actor is really an empathy with the camera. Consequently, the audience takes the position of the camera; its approach is that of testing."[80] The human affective dimensions of the actor are erased in the reproducible image, the latter flattening the former into another reproducible general "sameness."[81] The human in such an image thus loses, as Nancy would say, its mysterious singularity that can be found in every one of us. Additionally, and more specifically to the reproducible image of Whoopi Goldberg, the racial human other in such an image finds the disregard, dilution, dissolution, or denial of their rightful prerogative, as Édouard Glissant would want it, to flaunt, augment, and preserve their opacity.

I add here that the narrator in fact repeats this tendency to flatten out people around her into images of mechanical reproducibility with Reva too, even though she is not an unknown, racial other. Thus, when 9/11 hit, the narrator buys a new TV with a VCR to record the news coverages of the attacks on the towers. But what precisely keeps her in "awe" and makes her replay the tape is the image of the woman falling from one of the towers.[82] For the narrator, the woman "looks like Reva, and [she] thinks it's her, almost exactly her."[83] The narrator keeps watching also because she finds the falling woman "beautiful," because the latter represents for the narrator "a human being, diving into the unknown ... wide awake."[84] There are no doubt hints of a gesturing toward the aesthetic sublime with terms like "awe" and "beautiful,"[85] but I heed the Benjaminian warning here to say that such an aestheticization of this falling woman image with reparative aims arguably poses an ethicopolitical risk, since it blunts the tragic force of the event, encouraging us to see a supposed beauty of the image rather than to focus on and not forget the tragedy that lies behind it. Besides, what is "beautiful" here also bears a false promise. As we have already suggested, there is actually not much change or even positivity in being "wide awake" in either a pre-9/11 or post-9/11 world: again, it is to be awakened, or even "woke" in more recent parlance, to systemic racism in the world for which there is hardly any attempt at rectification. Here, there is definitely no "wake work," as Christina Sharpe calls it.[86] Moreover, the reiteration of the now reified "falling man" image, which has gripped almost every 9/11 consciousness, as that of a "falling woman" only insinuates a gendered perception of failure. As said, the narrator identifies the falling woman with Reva, and this seems to be the remaining image of Reva that she will have and replay in her memory. And given that we have proposed falling as perhaps the gesture or even image "proper" to failure, we could say that the image of Reva that the narrator retains and replays is the image of failure; Reva is stuck forever with the repeated or repeatable image of failure or failed existence. (This somewhat echoes what the narrator says earlier about Reva as she drones on about her failed love life: "She was just as good as a VCR.")[87] Put otherwise, it is this image of failure that will stay with the narrator in the wake of her sleep/hibernation project, where the sense of existential dread, existential failure, hopelessness, despair, nothingness, and ennui will continue to seep into her sense of existence. As the narrator says, "I continue to watch [the video of the falling woman], usually on a lonely afternoon, or any other time I doubt that life is worth living, or when I need courage, or when I'm bored."[88] Meanwhile, Trevor can afford to be away "on a honeymoon in Barbados" on that fateful day, escaping tragedy and very likely leading a more successful life from then on, escaping the loop of failure within which both Reva (even after death) and the narrator find themselves.[89]

At this point, we must state that the aestheticization of the narrator's flopping into sleep is no less problematic. Let us recall that in articulating a difference between genre (flopping) and form (sleeping) earlier, we have also suggested that the formal aestheticization by Ping Xi of the narrator's flopping into sleep fails the genre of flopping, and we will add here that it numbs the narrator's body to the affective depths of that genre. Aestheticization only leaves those affects—misery, anxiety, irritation, dread—at best like still-life: matter that is supposed to be of vibrancy and vitality but deathly frozen within the materiality and frame of an artwork. It leaves them stuck between aliveness and death. It prevents the narrator from fully immersing or dwelling in, or living out, the negative affects that accompany her sense of existential failure. The inhibition of affects applies to the producer of the work as well, in fact. As the narrator recognizes, the artist functions within an artworld and market propped up but by "a bunch of rich assholes" and the "persuasions of capitalism."[90] And racial capitalism underlies or drives this market, an activity in which the narrator, as said, is no less complicitous, if not in which she is invested, as she turns to Ping Xi for her project.

It is common knowledge too that it is through an exoticization of the other that this artworld and market have included the racial other first as mostly peripheral subjects of artworks and then in more recent history as producers of artworks. It is no doubt with this knowledge that Ping Xi produces his provocative pieces with no real aesthetic aim but, again, "to shock people," to elicit mere attention from them.[91] He very likely knows that such a fetishized attention never amounts to a real recognition of him as a person, as equal as any of the individuals that make up that artworld market, with all his complex multidimensional feelings and histories. This is why, according to the narrator (who, as seen, is also guilty of failing to recognize Ping Xi as a person), Ping Xi "wasn't interested in understanding himself or evolving."[92] By extension of the bracketing of his personhood, it seems that there is also the implicit need to self-censure his affects in his works. This is perhaps why the best he could do with respect to those affects is to transfer them onto a foreign medium for their expression, as he projects his mother's voice onto video images of the narrator. It is only then, on a white body in the artwork, that some hints of Ping Xi's affective murmurings, twice removed from himself, can find some outlet, albeit with little chance of them receiving the reciprocal work of understanding, not to mention deciphering, from spectators. In this regard, if we want to consider Ping Xi disaffected, we must understand this term once again in contradistinction to Yao's, because disaffectedness here has nothing to do with "a form of antisocial discontent about, if not outright defiance of, the compulsory norms for expressing feeling along with susceptibility to the feelings of others" by a racial other, as Yao would want it.[93] In Moshfegh's novel, it is, rather, an acquiescence or submission to the contempt (in Ngai's sense) of the personhood of racial others by racial capitalism.

Following the point on Ping Xi's disaffectedness, we could say that formal aestheticization ignores racial questions that the genre of flopping might actually be either highlighting or responding to. As I see it, the narrator's flopping actually calls into question who gets to embody and actualize this gesture or genre and who can afford to do so. This question might have been pointedly raised at the level of class when, with the knowledge of the narrator's sleep/hibernation project, Reva says, "I wouldn't mind taking time off from work to loaf around. . . . I just don't have the luxury."[94] The racial dimension comes into greater relief with the Egyptian migrants since, again, while the narrator is flopping to try to sleep, they cannot do likewise because they have to ensure that the bodega is "never closed."[95] This unfortunately reaffirms Nancy's point that there is no democratic equality to sleep unless everyone in the world sleeps at the same time, which is regrettably even further from any shred of possibility today, according to Crary's diagnosis of our 24/7 society.[96] Otherwise, as Josie Roland Hodson has also reminded us, we must not forget the racial history of sleep. For her, it is necessary to celebrate or advocate for what she calls "Black sleep," which holds the promise, on the one hand, of breaking the myth of "Black nonsomnia," which is the delimiting perspective and expectation of the diligent Black body as an automaton of "laborious endurance and resilience that defines racial capitalism's infinite extortions."[97] Hodson further tells us that such "fictive notions about Black people's ability to dispense with sleep" have their racist origins in holds of slaves ships, where the inhumane arrangements of Black bodies are only even more inhumanely torturous, rendering sleep almost impossible.[98] On the other hand, attending to the racial history of sleep also pushes back against the other more damning reductive stereotyping of Blacks as lazy, as "slothful, gluttonous" and an "overdependent ... welfare queen."[99] "Black sleep" becomes, then, for Hodson, a gesture of "a newly operable mode of pursuing Black liberation against practices of domination," "a mode of reparation against stolen time" of sleep deprivation accumulated since the epoch of enslavement "in the plantation economy to post-emancipation and present-day struggles against extractive labor practices and the stress of discrimination."[100] As evident, though, the concern for "Black sleep" or the sleep of people of color is glaringly absent in the narrator (and the novel).

—

What I am saying, then, is that in the novel the genre of flopping—notwithstanding the narrator's endeavors to soothe or smother it into a form of sleeping—actually exposes racial, class, labor, and gender problematics, underscoring the inequities that are underlying these issues. I would like to think that if stayed long enough with this genre, letting it flail in its full dimensions and complete duration, there might at least be some form of addressing these issues. I would indeed like to think that tarrying with flopping, if not seeing to a general flopping where everyone flops, could even potentially or even veritably challenge work cultures and ethics. To change how we think about work, to not let work subsume life to the point of rendering the latter a meaningless miserable drone, and to ensure that housework and reproductive labor get their due recognition or even recompense have been the critical labor from Marx to the autonomists and to the "post-work" feminists. Slightly more radical thinkers about work might even think of "breaking things at work" or else celebrate being a bum (as the narrator wants too), which no doubt has its debt to Paul Lafargue's "right to be lazy," with the aim to bring about a moratorium to, if not a break with or a rupture of, the relentless and ever more accelerating pace of unending work that has overwhelmingly outpaced living.[101] In a way, the COVID-19 pandemic, which we have listed as one of the more recent major "eventful" failures of our twenty-first century, did bring with it slivers of such possibilities through the phenomena of the "Great Resignation" movement, which included "rage" and "quiet" quitting, and the "lying flat" [躺平] movement in China that "degenerated," if not flopped further, into what is known as the "letting it rot" [白烂] movement. These are genres or gestures of flopping, in my view, which seek to posit a counterpoint to the ideology of work, to perhaps even bring about an end to work. This is also not to mention that the phrase "letting it rot" draws from basketball rhetoric in China—that is, the act of languishing or giving up when there is no way to win the game anymore, and this brings us back to the link between sports and flopping.

The previous examples of flopping can perhaps be said to push things— that is, work, work culture, and work ethics—to the point of breaking down, breaking apart, in response to how they have first pushed one to one's breaking point through one's labors. It is to make work fail, if we recall from the beginning of this chapter what break might signify, through our very failure to sustain any grit and resilience in us, letting our bodies flop instead. Break work before it breaks us to the point of death, as the Japanese case of *karoshi* or "death from overwork," or the French case of the France Telecom suicides between 2006 and 2011, have warned us, as well as Reva's case in the novel of dying at work because of her unfortunate aspiration of having "always wanted to work in the World Trade Center."[102] Here, perhaps we can also invoke a phrase from Harney and Moten's *All Incomplete*: "We do mind working because we do mind dying."[103] This is why they will call for the creation and the inhabiting of a break in the "flow line" or "assembly line" of the neoliberal political economy, which runs on nothing but the exploitative and oppressive logistics of settler colonial legacies and racial capitalism.[104] To be "in the break of the flow" is "to move wrong or not to move," which can be taken as, again, to flop or to languish; or else, sharing with our vocabularies, to fail, to fall and "to stay *there*."[105] All this is genre flailing no less, since it "won't return to form" by submitting itself to the neoliberal dictates of resilience and improvement.[106] All this is to "sabotage" work, if not to shit on work, as the narrator literally does before she leaves her workplace Ducat.[107] Break, then, like how the narrator's VCR breaks down, which is when "nothing was working," as the narrator would desperately cry out, when the images of a racial other no longer need to work repeatedly in the service of helping the narrator sleep.[108]

This would be, in my view, where flopping is not only flailing in perhaps its greatest intensity but also in its "im-potentiality," to borrow Agamben's term, which is to say, where the very fact of its being, without needing to do or enact anything, is sufficient to expose surrounding failures such as our problematic work culture or ideology and the systemic class and racial inequities that underlie or run through it. Of course, the imagining of an end to work is only naively utopian, a daydream. In less than two years after the pandemic, and as the world begins to recover from it, as the global economy picks up again, such flopping is now seen to be economically unsustainable.[109] Regrets of quitting have been reported, followed by the subsequent phenomenon of "boomeranging" back to previous jobs; pandemic-era remote work or "work from home" arrangements, which might demand online presence but which could allow one to slip out for some significant pockets of time to attend to matters of life beyond work, are also gradually being curtailed, just as the work economy has now mobilized Gen Z to post TikTok videos celebrating, if not aestheticizing (again in the Benjamin sense), physical office spaces, in addition to embracing having a stable, rather than a dream, job. Work never ends, therefore. Never has the sense of existence as inhabiting the absurdist world of an incessantly laboring Sisyphus been as hopelessly or eternally real as today. And sleep, as the novel suggests, does not bring any end to work either; sleep is even almost indistinguishable from work there. I have already pointed out how much work sleeping is for the narrator, as she has to resort to seeking out meds, watching movies or pornography, to get to sleep. Perhaps we should also recall one final time the narrator's words when the VCR broke—"Nothing was *working*"[110]—so as not to miss the irony in associating the notion of work with the attempt to attain the restive state of sleep. We also do not forget that she puts sleep to *work* by making it the remedy for her sense of existential dread. That it might just be difficult to separate sleep from work is also betrayed when the narrator had to tell Reva that she is "not making a career move" in undertaking her sleep/hibernation project.[111] Or else, when Ping Xi tells the narrator that he does not want her to "know what [he's] up to" in his curatorial acts, the offended narrator retorts by saying, "I'm doing important *work* on my own," with regard to her imminent sleep state.[112]

There is moreover an organized pattern or rhythm to her sleep/hibernation project: she wakes up upon every three-day "Infermiterol blackout," when she will also try to keep fit, as if to ensure that she will be physically ready to partake in not only the social but also labor economy upon the project's completion. There is no doubt an irreducible Protestant work ethic in this "WASP," as the narrator recognizes herself to be.[113] She also keeps a calendar to mark this progression, if not progress, and such a regulated timetabling, as many Marxist literary and cultural theorists have highlighted for us, is only the mark of the normalization or even naturalization of capitalist chronologics that regulate and manage labor, disciplining and surveilling the latter.[114] That she has no intention for her project to be any critique of capital but to sustain and perpetuate such a system is also evident through her economic arrangements, which include collecting rent, for the time during her hibernation period. As she says, she is committed to "stay in the black until my year of rest was up."[115] She also insists on holding on to her birth certificate, passport, and driver's license, even though Ping Xi suggests destroying them would be a truer commitment toward "a completely blank canvas" from which she would "emerge ... renewed."[116] Her capitalist mind is always alert to make the calculation that without them she will not be able to have access to "bank accounts, to go places."[117] To that, she would add, "I was born into privilege.... I am not going to squander that. I'm not a moron."[118] There is ultimately no true unproductive expenditure in the narrator's flopping, therefore, no matter that she gives away her designer clothes and jewelry to Reva and empties her apartment of things before entering the sleep/hibernation project.[119] Everything remains "on" during her sleep (and we keep in mind how she unconsciously maintains at times high levels of online communications and shopping during such times).

Sleep in the novel, in other words, is the dystopia that Crary fears in our 24/7 world. For Crary, real sleep—one that entails genuine "rest, withdrawal, [and] quiescence, all of which oppose the demands of 24/7 capitalism"— requires that we break with our consumerist position. Crary goes on: "We [must] stop buying what we are told we need, we must disavow the role of the consumer altogether. There must be a refusal of the deathliness of billionaire culture, and of all the debilitating images of ownership and material affluence with which we're surrounded."[120] Again, the narrator never does detach herself from such a culture. As Crary fears, capitalist activities and preoccupations have infiltrated sleep. To be sure again, too, it is not the narrator who effectively works while she is sleeping. It is always others— typically less privileged racial others—who work "in the meantime," as Sarah Sharma reminds us: the Egyptian migrants in the bodega; Ping Xi in his curatorial work.[121] And to reiterate, the issues of race, class, labor, and gender problematics, all raised as the genre of flopping is flailing, get largely forgotten after she wakes up from her sleep/hibernation project. We might also put it otherwise, then, to say that the genre of flopping in the novel reveals the narrator's failure—and perhaps the novel's too—in confronting those issues.

In the end, it is Reva who rightly says that the narrator is "not changing anything in [her] sleep" or that "sleeping all the time isn't really going to make [her] feel any better." Sleeping is a form through which the narrator is "just avoiding [her] problems."[122] In fact, the narrator also has the suspicion that her project essentially fails, that a sense of failure will always stay with her, as betrayed by the following pronouncement of hers: "It was lunacy, this idea, that I could sleep myself into a new life. Preposterous."[123] For Reva and her simplistic outlook on life, "a good cry" is what the narrator needs, even more so than meds.[124] Perhaps we could say that this might be one possible end of the genre of flopping: flopping till the point where the body is reduced to sobs, which can also be the point of one's breaking down, if not one's being broken, where one surrenders, abandons, or gives oneself wholly to the sense of failure, to flop. In this regard, I am not thinking of the cathartic cry that Reva undoubtedly has in mind, the "good cry" that allows one to get over with that which has led one to that state, after which one might feel purged of bad feelings then rejuvenated and optimistic to start again.[125] Rather, as said, it is one that precipitates into the unequivocal recognition with the sense of failure; that continues the sense of falling with failure; where, like the real flops mentioned at the beginning of this chapter that befalls certain sports people, one's world and the surrounding world are in shambles. This cry leaves one broken with no reparative horizon in sight. Or else, to cite Harney and Moten: "If you're fallen and you can't get up, all you can do is get down until you pierce the bottom of the broken world and its infinite crises in and out of regulation. So you ground, knowing that it's necessary but insufficient, until exhausted; with neither world enough nor time, earth be present and been gone."[126] Yet, as the novel also rightly underscores, all this may be easier said than done. It suggests, on the one hand, that when genres flail, they can do so such that they resist any rest, any approximation toward any end, even if it is their own end, which might be that natural, noncurated sleep that the narrator so desires initially, or a (noncathartic) cry. Or else, on the other hand, one's psychological upbringing, one's class or gender positionality, can also be the stubborn blocks for the genre to reach such an end. In other words, awash with a sense of failure and flailing in the genre of flopping that is in response to the former, one might still further fail in not allowing the genre to flail toward its own end.

As I have tried to show in this chapter, what happens then is that other failures such as the failures to rectify or even address systemic class, racial, and gender inequities, which also reveal how only certain groups of people are allowed to fail and flop throughout the duration of failure, are allowed to be sustained as collateral damage to one's failures and, perhaps worse, allowed to be perpetuated in the future. In the wake of such a failure, one reenters, as the narrator of Moshfegh's novel no doubt does, into a world of failures.

2

DRIFTING IN A WORLD OF FAILURES

FROM ROLAND BARTHES'S NEUTRAL TO RACHEL CUSK'S *OUTLINE* TRILOGY

What remains for failed existence when one fails to sleep through flopping, or, as unraveled in the previous chapter on Moshfegh's *My Year of Rest and Relaxation*, when sleeping reveals not only larger systemic failures but also more of one's failures because one might be complicitous with those systemic failures? In this chapter, I want to consider drifting as the next resort or genre. Drifting as a genre of failure has in fact been intimated in Moshfegh's novel in one of the narrator's later attempts at flopping to sleep. I quote the passage in question: "You get cold and sleepy, things slow down, and then you just drift away. You don't feel a thing. That sounded nice. That was the best way to die—awake and dreaming, feeling nothing. I could take the train to Coney Island, I thought, walk along the beach in the freezing wind, and swim out into the ocean. Then I'd just float on my back looking up at the stars, go numb, get sleepy, drift, drift."[1] I would like to think that drifting, in a way, potentially sidesteps the problems associated with sleeping because, even though drifting might assume a similar form to sleeping—that is, lying horizontally; it does not necessarily involve the shutting down of one's consciousness of the surrounding world. Drifting as such does *not* entail being blind to, or in denial of, one's failures and the failures of the world. Thus, even though one might seem disengaged from the surrounding world while drifting, appearing to be physically or physiologically indifferent to one's milieu, one can still be affectively plugged into, or awash with, the negative affects that surround oneself and the world. Besides, drifting can take on forms other than lying flat (and I use this phrase to make just one more nod to the movement that seeks to undo work ideologies and culture, since we will still be thinking about some form of "inoperativity" in response to the latter here). Drifting can take the form of walking, as a distracted *flâneuse* or *flâneur* does, wandering around without anywhere to go, without a place at which to arrive. To be sure, though, we are not considering drifting as a genre that compensates for the failures of sleep or alleviates the problems or troubles of failing to sleep. Drifting, as I see it, is an expression of surrender, an abandoning of oneself to the situation, letting the body move (along) in a quasi-involuntary manner, without purpose or even destination. I would even argue that drifting is the immersion in one's personal failure, where one does not make a scene about one's failure, where one does not inconvenience the world with it. Instead, drifting allows the world to go on with its everyday business, while one lives on after one's failure(s). In this chapter, I want to suggest that such a peripatetic drifting can be found in the narrator Faye in Rachel Cusk's *Outline* trilogy, and I will show how drifting in the novels only reaffirms the fact that the existing world has no space for failure, that it indeed tunes out failure and failed existence. At the same time, though, drifting also exposes how the world is in fact full of failures, but whose failures get to be articulated, in Cusk's perspective, can be determined by gender politics.

I will get to Cusk's works only in the later part of the chapter. Before that, I want to spend a little more time thinking more about drifting as a flailing genre. I also want to turn to Roland Barthes's notion of the Neutral, which involves drifting, no less, and which can have implications for both our thinking of failure and an understanding of drifting in Cusk's works. Now, drifting might be considered some sort of going with the flow or flowing along. Yet I want to draw a distinction here between drifting and flowing, especially if we are to think about drifting as a genre of failure. Generally, flowing is to keep pace with the rhythm of things that continue to function around oneself, the rhythm that continues to maintain the functioning of the world. Or, to recall from our previous chapter what Harney and Moten have emphasized for us, flow is (racial) capitalism's mode of capture of its subjects: it is the mode by which it appropriates almost everyone and everything to ensure its sustained operativity and perpetuity. To be in the flow is to bend to the dictates of this capitalist order, to be *com-pliant* (Harney and Moten's formulation) to its demands and expectations. Or else, as many cultural theorists of work have underscored for us, too, it is to accede to the neoliberal ideology of work that impresses upon one to be always untiringly efficient, productive, resilient, diligent. To be in the flow, therefore, is to hardly follow one's rhythm; it is to bracket, neglect, suppress, or repress the *sense* of oneself in that moment—and perhaps one should understand *sense* here according to the French *sens*, which indicates not only feeling but also direction. To be in the flow, again, is to follow the rhythm and direction of a larger entity beyond the self; hardly any deviation is allowed. Drifting, meanwhile, allows for some idiosyncrasies. One could drift along without bending to the demands of the surrounding world; one could drift along without following the rhythm of the latter. In this case, one could follow the general direction but one is detached from the general or dominant sentiment or pace of things: one leans into one's feelings, in touch with the affects about which one feels strongly, responsive to a "structure of feeling" that can be felt more intensely at the personal level before it disseminates itself beyond the personal and develops into a collective or historical consciousness. Otherwise, one could drift along in a direction deviated from the general flow, once again not bending oneself to the latter; here, one might be brought along by the flow of the currents, but the particular form, shape, and weight of one's body, with its limbs spread out or not, can veer one off, without deliberate navigation, toward another direction.

Drifting in the above sense could perhaps be articulated in terms of what Barthes, drawing from ancient monastic traditions, has considered a potentially ideal mode of living: *idiorrythmie*, which has been translated as "idiorrhythmy."[2] According to Barthes, idiorrhythmy must be understood to be different from rhythm. The latter is of a regular or regulating order, as it is typically executed in music, oftentimes metronomically too. And if rhythm provides a sense of movement, it is that of "the regular movement of streams," if not a "relentless regularity" (*implacable de régularité*), which gives rhythm, in Barthes's view, "a repressive sense."[3] It is as such that Barthes also regards rhythm to be on the side of power: "What power imposes before anything else is rhythm (of everything: of life, of time, of thought, of discourse)."[4] Power thus understood as a form of rhythm governs or regulates a largely homogenous collective; it is also power as rhythm that allows this collective to become dominant by imposing its rhythm onto other minor groups. Power is legible not only through the workings of the state, therefore, but it is also palpable through the social in its formation. Against such an imposing power, idiorrhythmy puts in effect a "mobile, free [*disponible*], supple rhythm," which corresponds to an entity that is "moving, mobile, fluid," one that bears "a form that has no organic consistency"—that is, a "modifiable, improvised form."[5] As such, this entity, escaping the delimiting norms and normativity of the social, is what the social finds difficult to call its own, reluctant to include within its general form. As Barthes sees it, what inheres in this outlier entity is more *rhuthmos* than rhythm, whereby "*rhuthmos* is by definition of the individual," pertaining to how the individual who is a "fugitive of the [social or dominant] code" moves within the "interstices" of the latter, if not "inserts itself in the social (or natural) code."[6]

Idiorrhythmy thus have bearings on "subtle forms of genres of life" with their "unstable moods and configurations," including "depressive passages,"[7] and we will say that examples of these may be failed existences that we are articulating in this present work or existences that choose to drift along with the sense of failure while the rest of the world tries to overcome or sublimate failure, perplexed by modes of living that bear with it. And if idiorrhythmy, as Barthes would want it, can be the fantasy of living with others, the fantasy of "the Living-Together of a group at once contingent and anonymous," a coexistence that is "fantastically [and] without contradiction a wanting to live alone and to live together," where "each subject has its own rhythm," perhaps we could add, with the help of Berlant's phrase to which we have referred in our introduction, that idiorrhythmy implies the possibility of a shared "inconvenience of other people" among all.[8] In other words, and for our case, it is the inconvenience of failed existences to the world of efficient productivity and its explicit celebration of cultures or ideologies of success coexisting with the inconvenience of such a world to the idiosyncratic preference, moods, affects, and genres of the former who prefer to retreat into a solitariness and wallow in their failures, allowing everything about and around them to fall apart.

For Barthes, the idealistic idiorrhythmy can take on "an idyllic, Edenic, utopian, median form," though Barthes will be precise to state that it will not be a "social utopia" since this implies a "search for an ideal way to organize power."[9] Our sense of drifting, however, recedes from such a utopian or idyllic contour. Like the other genres to which we are attending in this present work, we are not looking at a drifting that will bring us to a better place, as if setting us adrift toward a more positive horizon, even though it might take on the appearance of a tranquil solitariness or solitary tranquility such as floating on the ocean on one's back looking at the stars above, to follow the example of Moshfegh's narrator cited previously. There will be no idealistic idiorrhythmy here; there will only be the inconvenience of failed existence felt as an incursion into the world of positive futurity and the inconvenience of that world felt as the repression and/or suppression of failed existence. This is to say that the drifting that we have in mind will sink or even drown us anytime, and this would take us to the other meaning of drift in the geological sense, which signifies river deposits. In other words, drifting can also entail sinking to the bottom of the river, getting stuck there. To be sure, this does not imply any safe settling, because this is where erosion begins. It is in this sense that drift can be, to quote Moshfegh's narrator again from the earlier cited passage, a "way to die."

The (self)destructive tendency—and *tendency* is yet another meaning of *drift*—of drifting can also be found in the more popular context of motor racing or automobile culture. Here, drifting involves pulling the brakes on a high-speed car as it heads toward a bend, quickly turning the steering wheel toward the direction where the bend is supposed to take you, letting the car skid/drift. The aim is to release the brakes the very instant you see the road after the bend and step on the accelerator pedal and speed off straight on. Smooth or impressive as it sounds, there is no denying that this is a precariously dangerous move. Many things can go wrong: turning the wheel too sharply, hence sending the car into a tailspin; not releasing the brakes in time; the accelerator pedal not working at the precise time; gravity pulling the car away from the intended direction, etcetera. Drifting here always runs the fatal risk of sending the car over the bend, sending it off the cliff, especially on mountainous roads. Drifting in this case can quite literally be a death drive, which, according to Freud, would send us back to the state of nothingness or, in Jean Laplanche's reiteration, "the originary state of inorganic matter, a state where all forces are drawn into a final leveling-out."[10] Lacan would in fact translate Freud's drive or *Trieb* in German as *dérive* in French, which in English is "drift," and the function of this translation is to underscore the repetitive nature of *Trieb*, where memory is always bringing the subject back to the moment of desiring (through which a drive is generated) yet never finding the object of desire there.[11] Drift in Lacan's sense thus highlights the subject's eternal errancy in its searching for, and never reaching, the lost, impossible object.[12]

Drifting with Barthes's Neutral

Away from further considerations of the Freudian drive, I want to return to Barthes, who also mobilized the term *dérive* or drift for purposes beyond psychoanalysis. It is in his 1977–78 Collège de France lectures on the Neutral (following those on idiorrhythmy in 1976–77) where the term is invoked. Barthes's Neutral and its attendant drifting can have bearings on how we are trying to think about failure and how we can articulate or understand what transpires in Cusk's novels.[13] Barthes's Neutral is meant to free one from existing systems of meaning-making, which always found themselves on a paradigm according to which the meaning of one term is always set against that of another. Perhaps we could understand this paradigm in more general terms as the social or, recalling our introduction, what Raymond Williams, writing at about the same time as Barthes's lectures, has called "explicit" social forms: "Ideological systems of social generality, of categorical products, of absolute formations."[14] But to stay with the more specific sense of the semantic- or semiologically driven paradigm according to Barthes: this paradigm also brings us back to our challenge in the introduction to think failure outside any binary system, to think failure as something negative yet *not* in opposition to something positive. I did postulate the thinking of failure as such to be an all-out negativity, but perhaps Barthes's Neutral can also be a helpful complement to our endeavor. The Neutral, to reiterate, is meant to undo the will to meaning-making that not only sets itself up as an epistemological foundation but also predicates itself on a polemical binarism. Meaning within the framework of such a foundation, in Barthes's analysis, "rests on the conflict (the choice of one term against another) and all conflict is the generator of meaning: choose *one* and reject *another*, this is always to sacrifice meaning, produce meaning, allowing it to be consumed."[15] Again, this is how we have come to impute to failure a meaning that is undesirably negative, as long as it is always set against the meaning of success. In embracing the latter, we will always be sacrificing the former, never allowing ourselves to be exposed to the full range of the senses of failure, to receive what those senses can tell us about existence. The Neutral, however, refuses such a restrictive, oppressive, and terrorizing meaning-making paradigm; it rejects making a choice in the face of the terms set out by a binary system: it is the "suspension of orders, laws, prosecutions [*comminations*], arrogances, terrorisms, proceedings [*mises en demeure*], demands, seizures [*vouloir-saisir*]" of paradigms.[16] In this respect, the Neutral has its "irreducible No," which I would read as its negativity, which is also its ethics that is beyond choice (and this is perhaps also our ethics of giving discursive and affective space to those who stay with their existential ontology of failed existence, refusing to accede to the ideology of a failure/success dichotomy, refusing to choose to flip to the camp of success).[17] This is where drift or *dérive* is in effect, allowing the Neutral to sidestep, if not go beyond, the tiresome theatricality of antagonistic meaning-making, a drifting that "undoes" (*déjoue*) or "takes leave" (*donner congé*) of all oppositionality, leaving all paradigms ineffective.[18]

As such, the Neutral, as it drifts, also resists the conceptual. According to Barthes, the Neutral is not presumptuous to labor and elevate itself toward the status of a philosophical concept. The work of conceptualization only results in a form of hypostasis, one that seizes hold—from the German *griffen*, which is at the root of the German word *Begriff*, for concept—of a semantic field or position, from which opposing terms might then take on negative meanings, from which the concept then condescends to others that have failed to lay claim to this field.[19] Never aspiring toward the concept, which means resisting definition and explanation too, the drifts of the Neutral are at best descriptive "in a nonexhaustive way."[20] If not, they might even be, as we are intimating here, a flailing genre in response to a restrictive systematicity of thinking and existing. We have also noted how genres are of gestures, and the Neutral is no less gestural, which Barthes would argue to include those of care (*bienveillance*), fatigue, silence, sleep, and withdrawal (*retraite*). We will discuss some of these later. For now, we will underscore that the Neutral, unlike the arrogant, occupying concept or meaning but descriptive or flailing like a genre, moves via "non-provoking gentle drifts" (*dérives douces non provocantes*), a move that is no power trip, involving no power play, since Barthes will say that the Neutral "is not possible in the field of power."[21]

Perhaps we could say that the Neutral thus bears the contours of humility, which, according to Bradatan, is the critical lesson that we can draw from failure. Now, the descriptive drifts might outline that which stand against something that is dominant within a social order, against a normative entity or term, against a norm, yet Barthes will state that they constitute but "marginal, minor conflicts, visibly assured, instigated [*déclenchés*], not to 'win,' 'triumph over,' but to 'make manifest.'"[22] As Barthes further clarifies, conflict here must be understood as "the sign that I exist."[23] In other words, what these "minor conflicts" make manifest is existence, existence that has not been given full expression, and we will cite once more our example of failure, failed existence, or modes of living that do not dissociate themselves from failure. Otherwise, what the Neutral makes manifest too are affects: not those that are strong or forceful, such as anger, but weak or negative affects, such as pathos, to follow Barthes's examples.[24] And we can think of the pathos of not having one's existence that accepts its ineluctability with failure, or one's mode of living on with failure, recognized; the pathos of a "minimal existence" that can nevertheless be "the strongest" in terms of intensity because of the irrepressible affects of failure.[25] Yet, as affects are, nothing is defined or definite here, for pathos gives a body an "undecisive, vague unicity" "stripped of attributes."[26]

And if pathos is to be considered a "state," we must not think that things are, again, fixed or at rest. Instead, restlessness abounds, with a sense of "disorganization" emanating from its "lack [*carence*] of predictable rhythm," hence giving the body that assumes the pathos of the Neutral "a 'scandalously' incomprehensible image."[27] It is as such that the social regards the Neutral as "decadent, individualistic, ... depoliticized," someone who takes flight from responsibilities, someone ungrateful to what the social, the world, and life have to offer.[28] We can imagine how a body of failed existence, a body awash with a sense of failure, a body that tarries with its failures, which we have also acknowledged to have no political bearings or use since it is not invested in any world-building, to bear the "scandalous" rhythm and image of such a Neutral. "Normal" productive society will consider this body a mess, an entity that is unappreciative of all the positive things that life can give. This is how failed existence becomes relegated to the margins of the social, how its sense of existence is bracketed from the meaning of contemporary life; this is how failed existence is unappealing to the social, how the latter treats it as "the nonconcern [*le non-souci*] of the collective."[29] The intimate link between failure and the Neutral is definitely not lost on Barthes, as he will say that related to the Neutral are "always images" not only "of *nonpower*" but also "of *failure*."[30]

The "'scandalously' incomprehensible image" can also be said to be the "dive" (*plongée*) that the Neutral brings a body along (or else down) with it, not unlike the sinking feeling of failure that we have in mind throughout this present work, not unlike the sinking sense of drifting that we have noted earlier too.[31] With this "dive," we could also say that there is a depressive and even deathly sense to the Neutral. With a brief nod to the next chapter, we could add that this "dive" might even be close to Foucault's "plunging view" (*vue plongeante*) that lies at the edge of suicide and living on. Yet, to be precise, unlike Foucault's "plunging view," it does not concern suicidal ideation: the Neutral is "not a wanting-to-die."[32] Otherwise, it would only be an end of drifting. Or, to put it in the rhetoric of Barthes's text, that would be an arrogant decision against existence (not to mention a contradiction to the Neutral's manifestation as "I exist"). Here lies the Neutral's distinction from the Freudian death drive. The Neutral is arguably not even of any drive, since, if drive is all about desire, as Lacan reminds us, the Neutral, according to Barthes, in fact "desires nothing," or it is "the desire of nothing."[33] Furthermore, the Neutral seeks no oral or buccal satisfaction, which drives, as Freud understands them, do: unlike "the arrogance of the world" it makes no obligation "to eat, to speak, to think, to respond."[34] Drives presume and can entail a directed intentionality (unconscious or not); they are the putting to work of desire or they seek to actualize a certain potentiality (to be satisfied). To reiterate what has been said earlier, it does not matter if a drive reaches its object of desire. In fact, it does not, rendering the latter an impossible object and making drive a repetitive desiring-machine in this process or endless loop. But this is only to sustain what desire is, which, according to Lacan, is "the desire to desire." The Neutral, however, lies on the side of the Agambenian "impotentiality," which we recall to be *not* the negative opposite of potentiality but the freedom to be not-able-to, the freedom from any need to be able-to, hence wherein there is no sense of lack, shortcoming, or fault. Here, Barthes follows Daoist thought in calling this not-able-to 无为 (wu wei), which refrains from making any effort or calculated action and which actually involves drifting no less, given Daoist thought's emphasis on its eponymous 道 (dao), typically translated as "the way," according to which wandering is considered one of its modes.

We have already seen a manifestation of the Neutral's not-able-to in its resistance toward the philosophical work of conceptualization. In more general terms, we could perhaps say that the Neutral's not-able-to implicates a suspension of labor. But we should be precise again to say that the labor in question is one that has taken a disciplinary or institutional form with its specific regulations, regulatory norms, and regulating rhythm. In the face of such labor, the Neutral's drifting allows one to lose any form of concentration or focus that is always demanded of instituted or wage work. But what comes to the surface from this drifting, nevertheless, is fatigue: the fatigue of having lived within the dictates of organized work whereby existence must always systematically produce some valuable meaning according to the rubrics of the existing meaning-making regime, according to the valuations of existing epistemologies. This is why Barthes, right at the first session, will precisely raise the issue of fatigue and lament how university administrations will never take kindly to a professor's request to excuse oneself from lectures or classes because one is tired. Indeed, till today, fatigue is hardly accepted as a justified, medical reason for time away from institutional responsibilities. As Barthes recognizes, the institution will only punitively see such a request as flopping—to recall the genre of failure in the previous chapter—in the negative or derogatory sense, failing to understand that seeking time away from the institution does not mean the total abandonment of work but the desire to free oneself from the regulatory systematicity or the regularized "methodological rigor" of the institution.[35] For Barthes, such a taking leave of institutional labor still sees to work: the work of individual research and writing, with the "intensity and jouissance" of one own's rhythm, or rather *rhuthmos*, outside or beyond any productive metrics put in place by the institution, nonetheless work that will add to the research profile of the institution.[36]

At this point, we should not fail to mention that fatigue can also precipitate into sleep. For Barthes, though, he is not thinking about regular, everyday sleep, which can be useful or productive in terms of repairing, recuperating, and rejuvenating oneself.[37] That is the kind of sleep that Moshfegh's narrator seeks. The sleep that Barthes wants to drift toward is a "utopian sleep" (*le sommeil utopique*).[38] It is a veritable sleep where no work is done. It is even free from any dream*work*: it is without dreams.[39] And to be sure again that the Neutral is not a nihilistic drift, Barthes will state that this "utopian sleep" is "not ... a fall into nothingness";[40] it is not the case of to sleep perchance to die, the occasional contemplation of Moshfegh's narrator. There will be an awakening from this "utopian sleep," and Barthes calls it "the neutral, blank [*blanc*] awakening."[41] And even though Barthes might also describe this awakening as the "pure moment without Worry," it does not entail an optimistic outlook on life, giving life a renewed positive horizon of hopeful productivity, full of promising futurity.[42] Instead, upon waking from the "utopian sleep," one lives life "outside of wanting to live [*hors du vouloir-vivre*]," drifting in a suspended temporality (*temps-suspendu*) outside of regular, chronological time.[43] There is thus something depressive, pessimistic, or even negative that remains in and after this "utopian sleep." As I would read it, "utopian sleep" and its "neutral, blank awakening" continue to be traversed by fatigue, which Barthes also suggests to put in effect a suspended temporality by calling it a "durational idea" (*idée durative*), during which there is only the "infinite process of the end" without being an end itself, the sense of an incessant "bending over [*pencher*] and emptying of oneself."[44] It is in this regard that there remains fatigue, that Barthes considers his "utopian sleep" to be "unproductive" or "a kind of unconditional expenditure"[45] It is also in this regard that the not-able-to of the Neutral is not as idyllic as the free wandering of 无为 (wu wei) of Daoist philosophy.

After utopian sleep, one continues to drift, therefore. Again, one should not assume that things are better from then on. Life is no less difficult. One will still be drifting along a troubled or troubling existence. (Or, as Sidney

Dekker says in his analysis of how failure drifts from one system to another within a complex ecology of systems that is more than the sum of its parts, "Failure leads to failure."[46]) One need not be reminded that the world—predicated on and driven by organized work and traversed by an anxiety to make meaning out of every enunciation and every gesture, if not of everything—will not take too kindly to the drifting of the Neutral. All that have been said of the Neutral renders it, in the eyes of the world, something of an irrelevant banality (and I remind readers that the sense of failure that concerns us can be banal too).[47] The world is too packed or "full" for the Neutral as such to drift or "float" around freely or at ease.[48] But drift is what the Neutral does. In so doing, it does not seek to further crowd the world, to arrogantly proclaim its existence in opposition to the rest of the world. Neither does it deny its coexistence with the world by "distancing" itself from it or "putting a distance" between itself and the world; nor does it seek, for its self-affirmation, a negation of the world through the "desertification" of the social.[49] Drifting is a matter of "spacing" (*espacement*) which we must be precise to say that this is *not* about using one's body to thrash through space, thoughtless of what lies around oneself, negating surrounding objects, in order to make space for oneself.[50] Instead, drifting is where the body as it is, in its very existence in the world while respecting all that is around it, is already that spacing. According to Barthes, it is "a subtle practice of respectful distance [*la bonne distance*]" between oneself and everything else.[51] It drifts along the world in an unassuming silence.

Drifting from *Aftermath* to the *Outline* Trilogy

Let us finally approach Cusk's *Outline* trilogy, arguably Cusk's aesthetic response to the reaction by some readers against her preceding work, *Aftermath*, which is a memoir recounting her divorce. For Cusk, the breakdown of her marriage—which leaves her utterly "broken"—is nothing but a mark of failure, defining "where [she has] failed," and this sense of failure consumes her to the point that it permeates every aspect of her life, seeing it reflected in almost everything she does.[52] Thus, when she switched to a new (female) dentist and visited her practice only to witness a troubling scene of a semiconscious male patient groaning in distress while the dentist and her nurse were just helplessly flustered, Cusk "felt the presence of failure" overwhelming her, even though this entire situation was clearly no fault of hers whatsoever.[53] And when she bakes a cake for her mother's seventieth birthday, she is convinced, even before the cake is consumed by any at the birthday party, that "the cake is a failure," if not "failure itself."[54] A person consumed by, or awash with, a sense of failure can only see failure everywhere. Now, if *Aftermath* elicited a negative reception, particularly from readers in the United Kingdom, it is not because the latter are unsympathetic to Cusk's sense of personal failure surrounding the collapse of her marriage.[55] Rather, it is because of her simultaneous judgment of failure on the institutions of marriage and modern family life. In Cusk's feminist perspective, "marriage appeared . . . as a holding-in, a corseting, and it seemed to [her] eyes that the force of constraint was male; that it was men who imposed this structure, marriage, in order to make a woman unavailable, and with her the gifts of love and warmth that otherwise might have flowed freely out into the world."[56] For Cusk as a female writer, the modern family life that entails marriage essentially leaves her with barely any time and space to pursue her career or to fulfill her ambition or life purpose, since this family structure typically obliges, if not binds, the wife to unwaged housework and childcare responsibilities, which Cusk says results in "lost femininity" for her.[57] It is as such that Cusk sees marriage as a "compromise" as well as "an image of child-worship" that leaves the woman nothing much.[58] And Cusk indicts the rest of society, other women undoubtedly, for feeding this "lie" about marriage and modern family life.[59] If marriage institutionalizes the unequal power dynamics between genders, if it is the acquiescence to the tacit, formal division between men and women, a division that denigrates or even negates the latter, a society that still celebrates or embraces this institution "fails to recognize—and to take precaution against—the human need for war."[60] Or, as Cusk puts it otherwise, "civil unity," as represented by heteronormativity, is essentially "racked by the impulse to destroy" (the woman).[61]

Aftermath, then, is not just Cusk's feminist complaint against the marriage institution and the heteronormative family structure; it is also a complaint against the "female complaint" that, on the one hand, bemoans how a woman's love and her sacrifice of her independence for a domestic life never finds reciprocity and, on the other hand, holds on to "cruel optimism" through the consumption of sentimental fantasies about romantic love in popular culture, that things can be better for her.[62] It is arguably in threatening their fantasies, in disrupting the rhythm of the heteronormativity, that Cusk finds little sympathy from her UK readers. This is exacerbated by the pursuit of her idiorrhythmy of "having it all"[63]—that is, of wanting to be a writer with her own time, leaving childcare work to her husband, for which she demanded that he give up his career as a civil lawyer and to whom she refuses to pay alimony upon their divorce.[64] To follow through further with Barthes's terms, this is how she assumes a "'scandalously' incomprehensible image" in the eyes of the social, an entity that the latter prefers to disregard. This is not lost on her, as she feels that she, an "outcast from marriage," is set adrift away from the social.[65] As she says, while looking at other (married) mothers picking up their children: "I saw them as though from the annihilated emptiness of the ocean, people inhabiting land, inhabiting a construction."[66] Drifting in that ocean, she and her children are no longer "part of that story" of modern family life.[67] And she recognizes the precarity of such a drifting: "I imagine... [my children] like people sleeping in the cabin of a ship that has sailed off its course, unconscious of the danger they're in. We have lost our bearings, lost our history, and I am the ship's captain, standing full of dread at the helm."[68] Furthermore, any illusion that drifting might bring about a reconciliation with, or reintegration into, the social is quelled soon enough, something that she learns as she brings her children to stay with various friends and relatives. As she says: "For a while I thought that going elsewhere created possibilities of consolation, even of recovery, but I have discovered that every welcome is also a form of exposure. It is as though, in other people's houses, we become aware of our own nakedness. At one time I mistook this nakedness for freedom, but I don't anymore."[69] In other words, even though her fugitive drifting might allow her to slide in and out among the interstices of select modern families, it nevertheless leaves her with the uneasy sense that the exposure of herself through drifting is not so benign after all but actually opens her to the "risky disorder" of the world that is essentially "chaos, malevolent disorder."[70] We can undoubtedly infer from this that Cusk finds no real empathy or sympathy from others in her drifting but more likely hostility or antagonism. This is why she will also acknowledge that to drift or "to be stranded in that delirium" is in fact "frightening."[71]

We have said that *Aftermath* can be taken to be Cusk's feminist complaint, which includes the complaint against the sentimental "female complaint," but Sara Ahmed has also taught us that there is complaint in the first place because no one was listening before *and* that others might still not listen even after the complaint is made. In Ahmed's words: "To be heard as complaining is not to be heard. To hear someone as complaining is an effective way of dismissing someone."[72] Given Cusk's feeling that her experience is an unwelcome counterpoint to the story of modern family life, and given indeed the extratextual negative reception of *Aftermath*, Cusk's feminist complaint there, to put it in terms of this present work, failed. And when the first complaint fails, one just has to lodge another. As Ahmed would say, too, "Making a complaint is never completed by a single action: it often requires you do more and more work."[73] Cusk seems to be cognizant of this, for she will begin rethinking her strategy whereby she will no longer seek to attain the "inescapable knowledge" of "unbearable" failure by exposing her own failures to others, such as sharing her failed cake with others.[74] Instead, she goes on, "Now I imagine a different kind of knowledge, knowledge without exposure, without risk; the knowledge of the voyeur, watching, assessing, staying hidden."[75] In other words, in the wake of the failure of complaint, one not only complains again but one also drifts on, except one complains and drifts differently from then on.

The *Outline* trilogy, as I see it, is where Cusk experiments with a Neutral drifting. Put another way, given the pushback against *Aftermath*, a Neutral drifting is what Cusk sees as a remaining gesture or form of being in the world, of coexisting with the world in the wake of failing to get the world to understand her, in the wake of her failure to change how the world sees things, when one has to continue living in and with the world despite or in spite of her failed intervention in gender matters of the world. Let it be said here that I will focus on the first book of the trilogy in my reading, even though there are arguably as many drifters and failed existences in each of the three novels. This is because it is in the first book where a Neutral drifting is particularly marked; it is also where it tells us most about such a drifting.[76] Now, one could say that a trace of the Barthesian Neutral can already be found in *Aftermath*, for if the Neutral, as discussed earlier, is without possession or quality (hence needless for any adjective), Cusk in *Aftermath* seems to occupy a similar state, given that she says there, "Nothing belongs to me anymore. I have become an exile from my own history.... I no longer have a life. It's an afterlife; it's all aftermath."[77] Yet, to reiterate, *Aftermath* remains a feminist complaint, which is to say that Cusk still takes an explicit stand against social codes or structures predicated on male dominance and privilege.

In the *Outline* trilogy, however, Faye the narrator, likewise divorced with two children (sons, though, instead of daughters, as in Cusk's case) from the marriage, does not quite hold on to such a stand.[78] This is rather pronounced in the first book *Outline*, in her drifting as she heads to Athens to teach a writing class and during her time in Athens, where we notice a certain indifference toward the sexist heteronormative social order.[79] Here (and throughout the trilogy), Faye is not invested in explicitly calling out social structures for placing women largely in disadvantageous positions in relation to men and charging the male species for this implicit "war" against women, demanding that they be accountable or responsible for those actions. In this respect, Faye's words about her profession as a writer correspond no less to her approach to gender politics: "What I knew personally to be true had come to be seen unrelated to the process of persuading others. I did not, any longer, want to persuade anyone of anything."[80] Neither does she want to be affected by what the social thinks: "What other people thought was no longer of any help to me. Those thoughts only existed within certain structures, and I had definitively left those structures."[81] Between herself and the social, she seeks to maintain the respectful spacing of the Neutral. In other words, her drifting is more concerned with making manifest that she exists than seeking to win the war between genders or to triumph over her critics on the truth of the prison house of marriage and modern family life. To borrow the words of Maria, one of Faye's students in the writing class, she just "had to stay close to the line of things, close but separate, ... describing but never landing."[82] This is why we find throughout the narrative a general reticence in Faye in her encounters with others in her peregrinations, as if assuming the unpresumptuous silence of a Barthesian Neutral if not the Neutral's freedom of not-able-to or 无为 (wu wei) in the face of sexist heteronormativity.[83] Or, in Cusk's own terms, as one of Faye's interviewers put it in *Kudos*, the final book of the trilogy, Faye can be said to be seeking a "third kind of honesty" beyond one that takes leave of heteronormative systems and another—perhaps "a real honesty"—that remains within the systems to unravel the truths about them: an honesty, therefore, "to which no moral bias could be ascribed, that is interested neither in debunking nor in reforming, that has no compass of its own and can describe evil as dispassionately as virtue without erring on the side of one or the other, that is as pure and reflective as water or glass."[84]

In this Neutral or amoral honest reticence, there is passivity, which can be close to a desire for nothing, if not nothingness. As Faye would say, and I quote at length:

> I had come to believe more and more in the virtues of passivity, and of living a life as unmarked by self-will as possible. One could make almost anything happen, if one tried hard enough, but the trying—it seemed to me—was almost always a sign that one was crossing the currents, was forcing events in a direction they did not naturally want to go, and though you might argue that nothing could ever be accomplished without go-

ing against nature to some extent, the artificiality of that vision and its consequences had become... anathema to me. There was a great difference... between the things I wanted and the things that I could apparently have, and until I had finally and forever made my peace with that fact, I had decided to want nothing at all."[85]

Yet the passivity from drifting, from wanting nothing in drifting, does not necessarily amount to nothing. It can tell us something about failure in a world that is so bent on finding and achieving success, such as being a "famous writer," that is at the same time a "feminist of international renown" as Angeliki is, owning a publishing house as Faye's old friend Paniotis would want it, or tethering marriage to "the principle of progress" that involves "the acquiring of houses, possessions, cars, the drive toward higher social status, more travel, a wider circle of friends, [and] the production of children."[86] Through Faye's passive reticence in listening to such aspirations by the characters she meets, what comes to be unraveled is in fact a world traversed, if not undercut, by failure. Thus, Angeliki, caught up in her self-importance fed by her international recognition, fails the basic human capacity for humility, which can imply being sincere when seeking to know others, as she fails to remember that she and her ex-husband attended Faye's reading years ago in Athens and had met Faye then.[87] Ryan, the Irish writer who is also Faye's point of contact for the writing seminar in Athens, has failed to publish the bestselling thriller that some of his students had already done. Paniotis lost his publishing house and his marriage, "once there were no more things to add or improve on, no more goals to achieve or stages to pass through, ... he and his wife would be beset by a great sense of futility and by the feeling of some malady, ... which to both of them signified that they were no longer in love."[88] And Faye's Greek passenger-neighbor on her flight to Athens would say that his marriages and divorces not only "led him into such swamplands of failure" but also made him "the full disaster."[89]

Faye's writing class is suffused with this world of failure no less.[90] Her students would attest to having experienced all sorts of failures: Clio the failed musician, Georgeou who cannot get over his "failure to memorize the constellations of the southern hemisphere," and Marielle with her failed relationship, for example.[91] They recount these experiences through Faye's indirect prompts to talk about what they observed along their way to class or about animals, and Faye listens or tunes in to all these senses of failed existences. In this regard, the students are there not only for the "purpose of being recognized" as potential writers, as Faye suggests, but perhaps also for their failed existences to be acknowledged, legitimized. Or, to put it in terms of the title of the final book in Cusk's trilogy, they are also seeking "kudos," which Faye there learns from Hermann, a guide at a writer festival, that this Greek word "in its original form" can mean "recognition or acclaim."[92] According to Hermann, the word as it stands today—that is, "a singular noun that had become plural by a process of back formation"—is a "fabricated plural" where "the individual has been superseded by the collective."[93] In this respect, we can turn to Barthes again to say that there might be a yearning for an ideal idiorrhythmy here, where the *rhuthmos* or even inconvenience of one's failed existence seeks to coexist with a world attuned only to success.

In any case, Faye no doubt provides a discursive space that allows the negative affects associated with such existences to be articulated. Thus, we hear from another student Penelope who, after years of deferring to her apparently more successful sister, finally comes to the following reckoning: "I become aware of this feeling of having deserted my own life . . . and I was suddenly filled with the most extraordinary sense of existence as a secret pain, an inner torment it was impossible to share with others, who asked you to attend to them while remaining oblivious to what was inside you."[94] As Penelope tells it, the pain of failed existence or the experience of failure of the one listening is hardly met by an equal or corresponding sympathetic, empathetic ear. This is no doubt what Faye experiences too in her drifting. There seems no opportunity for her to share her pains and experiences with her class. Besides, when another student, Cassandra, lambasts Faye for teaching the class nothing, none in class seems concerned with how she feels even though Cassandra "caused [her] to feel like nothing, a non-entity," to feel "being negated."[95] In fact, throughout the trilogy, while characters such as the Greek passenger-neighbor, Ryan, Paniotis, Angeliki, and Anne (Faye's fellow UK writer teaching in the same writing seminar and living in the same flat after Faye's stint) in *Outline* are always way too ready to expound on their failed relationships, we do not find them asking in return, in kind, Faye's experiences of her divorce. There is no genuine or sincere desire for, or even attempt at, such a reciprocity. This is perhaps already betrayed in the early chapter of *Outline* where we are first introduced to Ryan, a chapter filled with Ryan's aspirations and his sense of Irish psycho-geographical failure by which a "sense of the self as a destiny and a doom . . . hung like a pall over his whole life."[96] Done with his rambling, Ryan would ask Faye, "What about yourself, . . . are you working on something?"[97] Yet this is where the chapter ends, and we never get Faye's response.

What drifting exposes, then, is the fact that others only want to narrativize their failures, and especially so in their own terms, but are never patient or willing to return the favor in listening to the failures of others.[98] This will to narrativize can also expose gender politics at the heart of the articulation of failure. This is apparent in the case of the Greek passenger-neighbor. While narrativizing the failures of his first two marriages, we find him faulting his first wife and demonizing the second. He not only has contempt for the latter in being "absolutely ignorant" but also accuses her of mistreating his son from his first marriage.[99] With regard to his first wife, he deems her a perfectionist, but this is made to seem a fault when he considers this trait to render her unsympathetic to, and unforgiving of, any slight hint at failure. In his first narrativizing of the breakdown of this marriage, no detail of this failure is given except referred to in rather vague terms as "the argument in which everything between them was broken."[100] He faults her further by saying that in failing to "tolerate" this failure,[101] her abandonment of the marriage sent him spiraling into an existential/identity crisis: since "it was with her . . . that his identity had been forged" before and throughout the marriage, after the divorce, "she could not be called upon to recognize him," which led him to question, "If she no longer recognized him, then who was he?"[102] It is only in a later narrativizing where we learn that the "failure" in fact stems from his having an affair, which he downplays or shrugs off as "nothing" or "a piece of stupidity, an office flirtation that got out of hand."[103] What becomes evident, then, is that in the narrativization by a man of a marriage's failure, the woman is often made to bear more of the fault/failure while there is barely any serious or sincere accountability on the man's part, he who furthermore portrays himself as a victim. Faye is certainly not ignorant of the ruse of such a narrativization. As she says, in this case, "The narrative invariably showed certain people—the narrator and his children—in a good light, while the wife was brought in only when it was required of her to damn herself further."[104] Consequently, "this was a story in which . . . the truth was being sacrificed to the narrator's desire to win," and indeed, it will be revealed later that the Greek passenger's son does have his problems and that there is no certainty at all that his second wife mistreated that son.[105]

The refusal to reckon with the truth of one's failure in one's narrativizing plays itself out again in the diplomat whom Anne meets on the plane—an encounter that seems to be a reiteration of Faye's meeting of her Greek neighbor. To be sure, the pompous, presumptuous diplomat is in fact more enthusiastic to describe his successes surrounding his career and family, including his talent for learning languages. Anne quickly senses, however, a negating affect dissipating from such descriptions and descending upon her. According to Anne, "He was describing... what she herself was not: in everything he said about himself, she found in her own nature a corresponding negative."[106] In this situation, as if in critical counterpoint to Barthes's advocation for description in the Neutral, description can potentially *not* be benign or benevolent but antagonistic. Anne calls such a description "anti-description," which "made something clear to her by a reverse kind of exposition: while he talked she began to see herself as a shape, an outline, with all the detail filled in around it while the shape itself remained blank. Yet this shape, even while its content remained unknown, gave her for the first time since the incident [of her assault] a sense of who she now was."[107] "Anti-description," in other words, can conjure the failures of another—failures that the latter might not even have perceived until then—and thereafter empty out the other's sense of existence, rendering the latter a blank. (We are no doubt reminded of Penelope's pain of existence here while being the passive listener of her sister's success stories.) Meanwhile, when the diplomat begins revealing how Greek is the only language that escapes his grasp, Anne offers the hypothesis that this particular failure is possibly an effect of (or an affect from) his being away from his family. But he "refused to take the blame for his own failure"[108]—that is, he does not acknowledge his need to have his wife and children around him for him to succeed, insisting rather that his failure, if it is one in his perspective, is but a sign of the uselessness of Greek as an international language. He senses that Anne is undoubtedly right, though, and to continue the conversation with her would only further threaten to burst the bubble of "his own view of his life," a bubble that counts on denying any failure on his part.[109] He thus places a silence between himself and Anne, disregarding any civility or politeness to ask after Anne about herself after speaking so much only of himself. As Anne sees it, this silence is one that "put people out of one another's reach."[110] In any case, the diplomat's narrativizing of his failure can have a negating effect on others—the Greek language and Anne—especially others who only reaffirm his failures.

Outline, however, forewarns of the karmic risk of not observing the ethics of a reciprocal listening or attentiveness to stories or even senses of failure. This is the lesson that Faye gleans from her meeting with Paniotis, who recalls the last time they had lunch in London when Faye was still happily married. At that time, to Paniotis, Faye was an image of success, giving him the "feeling that [his] own life had been a failure."[111] Faye then was "so immersed" in the moment that she did not notice Paniotis's sense of failure.[112]

Meeting Paniotis again and finally knowing how he felt then, and now with her happily married life being a remnant of the past, a guilt-stricken Faye thinks that her inattention to Paniotis's sense of failure at that time had precipitated into failure befalling her thereafter. According to Faye: "Sometimes it has seemed to me that life is a series of punishments for such moments of unawareness, that one forges one's own destiny by what one doesn't notice or feel compassion for; that what you don't know and don't make the effort to understand will become the very thing you are forced into knowledge of."[113] In this regard, failure can be said to be like an affect that is circulating or drifting in the world and making its rounds among individuals, with the likelihood of it sticking to those who had been insensitive to the failures of others. There will, however, be those who, in their hubris, will nevertheless not fully reckon with the full force or weight of failure upon them: those, such as the diplomat, "who are certain to remain unenlightened by suffering to the end of their days."[114]

—

What, then, are the ends of drifting, besides the ethics of listening and tuning in, for some, to stories and senses of failures? Like what we have said about the genres that interest us in this present work, drifting essentially serves no utilitarian ends. A failed existence that drifts, in full exposure to the rest of the world, will barely succeed in getting others to understand their sense of existence, rarely elicit help from others. And even when a failed existence senses or meets another in the world, there is little they can do for them either. There is hardly any "kudos," therefore, in the sense of recognition, of failed existences by the world, no ideal idiorrhythmy between the inconvenience of the former and the aspirations of the latter. Paniotis's thoughts are revealing here—thoughts that are actually reflective of marriage but applicable no less to how most of us view or not the veracity of failure in the world: "We never ... discovered the true nature of the things we saw, any more than we were every in danger of being affected by them; we peered at them, at people and places, like people on a ship peer at the passing mainland, and should we have seen them in any kind of trouble, or they us, there would have been nothing whatsoever either one of us could have done about it."[115] And if we still insist, after drifting, on some narrative of progress or positive or optimistic development after failure, drifting, should we come to terms with it, presents us with quite the impasse in or with which we will always be stuck, a genre with which we will find ourselves always flailing. We will borrow the words again of Paniotis while recounting how he and his children "drifted around and around" in a deep pool made by a waterfall during a trip they made after his divorce.[116] According to Paniotis, "Those were moments so intense that in a way we will be living them always, while other things are completely forgotten. Yet there is no particular story attached to them." He continues: "That time spent swimming in the pool beneath the waterfall belongs nowhere: it is part of no sequence of events, *it is only itself,* in a way that nothing in our life before as a family was ever itself, because it was always leading to the next thing and the next, was always contributing to our story of who we were.... There was no sequel to that time in the pool, nor ever will be."[117] Drifting, to follow Paniotis, "is only itself" (just as how we have said of failure too in the introduction). Put another way, drifting as a genre of living on after and/or with failure is but to stay with failure, to be immersed in the intensity of failed existence, where existence prior to the experience of failure *and*—if ever possible—existence relieved of failure can never erase or overcome this troubling drifting. Otherwise, drifting circles one back to failure, once again emphasizing failure as an impasse.

There is indeed the possibility of drifting (back) to a place in the world that reminds one of his or her failure. This is again the psycho-geographical sense of failure as inhabited by Ryan and the Greek passenger-neighbor. For the latter, as he was undergoing his first and second divorces, "Athens at the time seemed full of his failures."[118] In response, he can attempt to drift away from Athens to seek fortunes and other successes elsewhere, even taking up a job in London. But, as he acknowledges, this "only results in him becoming lost," and after a "long, directionless detour" in all the drifting, finds himself back in Athens.[119] This leads him to the following conclusion on the inextricability between Athens and his failed existence: "It seems success takes you away from what you know,... while failure condemns you to it."[120] Ryan, on his part, can drift away from his small Irish town of Tralee to America or the bigger and famed Irish city of Dublin, but he will reckon with how memories of growing up with existential failure in Tralee will always stay with him or how he will be reminded of them by his parents. He would say, then, that "your failures keep returning to you, while your successes are something you always have to convince yourself of."[121] In drifting, we will only come to recognize how visceral and enduring failure is while success is something transient or even illusionary. Of course, when it comes to *Kudos*, Ryan would find success in finally having a book that "sat at the top of the *New York Times* bestseller list for six months."[122] We have to be precise, however, to state that this success actually needed another: "A writing partner, a female ex-student as it happened" named Sara.[123] Ryan's supposed success, then, is more like "kudos" in the sense of a "recognition or acclaim... falsely claimed by someone else," for the bestseller in fact "had originally been [Sara's] PhD thesis," and all Ryan did was "[give] her all the sterling commercial advice he'd never quite managed to follow himself."[124] And while Ryan fails to acknowledge his essential failure to produce a bestseller that is of his own idea and writerly craft, he has no qualms in regarding Faye as quite the failure. So, even though Faye never stops getting invited to writers' festivals in various European countries, drifting in and out of conversations with the people she meets along the way and tuning in to their failures, she has yet, in Ryan's view, to be among the "big names" included in an anthology he put together.[125]

Throughout the trilogy, then, Faye is always drifting amid a failed existence. And drifting as such in the world can also mean taking on the latter's senses of failure—failures that are both openly declared and those that are drowned out by narratives of success. We have seen this in Penelope and Anne. There is also the experience of Oliver, the young companion of one of the writers in *Transit*. Drifting around in Europe, he realizes that the world around him is drifting too. But not only that: "He had found not the intact civilization he had imagined but instead a ragged collection of confused people adrift in an unfamiliar place. Nothing had seemed quite real, in the sense that had come to know reality: yet he experienced the failure as his own."[126] We could say once again that that is Faye's experience too. Yet, to reiterate, assuming the role of a receptacle of the world's failures and bearing those failures as if her own does not entail reciprocity. So, if she hardly finds respect or recognition from the heteronormative world, she would seemingly find little solace from the queer community likewise at the gay beach she visits at the end of *Kudos*.[127] There we see that Faye's drifting in the world does not go undisturbed; she is not left to herself to a tranquil drifting. After entering the ocean, in her "suspended distance" from the rest of the world, she sees one of the gay men walking to the water's edge and with eyes "full of malevolent delight," looking at her with "cruel, merry eyes," pisses into the ocean.[128]

3

EXSCRIBING A DARK CARE OF THE SELF OF FAILED EXISTENCE

EVE SEDGWICK'S *A DIALOGUE ON LOVE* AND ÉDOUARD LEVÉ'S *SUICIDE*

The Failure of Care

What the previous chapter reminds us is not only that we exist in a world of others but also that this world is where others fail equally, if not more. It is in the face of such a world that we sometimes see only a world of failures, a world where there can be little hope in alleviating our own sense of failure, a world that offers little comfort to our failures. Seeing a troubling or troubled world of failures, it might even reinforce our pessimism of there being no escape from the sense of failure. Leaving aside the problem of failure for just a little while and to take into account this world of others, we heed once again Jean-Luc Nancy's insight that existence is always already coexistence and, correspondingly, all ontology a co-ontology: in our existences, there are not only others who come into presence in this world alongside us but also others who have had come before and others who will come after. Even at moments when we want to retreat from the world, when we want to drift silently at the margins of the world, we can never stop the world from encroaching or imposing, and intruding, upon us. Even when we just want to quietly dwell in our own failures, we can never block out the noise of the world, and this is what the previous chapter on Cusk's *Outline* trilogy has underscored. This is existence as *ek-sistence*, as Nancy would say too after Heidegger, where the prefix *ek-*, signifying outside, marks how we extend beyond our selves, beyond our carefully conjured subjectivity, in our being-in and/or being-with the world; but it also serves, we would add, to remind us how the outside world is constantly infringing upon our interiority in our daily existence. Put another way, as long as we accept reality—and perhaps nothing is more real than living on after failure while still tarrying with failure—we will have to accept the fact of us knocking against the real world and vice versa. In this regard, and to reiterate, there will always be elements in the real world that will constantly remind us not only of our failures but also the failures of others; oftentimes, they will even make us focus on the latter, making us attend to them more so than ours. The fact of a co-ontological ek-sistence thus also compels us—especially those of us who are humbly mindful of others—at times to care for others, placing others before us, giving voice to them while bracketing our own thoughts and feelings about our very sense or experience of failure.

Some might see the deferral to others as an Asian disposition or reflex, a naturalization of Confucian ethics that teaches selflessness as a virtue, which has no doubt become an ideology undergirding Asian societies for many centuries. Yet, as Michel Foucault has highlighted for us, such an erasure of the self also has a long history in Western culture. In the "Technologies of the Self" seminar held at the University of Vermont in 1982, which extends from the 1981–1982 *Hermeneutics of the Subject* lectures at the Collège de France, Foucault pointed out that 1980s Western culture and society still predicated themselves on two major strands of thought that had driven Western civilization: Christian ideology, which presented itself as a paradigm of morality that demanded a certain renunciation of the self, and theoretical philosophy from René Descartes to Edmund Husserl, which placed a premium on knowledge rather than care of the self. The respect for "external law" during that time, too, as Foucault saw it, was a further expression of moral deference to others.[1] The idea of a care of the self then was seen as incongruent with social, cultural, and intellectual codes, if not "immoral."[2] Any care of the self then had to take a back seat—and not for the first time in history. As Foucault reminds us, Socrates and Plato's reading of the Delphic oracle of "know thyself" (*gnothi sauton*) always meant a quest for a knowledge of the self and hardly ever a matter of a care of the self (*epimelēsthai sautou*). To Foucault's observations on the reservations toward a care of the self in the late twentieth century, I would also add French thought's own ethical project since the late 1960s of affirming others and differences, which was strongly promulgated by Foucault's peers and/or predecessors such as Emmanuel Levinas, Hélène Cixous, and Jacques Derrida, including Foucault himself, and which saw its wider political reach in more global feminist and postcolonial movements, especially from the 1970s onward.

A care for others, however, can prove a real challenge to its sustainability. The spirit of altruism wears thin, or any endeavor at an "aneconomical" ethics—as Derrida calls the form of absolute giving that does not expect anything in return, which he sees as necessary but at the same time acknowledges its impossibility—becomes intolerable, when the self that has been asked to give receives incommensurably less, when the self sees one's supposed privileges seemingly diminish or "replaced" in the face of rising "identity politics" by minority groups. As Freud had already cautioned, greater violence will only erupt from the disenfranchised self when one's interests are repressed. And erupt it did, as we have seen in the hate crimes of recent years: the mass shooting at the gay club Pulse in Orlando in 2016, the synagogue shooting in Pittsburg in 2018, the shooting of female Asian American spa workers in Atlanta in 2021, the racially motivated grocery store shooting in Buffalo in 2022, etcetera. All these, in a way, are no doubt extreme violent pushbacks against any endeavor at respecting others and differences. Without justifying (and definitely not excusing) any of these hate crimes, these expressions of extreme violence may nevertheless be symptomatic of how a self might snap when one perceives too much pressure mounting on oneself to care for others. Aside from taking into account hate crimes perpetuated typically by those who also presume a sense of entitlement (which is to say, they would hardly care for others), we must nevertheless acknowledge that care can cut both ways: a show of care for some can no doubt be perceived by others as a carelessness toward, or even disregard for, them: "Our cares can perform disconnection," as María Puig de la Bellacasa reminds us.[3] Thus, in the serious case of hate crimes where an ethical care for others can indeed create violent political rifts leading to fatal casualties, in less severe situations, our care for some can generate jealousy or envy in others, leading them to read our care for others as an abandonment of them, hence letting them drift away from us. Or, as Hil Malatino sees it, "We are often triggered by one another in the act of caring but nevertheless need one another, in both specific and abstract ways, to get by."[4] In whichever case, one must recognize a certain violence of care.[5]

The violence of care can be articulated in another way: care fatigue. For advocates of hate crimes, it is seeing how care is distributed to others that becomes tiresome to them. But even when care is well-intended, given either willingly or by vocation of choice, especially in the case of caregivers for the sick, the old, or the dying, it can bring about both physical and emotional exhaustion. "Too much care can be consuming," as Puig de la Bellacasa will say, following decades of scholarship by Marxist feminists on care work by female labor; care fatigue can smother, if not denigrate or negate, any sense of self, individuality, and even personhood for the caregiver.[6] I do not need to remind readers that this is what effectively comes through in Cusk's trilogy for the narrator as other characters pile their stories of failures on her while barely demonstrating any genuine interest in hers. The danger of care is that it can be so overwhelming that too little space is left for any care of the self. This problem of care has been made especially acute by the COVID-19 pandemic, where medical/health workers and social workers have worked incessantly for at least two years, caring for highly and/or fatally contagious patients despite serious burnouts and in spite of unjust discrimination or ostracization by others. To say the least, real material and even psychological care for these workers—not to mention commensurate remuneration for their labor—have not been sufficiently forthcoming or available. As the Care Collective has pointed out, such a "crisis of care" or the systemic shortcoming of care apparatuses in society has in fact already been in place decades prior to the pandemic because of the dominance of neoliberal capitalism. The "market logic" of the latter, in the words of the collective, "has meant systematically prioritizing the interests and flows of financial capital, while ruthlessly dismantling welfare states."[7] Consequently, it "normalizes endemic care deficits and abject failures to care at every level by positing them as necessary collateral damage on the road to market-oriented reforms and policies."[8] Careless about care, especially (and cruelly) during a serious global crisis such as the COVID-19 pandemic where both the vulnerable and unwealthy patients and the medical and social care workers who attend to them need critical care, this "market logic" has only continued to exploit the long history of the devaluation of care—partly through its past relegation to the undervalued female workforce and the bias against care work as "unproductive" or rather unprofitable in order to "consistently subject [the work of caring and care workers] to less pay and social prestige."[9]

At the same time, though, Puig de la Bellacasa and the Care Collective have also noted a putting to work of a normative "care" of the self by neoliberal economics, one that, as we have mentioned in our chapter on flopping and Moshfegh's *My Year of Rest and Relaxation*, effectively leaves us to our own devices to remain physically and mentally healthy only so that we continue to be able to maintain our keep. In Puig de la Bellacasa's words,

"Neoliberal governance has made ... caring for *the self* a pervasive order of individualized political morality."[10] On the one hand, this has only created a new worry, which is the stress of resiliency and which demands the hasty recuperation of the individual as a high-functioning subject of this very political economy instead of fostering real rest and healing of the body and mind. On the other hand, this order has also translated itself into an immensely profitable "self-care" industry, the benefits or luxury of which, and the time for which, are affordable only to the rich. Meanwhile, the rest of us, because given the stressful imposed need to "care" for the self for which we actually have not much financial resources or the luxury of time, are, as the Care Collective has highlighted, "less able to *provide* care as well as less likely to *receive* it."[11] "We have," the Collective reminds us, "for a very long time, been rendered less capable of caring for people even in our most intimate spheres, while being energetically encouraged to restrict our care for strangers and distant others."[12] At best, or actually worse, we are made only to "rearticulate and reorient our caring inclinations toward 'people like us.'"[13] In other words, if there are care communities, they are largely comprised of those of similar socioeconomic classes, those who can buy into the "hype" or "current commodification" of care.[14]

    I recall that French thought from the late 1960s till the '80s had tried to break with any sense or order of an exclusionary homogeneity. The Care Collective undoubtedly also seeks to counter such a homogeneity with a more encompassing or inclusive global politics of care, where none is left behind in any care economy. Puig de la Bellacasa's endeavor to think about care bears a similar spirit no less.[15] And perhaps echoing French thought's "aneconomic" thinking about care with differences in mind, she would state that care "cannot be enacted by a prior moral disposition, nor an epistemic stance, nor a set of applied techniques, nor elicited as abstract affect."[16] In other words, for her, care cannot discount, disregard, or be abstracted from the particular or empirical situatedness in which it is needed: specific cares must be given or catered to each specific case, even though the technics of some of these cares have not been practiced or thought of before, and they surely must not be given as an afterthought following some moral calculation. (Or, according to the editors to the volume *Care Ethics in the Age of Precarity*: "Care is always a response to the particularity of someone's circumstance that requires concrete knowledge of the situation, entailing imaginative connection and actions on behalf of their flourishing and growth."[17]) The attention to the specific situatedness of care, I believe, allows Puig de la Bellacasa to sidestep a certain failure in French thought in fostering a more universal acceptance of the ethicopolitical project of affirming and respecting others and differences. That failure might be because of French thought's insistence (as mentioned in our introduction) on a structural and hence impersonal mode of thinking, which can indeed come across as unfeeling and which can place the notion of otherness in an abstract horizon, which in turn can have the unintended effect of obscuring the other's corporeal and affective particularities, thus further foreclosing any real care for it.[18] Picking up from John Dewey, Puig de la Bellacasa would insist, however, that thinking can always have the potentiality for a mindfulness of others, hence a dimension of care.[19]

And yet, as I have already forewarned about the violent danger that can possibly entail from the fatigue of caring for others, thought must be equally mindful to maintain the very delicate or fragile, if not precarious, balance between a care for others and a care for the self. But even without thought, given care fatigue, and given that everyone/everything needs care, there will be moments when a care of the self—other than the ideological and/or commercialized "self-care"—becomes inevitable or even necessary.[20] Foucault had noted that there was indeed such a turn toward a care of the self in the Hellenistic period that followed the era of Socrates and Plato. According to Foucault, this turn was signaled by a particular writing practice through which there was the recognition that "the self is something to write about, a theme or object (subject) of writing activity."[21] The question of writing will be critical for the kind of care of the self with which we will be concerned in this chapter, and I will say more about this soon. For now, and just to stay with the Hellenistic writing practice, Foucault observed how it paid "attention ... to nuances of life, mood, and reading."[22] Put in more contemporary parlance, it was concerned with the self's "ordinary affects," to borrow Kathleen Stewart's phrase. Or more simply, it was attuned to common everyday life, an attunement that could be as banal as noting down ordinary routines rather than proceeding with a view of pedagogical ends, as was the case with texts produced in Socrates's and Plato's time. This is also not to mention that in the latter epoch, it was the case too that only the elites had the luxury to think about a care of the self. By contrast, in the Hellenistic period, as long as one knows how to write, a care of the self predicated on writing could more democratically be available to anyone. And yet, for Foucault, the conversion toward a care of the self in the Hellenistic period was not exactly comprehensive. As he argues through a reading of Marcus Aurelius's letter of 144–45 to his teacher Fronto, the question of sexuality, along with other forms of existence such as the self in sickness or madness, were after all bracketed from the exercise of a care of the self at that time.[23] From such a reading, Foucault envisioned a reanimation of the discourse on the care of the self with a particular focus on the self's deviant sexual desires. This would constitute for Foucault a revolutionary conversion that would allow for the articulation of a self, or even selves, that could potentially defy heteronormativity, and his texts of the period between 1981 and 1984 were no doubt formative of a revolutionary queer conversion toward a care of the self that dared speak the truth of one's sexual desires and practices. It is not the interest of this present book to chart the development of this Foucauldian trajectory, but allow me to just say that it is very much in our present century that written discourses on such a care of the self have really come to the fore and proliferated in literary and/or theoretical domains, especially in the genre that has lately come to be known as "autotheory," with celebrated examples such as Paul B. Preciado's *Testo Junkie* and Maggie Nelson's *The Argonauts*.

In this chapter, I want to elucidate a darker or even more perverse care of the self, one more radical than Foucault envisioned and accomplished by writers such as Preciado and Nelson. In a way, Puig de la Bellacasa also has an ambitious or radical end in sight for her thinking of care. She wants care to "disrupt the status quo and to unhinge some of the moral rigidities of ethical questioning"; she wants care to be "a critically disruptive doing that can open to 'as well as possible' reconfigurations engaged with troubled presents."[24] For Puig de la Bellacasa, "troubled presents" include nonhuman and nonorganic entities that she perceives to even deserve the value of care as much as humans do. The care that I want to talk about here, even though it returns to the human self, is even more troubling or messier than Puig de la Bellacasa would want it. I am speaking about a care of a self that seeks its extinguishment, a self that desires an exit from existence. Let it be said at the outset that such a care, not surprisingly, barely promises anything positive; its outcome is hardly recuperative; it can even head toward "bad" endings in normative terms. Yet I would argue here, through readings of Eve Sedgwick's *A Dialogue on Love* and Édouard Levé's *Suicide* and *Autoportrait*, that such a care is necessary for those who feel that their existence is essentially, irreducibly, or hopelessly a failed existence, either because of an underlying but undeniable sense of ontological failure or because of bodily failures.

In other words, I want to consider this dark care of the self a genre flailing in response to demands of care to be given to others—the care for their stories of failure, the care for their positive or optimistic worldviews, the care to not inconvenience them. (Or, to recall the previous chapter, such a care of the self might even be considered the gesture of the Neutral, where what is at stake is to make manifest the existence of the one who had cared too much about, or for, the world but now needs to turn the attention to oneself.) Care in this case, I would say, is "a nonnormative necessity" way more radical than Puig de la Bellacasa would allow care to be.[25] And this care can only be given to oneself by oneself, because no existing morality—normative or otherwise—can possibly allow it, not to mention that legally such a care coming from others can amount, in many places, to the crime of assisted suicide. To borrow Puig de la Bellacasa's words again, and to bring them beyond the semantic contour she has circumscribed for them, this is care "as an everyday practice that refuses moral orders that reduce it to innocent love or the securitization of those in need."[26] This care needs a complementary, or even supplementary, genre too, and the other genre that is also flailing here is one that is more conventional—that is, one according to which we understand genre in its classical sense.[27] It is a genre that Foucault had already underscored that could accompany his idea of a care of the self: writing.[28] More specifically, though, it would be a writing that attends to the desire for the exit, if not the very exit itself, of existence. To understand such a writing, I will borrow Nancy's term of "exscription," but like how I mobilized Puig de la Bellacasa's phrase of "nonnormative necessity" to describe my dark, deathly care of the self, I will take its meaning further than that for which Nancy had intended.

Dark Narcissism

As mentioned, the care of the self with which we are dealing here is darker in tenor. Perhaps inevitably it also implicates a form of narcissism, as do all cares of the self, although I will underscore here that it will be a somber and, again, perverse narcissism in our case. Now, the phrase "perverse narcissism" might recall a problematic understanding of narcissism that Freud identified during his time. In the essay "On Narcissism: An Introduction" (1914), Freud notes of "psycho-analytic observers ... struck by the fact that individual features of the narcissistic attitude are found in many people who suffer from other disorders—for instance, as [Isidor] Sadger has pointed out, in homosexuals."[29] According to this skewed view, queer narcissism involves libidinal cathexes no longer being distributed to others out there in the world but flow back entirely into the ego, leading to a certain "end of the world" condition for the narcissist in the sense of extracting the latter away from the world of others.[30] In this regard, the narcissist refuses, or fails to acknowledge, the co-ontology that connects each and every one of us in the world. More than a century later, and certainly with the benefit of an immense and growing archive of queer texts and theories, this point is easily debunked today. Indeed, the aforementioned *Testo Junkie* and *Argonauts* would testify that there are cases where the queer self does not shy away from the endeavor to negotiate with the heteronormative world, with either a queer community (in the case of *Testo Junkie*) or a queer family unit (as in *Argonauts*). In any case, against the homophobic pinning of narcissism to queer subjects, Freud wants to recuperate narcissism from its pathologizing as a queer "disturbance."[31] For Freud, this involves recognizing that not just queer subjects but all of us have a "primary narcissism": there is "a primary narcissism in everyone."[32] This is how narcissism "would not be a perversion, but the libidinal complement to the egoism of the instinct of self-preservation, a measure of which may justifiably be attributed to every living creature."[33] As Freud argues, "primary narcissism" can be traced back to childhood "auto-eroticism" or "early state of the libido," but it becomes repressed through processes of socialization as one internalizes the moral codes of (heteronormative) family and social institutions.[34] Through the latter, one imagines an ego ideal, which is really "imposed from without," and precisely through which there is the "departure from primary narcissism," if not its sublimation, by which there occurs the "instinct's directing itself toward an aim other than, and remote from, that of sexual instincts."[35] According to Freud, though, one could revolt against the repressive mechanism of the ego ideal "out of the subject's desire ... to liberate himself from all [the familial and social] influences, ... and out of his withdrawal of homosexual libido from them," which would suggest a reclaiming of "primary narcissism."[36] According to Freud, too, the narcissistic love-object could be "what he himself is (i.e. himself)," "what he himself was," "what he himself would like to be," or "someone who was once part of himself."[37] In whichever case, "the aim and the satisfaction in a narcissistic object-choice is to be loved"[38] or, in terms of the concern of this chapter, to be cared for.

As said, though, we are seeking a *darker narcissism*, one that is no less ontological, and for this I would suggest Ovid's Narcissus story to be more instructive than Freud's libido theory. If Freud's take on narcissism builds on, and moves away from, one with a homophobic perspective, turning to Ovid might even be a more radical move since Narcissus is very much the queer subject. Narcissus is attracted to, and desired by, both males and females. Yet he never yields to any of them because of an unwavering pride in his own beauty. It could be said that Narcissus's way of going about his life as a pococurante seducer is an art of living that takes care of his self's sexual desires and pleasures, albeit in solipsistic ways. This sees to his rejection of Echo, making her flee to the caves where, with "unsleeping grief,"[39] her body wasted away, leaving her with nothing except her voice. As if in line with poetic justice, there is no happy ending for Narcissus either. His eventual demise could be attributed to Nemesis, the goddess of vengeance, when she grants the wish of one of Narcissus's spurned admirers for Narcissus to likewise never attain his beloved. However, prior to Nemesis's intervention, Tiresias had already foretold that Narcissus can live a long life only on the condition that "he knows himself—not."[40] (There is no doubt a semantic distance between the Latin original of this utterance—*si se non noverit*—and the negative form of the Greek *gnothi sauton* or "know thyself," but it is nevertheless interesting to note that already in Ovid, prior to Foucault, there is a caution against knowledge of the self.) Narcissus's fatal "know himself" moment arrives when he realizes that the reflection in the pool, that "singular boy" whom he desires so much, that "immaterial hope" with which he is obsessed, is none other than himself.[41] The image, unlike the Freudian ego ideal, is not a repressed self excavated from Narcissus's past; neither is it an object of sublimation since it is not a desexualized other—in Ovid's tale, Narcissus does make himself sexually attractive and available to the image. Instead, the image is a part of Narcissus's always present self that he had never known or encountered before, apparently altogether different from any image of himself reflected in other pools.

What Narcissus comes up against, then, can be said to be the "not-I" or "not-me" that nevertheless is still very much part of the self. And it does appear that Narcissus practices some form of care of the self obsessed with this not-I or not-me: a perverse care no doubt, for it involves ignoring his hunger and fatigue. He is willing to let his existence slip away while obsessing over his image:

> neither his hunger nor his need for rest
>
> can draw him off; prone on the shaded grass,
>
> his insatiate stare fixed on that false shape,
>
> he perishes by his own eyes.[42]

And even after he knows that the image is essentially his own, there is still no abandoning this form of care for the obsessed self: he remains prone on the ground, the body still in pain from yearning for the image and now grieving over the impossibility of ever attaining it.[43] As the story goes, this is how "he dissolves, wasted by his passion."[44] In my reading, there is another more desperate and potentially fatal gesture on Narcissus's part: his desire "to plunge / his arms into the water."[45] Certainly, it is but a "shallow pool" and one would hardly drown just by diving into it.[46] However, given that Narcissus's goal was to embrace the image, to be with the image, it would not be surprising if he would renounce coming up for air again should he be able to grasp the image in one of his dives. Besides, upon recognizing his own image, Narcissus also says that "death is no grave matter" and looks toward death, since he is convinced that it is "in death" that he and his image will "merge as one."[47]

Narcissus's plunge thus goes further than "the plunging view" (*la vue plongeante*) that Foucault had identified as another element of a care of the self. Not unlike Narcissus's staring into the image at the pool's edge—that is, languishing in a position between life and death—"the plunging view" according to Foucault is one that is adopted "at the point where one is at the edges of life and death, where one is at the threshold of existence."[48] At such a point, one deliberates on whether "to kill oneself or continue to live."[49] This is the point of symmetry between suicide and living on. In Foucault's view, the plunging view acknowledges that while there are "a thousand scourges of the body and the soul, wars, banditries, death, and sufferings" on earth, there are also "all the splendors" in this very same world, and this very reckoning encourages one to keep one's gaze "on this world" rather than on another (above, typically).[50] This is how the plunging view actually has an optimistic horizon, leading one away from any melancholic or depressive view of existence toward a perspective that is hopeful and committed to living on.

In contrast to Foucault, I want to take into consideration here the pessimistic side of the symmetry—that is, the plunging view that precipitates into suicidal ideation if not the act of suicide itself, thus pushing the plunging view deeper into the dark recesses of existence. I would like to think that adopting this dark plunging view constitutes no less a care of the self, and this is the lesson gleaned from Narcissus's story, where we have a care of the self that heeds the self's desire to depart from existence, a care that is willing to renounce life.[51] Such a consideration takes into account that some of us, especially those of us whose sense of existence is cut deeply by an unshakeable sense of failure, we who feel life to be largely a failed existence, oftentimes without reason, do desire a departure from existence, a real out of ek-sistence—this time literally living out the *ek-* of existence. Some of us see, understand, feel, and accept such a desire as an irreducible part of ourselves: a part of the self that, as said in the introduction, no talk therapy, no cognitive behavior therapy, no psychiatric or pharmaceutical intervention can ever absolutely dispel. For us, to be attentive to this part of the self, to allow it to articulate the desire of this ek-sistence, to articulate all the struggles and failures of ek-sistence, would be a real care of the self, a freedom of being in this world, no matter if what is being opted for or looked toward is an exit from this being. No doubt, attention to all this generates a rather depressive discourse of a care of the self. Yet, as Timothy Morton has said, "Trying to escape depression is depressing."[52]

Ek-sistence: Eve Sedgwick's *A Dialogue on Love*

A depressively narcissistic care of the self can even be found in Eve Sedgwick, whose theoretical/scholarly project is to bring some kind of uplifting relief to the field of literary criticism, which has had for a long time been burdened by a disciplinary practice grounded in what Paul Ricœur calls "a hermeneutics of suspicion." As we all know now, Sedgwick has revealed the "deep pessimism" (in the epistemological sense rather than an ontological or experiential one) of this practice, seeking to balance it out with what she calls, following Melanie Klein, "reparative reading" where instead of the anxious need to expose imminent "bad surprises" everywhere through a generally apocalyptic lens, the aim is to elucidate possibilities of pleasure and nourishment (and Sedgwick cites Foucault's "care of the self" on this), optimism, hope, and love.[53] The pendulum swings to the pessimistic shade, however, when it comes to writing about the self that perceives itself not to have been successful in various ways or situations, the self whose body has fallen susceptible to illness or disease (or the self with a failing body), the self whose mind has not been able to rid itself of the negativity of things. The discourse on a dark, depressive narcissistic care of the self thus writes itself out in Sedgwick's *A Dialogue on Love* (1999). No longer the conventional scholarly/theoretical text with which Sedgwick's œuvre is filled, *A Dialogue on Love* is mostly a memoir of her recuperative process with her therapist Shannon Van Wey to treat her depression in the wake of her breast cancer diagnosis. Taking on a hybrid form of prose, poetry, and notes written by Shannon, *A Dialogue on Love* seeks to make sense of both Sedgwick's experiences in therapy and her relationship with her therapist. On the one hand, then, it is a text written by a body that is, like Narcissus, in pain. As the narrator says of her body, it is one that is "bursting out of my / eye sockets with pain."[54] On the other hand, a narcissistic self-absorption is clear for all to see, through both her relationship with her therapist and when the sessions touch on her childhood. During the latter, Sedgwick recounts her struggle to feel adequately loved by her mother, constantly frustrated by not being the "favorite daughter" in comparison to her sister Nina.[55] Sedgwick reiterates this desire to be the most well-liked with her therapist: she wants to be "truly *exceptional among his patients*" and even often wonders if he is in love with her.[56] To feed this narcissism, she asks a lot of Shannon's time and attention, which she admits is aimed at taking Shannon away from his wife.[57] And if Shannon evaluates her as "transparently narcissistic,"[58] and even though this evaluation comes after Shannon is made to understand that he "completely missed" recognizing Sedgwick's personality as "demonic, powerful, and unique (in an anomalous sense)," such a claim about Sedgwick here in this text is hardly contestable.[59] And despite Shannon's failure to recognize Sedgwick's exceptional personality, the sessions with Shannon, for Sedgwick, "let [her] indulge that desire ... to *show oneself to be loved*,"[60] in contrast to past sessions with other therapists where she only felt "a particular impasse ... wedged so firmly between them."[61]

Sedgwick's sessions are no doubt occasions for the self that wants to be the "favorite daughter" or the "exceptional" patient to come to be loved. Yet, with regard to *A Dialogue on Love* as a whole—that is, as a text or discourse that sees to a care of the self—there is another self at stake: a self that desires the darker ek-sistence as mentioned earlier, which is to say, a self with the "wicked thought" of wanting to die.[62] For Sedgwick, this self is ineradicable. In fact, it structures her being; it constitutes her "ontological problem."[63] To be sure, it is a "problem" only in the eyes of psychology and psychiatry. Otherwise, as *A Dialogue on Love* attests, this self is what Sedgwick desires to sustain. This is why when she postulates that the mark of successful therapy might be when she would "stop feeling the want of being dead," she immediately regrets such a possibility, reasserting that this very feeling is "such a deep, old fact about [herself]," suspecting that being freed from the desire for ek-sistence "could be a *terrible* index of what might change."[64] That no therapy will be able to dispel or dissolve such a self becomes rather evident toward the end of the text, when Shannon believes that Sedgwick "is experiencing a change in her relationship with death—somewhat that it is a simple fact, not that it waits soon for her, or that it is something she seeks."[65] However, Sedgwick has a quick rejoinder that states that "one of the main ways [she is] using Shannon is as an excuse to be more withdrawn," by which the "return to [her] unskilled, unsociable demeanor feels just right," and that "there were something true, or vital, in all that old shyness."[66] In other words, the self that wants out of existence is that which Sedgwick wants to see remain through and after therapy. It is this self that she wants to see unraveled in *A Dialogue on Love*; this is the self for which the text is a care. Thus, when Sedgwick says at the end of the text that "I love that his care for me was not care for *me*,"[67] we must recognize that the latter "*me*" is the self with "the longing for death."[68] And this "care for *me*" can be in effect only as the written text or discourse that is *A Dialogue on Love*; this care cannot be provided by anyone else or by some external psychotherapeutic intervention. The text is where the self that seeks an exit from the world can be articulated, where such a desire can be expressed, where all the affects of failed existence and/or failed ek-sistence can be inscribed. Through this text, then, Sedgwick can stay with her "groundstone" of sadness,[69] through which she can say to herself, if not her other self:

"That's enough. You can

Stop now."

    Stop: living, that is.

And *enough*: hurting.[70]

While the text offers a space within which she can comfortably or reassuringly say (to herself), "You don't need to live anymore,"[71] it also records no less her sense of failure in not dying, in not being able to "die at the right time" as Nietzsche would say, despite or in spite of the desire to exit life.[72] Sedgwick calls this a "different failure" from the failure to feel really alive, but it does not stop her from feeling already dead.[73] This is why she will, while looking back at an incident where Shannon unknowingly retraces a path she had taken earlier, consider herself a spectral being, which is also that "*me*" for which Shannon can never care.[74] In all, *A Dialogue on Love* carves out a textual space in and through which it is possible to express the truth of longing to die or feeling already dead. Put another way, it serves as a space of *parrhesia*— another term Foucault highlights in discourses on the care of the self in *The Hermeneutics of the Subject*. Yet the parrhesia in *A Dialogue on Love*, in bespeaking the brutal honesty of wanting to see to the extinguishment of the self, is clearly more radical than daring to speak the truth of one's deviant sexual desires as Foucault wanted it. In this regard, the discourse on a care of the self in *A Dialogue on Love* can hardly deliver any pleasure or happiness that Sedgwick might want to bring to surface in her theoretical thinking.[75] One will indeed be hard-pressed to elicit from this text any real hope or optimism that Sedgwick seeks for "reparative reading." Otherwise, one could say that *A Dialogue on Love* bears a "cruel optimism," except it does not keep faith with the promise of the capitalist good life as outlined by Berlant. Instead, it perversely believes in another chance, another day, for ek-sistence. It extends, as Sedgwick says, "the thread for the labyrinth," which, to be sure, does not lead one out of the labyrinth but keeps one deeper and even more lost within it.[76]

Exscription: Édouard Levé's *Suicide*

Given both the memoir dimension and the poetic—hence creative or fictive—elements of *A Dialogue on Love*, one could no doubt call it an "autofictional" text, if not, as I have done elsewhere, a text of "auto-thanato-theory."[77] Yet, to better correspond to the trajectory of ek-sistence in such a discourse on a darker care of the self, perhaps Nancy's term of "exscription" [*excrit*] is more apt. As indicated by the morphological stem *script*, one could rightly guess that the term has something to do with writing, though it has to do with something more *and* less than writing as we know it—that is, writing that we see scribbled or printed on the page. From Nancy's early eponymous essay in *Une pensée finie* (1991), through *Le sens du monde* (1993), to *Corpus* (2000), one could say that exscription is writing that is both the trace of sense *and* on the trail of sense. It is a matter of sensing—and this includes reading, as we will see—sense that gives us a sense of our existence in the world. To be sure, this sense is not henceforth exhausted in us, as if we were its terminal point. Instead, sense is always already traversing (out into) the world, which thus allows our existence to make sense to others. Furthermore, Nancy also understands this sense in all its senses: not just common sense, or intelligible sense, or even nonsense but also sense that can never be captured by these registers, which nevertheless, again, traverses all of us, coming from and going in all directions beyond our determinations. Exscription is very much in the order of the latter sense, surpassing common-, intelligible-, and nonsense, yet not excluding them at all but can subtend them too. (We have suggested in our introduction how the irreducible sense of failure can be understood in this sense too.) According to Nancy, such a sense is coextensive with the constant movement of existence in its very transitivity: it is the sense of ourselves exist-*ing*, pushing our bodies forward, extending us beyond the stubborn weight and formal limits of our corporeal bodies. It is also the sense of us *ex*-isting—that is, as already mentioned at the beginning of this chapter, our existence as always a movement to the outside, as ek-sistence, always outside of, or exiting, any supposed essence, sending existence back to its proper exist-*ing*.

This sense of exist-*ing*, precisely because of its constantly transitive aspect, never waits for us to make sense of it, not especially for us to scribble down our sense of it. No matter how agile our minds, how dexterous our writing technics, this sense by and large escapes our meaning-making or signifying capacities and strategies at the moment of its passage, and after, too, as is often the case. In other words, all our attempts to inscribe it generally fail on two counts: failing to inscribe it at the very moment it passes and failing to inscribe it in a precise and comprehensive (or even total) manner. Not all is lost, though. As long as we are committed to writing, or, more simply, as long as we write, we never fail to trace a sense of the sense of exist-*ing* or ek-sistence. As Nancy writes in *Corpus*, "Exscription passes through writing," except that exscription is the "outside-text" (*hors-texte*) of every writing.[78] This "outside-text," according to Nancy in his early articulation of exscription, is but "the being of existence," and this must be understood precisely as ek-sistence as outlined previously. And ek-sistence finds its trace in writing because the latter, "in inscribing signification, . . . exscribes the presence of that which withdraws from all signification."[79] In other words, writing can paradoxically bear the trace of that which escapes all that writing seeks to circumscribe; there can be an exscription or "outside-text" in every writing. Exscription, then, is also ek-scription, meaning it slips outside, if not writes itself outside, of every signifying process, in tandem with ek-sistence; or else, subtending all inscription or signification, it names or recalls ek-sistence. Or else, to put it in terms of the topic of care that is the concern of this chapter, exscription takes care of ek-sistence through writing.

It is in *Corpus* that Nancy further gives a bodily dimension to ek-sistence, and he makes clear that this body, even though it is still ours, is different from the visible, material body that gives weight to our endeavors in granting substance or essence to our subjectivity, individuality, Being, or any other appellation we conjure to think ourselves as fixed, complete, permanent, and hence representable in our own terms. To be sure, the body of ek-sistence is never completely separate from the visible, material body, but it is stretched out from the latter to ek-sistence. It is through Nancy's explication of ek-sistence in terms of bodies where we find Nancy saying that exscription bears a "double failure."[80] This "double failure" marks, first, our inability to articulate and inscribe, in a timely manner, the body that escapes fixed presence and representation, this *other* body that is still our very own body but has already extended itself beyond the formal, material, and visible limits of physical presence in its ek-sistence. The second failure is that we are in fact not able to silence this *other* body of ours. Not being able to represent or even articulate this *other* body, we cannot, however, not feel its presence. We fail to leave it be, as if we could be indifferent to it, as if we could put it aside and not be disturbed by its absent presence. Something—a body—always cries out to us, even though we cannot see or grasp it, even though we fail to find the exact words for it; it cries out in and through our writing. We always fail to silence exscription.

Despite Nancy's pronouncement of the "double failure" of exscription, I suspect he still brackets a sense of failure, particularly the sense of failed existence—one that fails to continue wanting to exist, one that seeks a literal out of existence as in Sedgwick's ek-sistence, as seen earlier—in his elucidation of existence through exscription. He seems to want to overcome this particular failure that motivates the corresponding dark ek-sistence through his undeniable insistence, not unlike Gilles Deleuze, on affirming life and/or the continuation of life in existence throughout his philosophical writings. He does not quite follow ek-sistence through to its end, in other words. Certainly, Nancy in elucidating exscription would consider the "body sending itself out" (*être s'envoyant*); the body "always on the point of departing, in the imminence of a movement, of a fall [*chute*], of a distancing [*écart*], of a dislocation," "a suffering body," the body of "fatigue," the body that "expels itself" or is "expelled," and the body that registers its "degradation . . . up to its paralysis."[81] However, Nancy does not expand exscription to include the body that is burning out, totally exhausted, if not exhausting itself, not only by ordinary failures but also *by existence itself*: the depressed, anxious, catatonic body; the insomniac body; the body fumbling, in shame, shattered; the body abandoning all wills to live on, to struggle on, to be resilient, to pick itself up after it has failed, fallen; the body just desiring to disappear, to fade out, to extinguish itself; the body either having done with its pains, or else the body that has learned to live with its pains, to accept its pains, to accept them as but part of itself;[82] the body that, like Sedgwick in *A Dialogue on Love*, really wants *out*—a real out—in or through the *ek-* of ek-sistence; the flopped or flopping body; the body crying out mutedly; the body that undoes itself (*se désœuvrer*); the suicidal body; the body that is indeed a black hole, which, to borrow Nancy's words, is the body as "a star that extinguishes itself and collapses into itself."[83] These are bodies that no philosophy against suicide (Camus), no philosophy combatting for the affirmation of life (Deleuze), no philosophy of sense of existence that establishes life as unsacrificeable (Nancy), no psychoanalysis, and especially no talk therapy can console or talk out of their affective states. Not even pharmaceuticals. Not even all the love in the world (Woolf).[84] Not even the other fellow bodies of failure: here, Nancy is precise in saying that for a body that "rejoices [*joui*] in pain," this rejoicing is but an "unshareable sharing" (*impartageable partage*).[85]

All the above bodies, like any other body that Nancy considers, certainly do not stay silent, despite or in spite of the fact that they actually tend not to inscribe all the sensations or affects accompanying their failures in writing. They nevertheless cry out for care; they seek a care of itself, a care that is undoubtedly as dark as the one in Sedgwick's *A Dialogue on Love*. This is why these bodies exist/*ek-sist* no less as exscription. In a way, this also means that they demand a particular mode of reading, and Nancy has given us an indication of the approaches to such a reading. In the earlier iteration of exscription, Nancy proposes a mode of reading that is not committed to any commentary of a text, "neither seeking nor positing to interpret, signify."[86] In the later *Corpus*, he will say that if it is possible to read exscription, it will be a kind of reading that has nothing to do with "deciphering"; instead, it will be a matter of "touch and being touched."[87]

But how exactly do we touch, and how are we touched by, the bodies of, or in, exscription? According to Nancy, it has to do with "feeling the weight" (*être pesé*) of the "infinitesimal expenditure of some grams" of these bodies.[88] And this, in line with Nancy's philosophy of touch, must be done with tact. In other words, touching here involves touch that knows how to withdraw itself, touch that knows not to touch too much, if not touch that we can say proceeds with care.[89] In a way, there is already tact on the part of bodies in exscription, since they step away from signification, withdrawing from any full and fixed presence in writing on the page; they also certainly do not make it an imperative for anyone to read or decipher them. Tact or a careful touch, on the part of the reader of exscription, then, perhaps entails some form of reserved hermeneutical interpretation, if not a resistance against, "paranoid reading," which, as Sedgwick tells us, only displays the reader's ingenuity for close reading or which mimics the underlying idea in the text at hand in order to reiterate it as a "strong theory" that typically claims to explain everything, or which preemptively closes off any "bad surprise" that might pose as a pushback against itself as a "strong theory." I would go further here to say that this tact might even refuse a "reparative reading" as Sedgwick would want it, only if such a reading means imposing upon all the senses and affects of failure a recuperative horizon. Perhaps, then, it is a mere matter of listening to, and letting resound, the pain that inheres in writing or language, as Werner Hamacher tells us in one of his last unfinished and posthumously published texts.[90] It is to be sensitive or attuned to the lingering pain of bodies of failure in exscription, the pain of existing passing through ek-sistence, as we have done with Ovid's Narcissus story and Sedgwick's *A Dialogue on Love*. After all, there can be muscle memory in language or writing, and Nancy recognizes this as much when he says, "If I write, this strange hand [of my body in ek-sistence] has already slid into my hand that writes";[91] and muscle memory no doubt also includes sensations of pain.

To be sure, pain abounds no less in Nancy's discourse on exscription. The writing of bodies, according to Nancy, is "without anguish, perhaps, but not without pain (or trouble [*peine*])."[92] Pain renders the material body undeniable. As Nancy continues to say, the "limit of pain" is what "offers an intense evidence" of the body, of "the body in sorrow" (*le corps en peine*).[93] But he will also write further on: "Pain does not present itself as meaning. We are in pain for we are *organized for meaning*, and its loss hurts us, hollows us [*nous entaille*]. But no more than lost meaning, pain does not make meaning of loss. It is only sharpness, the burn, misery."[94] This seemingly implies that the pain that Nancy seems keener to acknowledge and elucidate is more an epistemological pain than an experiential one: we are in pain primarily only because we fail to construct a legible system of knowledge of bodies in exscription, to ascribe meaning—through signification, through the inscription of common and intelligible sense—to the bodies in exscription, whose departure or "loss" is but a secondary pain for us.[95] But, to reiterate, there are indeed other real pains beyond the pain that follows from our (failed) will to make meaning, pains that cut deeper into our sense of existence and push us toward a real out of ek-sistence. There are affects of these other real pains, of pains resulting from more personal failures, each of them different in themselves, no less registered or traced out in exscription. In this respect, I would like to think that exscription is also the memory of such pains: it brings up the pain in our existence, in our ek-sistence.

—

Such an exscription can be found in Édouard Levé's *Suicide* (2008). Levé is no major French writer, but he did receive some posthumous attention with *Suicide* because of the circumstances surrounding its publication—namely, the fact that it was published in the wake of Levé taking his own life ten days after submitting the manuscript to his editor. At this point, I underscore how the institutional culture of close reading methods, still dominant today, is always accompanied by the paranoia of committing intentional fallacy, hence generally averse to allowing the fact of Levé's life or extratextual biographical information (if not, Levé's *hors-texte*) to influence or affect any reading of *Suicide*.⁹⁶ Yet, in light of what we have learned from Nancy on exscription, I would argue that taking into consideration the fact of Levé's exiting existence can be critical for understanding *Suicide*. Besides, Levé's earlier *Autoportrait* (2005) seems to allow for such a consideration of *Suicide*. Yet *Autoportrait* actually problematizes any reading of *Suicide*. The narrator in *Autoportrait* will say, "I do not write narratives. I do not write novels. I do not write short stories. I do not write plays. I do not write poems. I do not write detective fiction. I do not write science-fiction. I write fragments."⁹⁷ *Suicide*, however, is not composed of fragments.⁹⁸ How, then, do we make sense of *Suicide*? On the surface, *Suicide* is a text about, and addressed to, a childhood friend of the narrator's who committed suicide at the age of twenty-five. The text attempts to make sense of this suicide, which the narrative does by assuming the friend's point of view on life. Yet, as the narrator recognizes, this task is doomed to fail since there can never be "good reasons" for understanding such an act.⁹⁹ Nonetheless, something does get written. And one could ask: Why write on? Why leave something written (out) if the narrator knows it is a failed project from the start?

As I see it, the manuscript is written—or, rather, it is necessarily written—because of the irresistible and irrepressible force or affect of exscription that is taking place through the narrator's ek-sistence. We can sense the latter if we recognize the uncanny resemblance between the friend and the narrator himself. That the narrator is actually not much different from the friend becomes more evident if we take into account *Autoportrait* here. Supposing that both narrators in *Autoportrait* and *Suicide* are the same, which then entails that *Autoportrait* arguably gives us a sense of the narrator in *Suicide*, we can assume the latter to be, like the friend, an insomniac body, an evasive body that shies away from new social groups, a body that feels difficult to be loved by both others and itself,¹⁰⁰ a body that feels alone in the world despite the love of others, a body that has difficulty feeling happiness, a body that is fearful of getting old, a body that refuses to pathologically reduce itself to being ill, a body resistant to psychoanalysis and psychiatric and/or psychological interventions, a body that feels some strange affinity to tramps (*clochards*), to the unhappy lot, to "those who have failed at everything, or succeeded at nothing."¹⁰¹ Both the narrator in *Autoportrait* and the friend are furthermore bodies that feel the pull of ek-sistence: bodies that, after a shower, feel separated from themselves, "relaxed to the point of being insensible"; bodies that subject themselves to intensive sport, running, expending themselves (*se dépenser*) to the point of "physical excess" such that in the state of extreme exhaustion thereafter, what passes between the temples, the eyes, and the back of the skull no longer belongs to them; bodies that ask themselves if they were themselves.[102]

More pointedly, the narrator in *Autoportrait* acknowledges that, having been tempted four times to commit suicide, he did attempt once. In this regard, it is not difficult to recognize in the narrator of both *Autoportrait* and *Suicide*, not unlike Sedgwick in *A Dialogue on Love*, one who has failed to die at the right time. Avoiding the narrow, probing, and paranoid vision and method of close reading (as any reading of exscription does as much as a "reparative reading"), I would then like to more tactfully posit the possibility of *Suicide* as exscription in the sense of *also* "exscribing" the body of the narrator, the body that wants a real out in ek-sistence, the body that believes in suicide to be able to calm, if not expel, "the painful agitation" of life.[103] Put more simply, *Suicide* is the text that allows the narrator to exscribe his ek-sistence through the recounting of his friend's ek-sistence. Ek-sistence like the one in Levé somehow finds its way into writing; or else, the exscription of writing, or what Al Alvarez had once called "quasi-literary forces," can constitute the propelling force of ek-sistence.[104] What remains for us to do, then, is simply to listen to this body in ek-sistence as it exscribes itself, to let it speak in its exscription, to be open to, and accepting of, all its affects, and perhaps even let it go, according to the dark abyss of ek-sistence. As exscription, this also means that we can only read or listen to the body in ek-sistence in either a belated or retroactive manner; we can read or listen to its affects only after the fact, as echoes, as reverberations that return only posthumously. Perhaps this is the least or even best care we can give to the selves seeking ek-sistence. To be sure, exscription, at least in the case of Levé's, does not call out for any form of care by others. Exscriptions like Levé's do not appeal for any intervention whatsoever from others; they do not need others to act on anything, except, as said, perhaps to give them space, read them, and recognize them as a legitimate discourse that takes care of the self of ek-sistence. And yet, even in this regard, it has to be acknowledged that exscription as such is not only a resonance of the sense and affects of failure, of a body that has failed to die at the right time, but also a mark of *our* failure to have read, listened to, and sensed those senses and affects at the moment when the body is flailing in failure to die at the right time.

4

THE MELODRAMA OF FAILURE'S SHARED UNSHAREABILITY, SUICIDAL IDEATION INCLUDED

YIYUN LI'S *DEAR FRIEND, WHERE REASONS END,* AND *MUST I GO*

The Shared Unshareability of Failure

In chapter 2, we saw the narrator in Cusk's *Outline* trilogy assuming the role of a receptacle for all the narratives of failures recounted by other characters she meets in her peregrinations following her own failed marriage and/or family life. We have also noted how the narratives of her own failures were never shared with the characters, not that the latter initiated or even demonstrated any genuine or sincere desire to know or listen to them. Chapter 3 underscored, though, that such personal narratives of personal failure nevertheless need to be inscribed: the sense of failure always seeks its articulation; it "exscribes" itself in existence. Silence is not really an option. We have thus been careful to state in the chapter on Cusk that while the Neutral drifting of Faye involves reticence, it does *not* at all mean absolute silence. Or, as Anne the playwright, and Faye's fellow English instructor at the writing course in Athens, would express her concern about silence: "If people were silent about the things that had happened to them, was something not betrayed, even if only the version of themselves that had experienced them?"[1] She would go on to say that this silence might also entail forgetting, and "there was something worse than forgetting, which was misrepresentation, bias, the selective presentation of events."[2] To bring this to bear on our present work, we will say that to confine failure to silence is to risk us failing to recognize, accept, and respect the modes of living of failed existence; us imagining wrongly what it might be to live on after failure; us failing to understand that it is actually difficult, if not impossible, to snap out of the sense of failure and get on with life. The experience of failure, of the difficulty to live on after and/or with failure, has to be written.

Yet, even though the inscription of failure implies that these narratives of failures are from then on shared with the rest of the world, it does not mean that the sense of failure is understood or similarly felt by others. To be sure, and to be fair to others, this is not always their fault. It is not always their lack of sympathy and/or empathy as made manifest through their unwillingness or noncommitment to listen, as is the case with the other characters in Cusk's novels. As the selected works of Sedgwick and Levé suggest, no one else but oneself feels the full impact of one's sense of failure, bears the weight of one's failures, and inhabits the moods of the negative affects that linger in the remainder of one's failed existence. Furthermore, in these cases, hardly any sympathy and/or empathy from others can alleviate or dispel the sense of failure felt by the individual. We come back, then, to an aspect of failure mentioned at the beginning of this book: its *shared unshareability*.[3] The experience of failure—even that of a same or similar failure—can be unique to each and every one of us. Each of us experiences differently how that failure befalls us, the duration of that sense of failure in us, and how the afterlife of that failure unfolds. Only we ourselves know and feel the full force of failure in us. In other words, no matter how much of that failure is shared with others through conversations or writing, something of that failure will be reserved only for ourselves, forever uncommunicated or uncommunicable in any absolute sense to others. This is how failure, at the end of it all, bears some irreducible shared unshareability in us all. With failure, then, we go (with) it alone, ultimately. Or, as Virginia Woolf once said of depression, which may be considered the failure to go about life in a "normal," "healthy" way void of negative thoughts swarming the mind, it is even preferable as such.[4]

The affirmation of failure's shared unshareability here runs counter to a common trajectory in "failure studies." As mentioned in the introduction, many works in failure studies tend to perform some kind of recuperative or reparative reading of failure. Part of this reparative move is to also give failure a communitarian contour or horizon. This is rather evident in Halberstam's *The Queer Art of Failure*, where failure is claimed to be a queer characteristic or property: "something queers do and have always done exceptionally well," if not, following Quentin Crisp's claim, something that constitutes their "style."[5] It can also be found in Shawn Graham's *Failing Gloriously*, where he says that "failing gloriously is a collective endeavor" and—with added altruistic spirit—"an exhortation to build spaces that make it safe for others to have the same freedom to make mistakes, tinker, iterate, and imagine better."[6] With shared unshareability, I am resisting this communitarian move. I believe that the literary works discussed in this book so far do likewise and so will those that I will look at in this final chapter.[7] They all suggest that the sense of failure, especially with regard to personal failures, can never find its sharing with another. Such failures even resist leaving the domain of the personal. Reckoning with failure's shared unshareability, as I would argue, helps us come to terms with the full dimension of the sense of personal failure: how inescapable that sense of failure really is for the individual, how there can be no relief to it, despite whatever external help. It also makes us recognize, accept, and respect the desire of those who prefer to keep their sense of failure as such to themselves, who want to dwell or wallow in it, and who refuse any project that endeavors to turn failure into a reparative object or collective pedagogy.

In this chapter, I want to give further elucidation to failure's shared unshareability through a reading of selected works of Yiyun Li. I will start with *Dear Friend, from My Life I Write to You* (2017), a hybrid genre of memoir writing and essays, and then work through the two novels that follow—namely, *Where Reasons End* (2019), an undoubtedly "autofictional" work, and *Must I Go* (2020), which returns to a more conventional fictional register. In my view, they provide nuanced depictions of how one negotiates with the shared unshareability of existential failure particularly—that is, of the failure to want to live (on), more commonly known as suicidal ideation. Quite immediately, the different genres (in the classical sense)—the memoir versus the novel—and the different forms of the same genre—the "autofictional" novel versus the more traditional fictional novel—with which Li experiments across these works make manifest the implication of writing with regard to circumscribing the sense of shared unshareability. In other words, her experimentations only betray a dissatisfaction with these genres or forms: one is always left desperately seeking a mode of writing that could adequately manage the sense of shared unshareability. Or else, more precisely perhaps, this seeking only bespeaks the unmanageability of shared unshareability. This desperate seeking is certainly not short on histrionics or, as Li prefers, melodrama. One could say that melodrama is the genre—and we return to the sense of bodily or gestural genre here—that flails in Li's works. As will be seen, melodrama in Li can oscillate between, on the one hand, the more common form that manifestly overflows with sentimentality and, on the other, an idiosyncratic, reserved form exercised with reluctant sentimentality. Let us say at the outset that such a wavering between melodramatic forms, just like the inability to settle on a literary genre for the inscription of failure's shared unshareability, betrays the inadequacy or even precariousness of melodrama as a genre of living on after failure. The flailing of both genres in the classical sense and in Berlant's terms in Li's works, then, points to the enduring existential struggle with failure's shared unshareability. It is a reckoning with an existence wrought with the irreducible mark of failure, one that, as will be seen, threatens to overtake existence anytime.

Li's works will also show furthermore how even for those particularly attached to their sense of failure and who also desire failure's shared unshareability, they nevertheless struggle much with the latter too. As *Dear Friend* intimates, many of this lot feel exclusively privy to failure's shared unshareability, believing that no one else gets it, which is also why, in immersing themselves in it, they are more than ready, or even glad, to further follow it down the rabbit hole alone. This shared unshareability is felt as their sanctuary, a bubble to which they believe to have exclusive entry, access, and right to occupancy. They would thus even refuse recognizing it in another whose existence is likewise awash with an overwhelming sense of failure (which only reaffirms failure's shared unshareability even between those who belong to the lot that acknowledges failure in themselves). So, when another effectively lays claim to it as well, if not first, the assumed sanctity can be easily shattered, the bubble burst. Shared unshareability henceforth becomes an uncanny phenomenon or concept that is difficult for them to come to terms with, if not an affect not unlike Sianne Ngai's "ugly feeling," which imbues them with a "suspended agency," leaving them not knowing how to act or react.[8] This is especially so when that other is someone particularly close; for example, a mother's child, a mother's pride, as we will see in *Where Reasons End*. To see it in someone close as such is heartrending, to say the least. But for those who had the illusion of solely possessing failure's shared unshareability, the reckoning of this shared unshareability in a loved one also amplifies their own sense of failure, multiplying the series of failures in them: to what they might have considered the very last thing in life to hold onto, or that one thing in life that they might finally be able to call their own, they fail to lay exclusive claim. The elusiveness of an exclusive shared unshareability thus becomes yet another failure of a failed existence, marking existence as failed through and through. This does not mean, though, that failure's shared unshareability has left them. One might be distracted by its presence in another, but one's own sense of failure and its shared unshareability, as will be seen in *Must I Go*, will always resurface from within, reasserting its persistence, relentlessly cutting across and troubling one's existence.

Dear Friend (2017)

Let us begin with *Dear Friend*. This text tracks Li's writings across two years after her two-year bout of suicidal depression and hospitalization for it. Suicidal ideation arguably bespeaks a certain sense of failure: the failure to want to live, the failure to sustain the desire to continue existing. In this respect, *Dear Friend* touches on undoubtedly the most unshareable of all the senses of failure, if we keep in mind how society tends to discourage or even repress the discourse of suicidal ideation: the typical response, according to social practices, to someone who expresses suicidal ideation is "don't say that."[9] Even before reckoning with this particular failure, many will find it hard to discern *any* sense of failure in Li, though. Her switch from a career as an immunologist to a recognized writer and professor of creative writing and the successful transition from a life in China to a new one in America, all recounted in *Dear Friend*, have led some of her readers to consider her "an example of the American dream" if not, in the words of Rachel Cusk, "to belong to [the] narrative of success."[10]

Yet, Li is left nonetheless with an inextinguishable feeling of emptiness, one that poses as an uncontestable negating force to her existence: an "emptiness that says: you are nothing."[11] There can be no logical explanation for whence this feeling comes or why it hits her (which perhaps also explains why it is difficult for her to articulate this sense of failure to readers for the most part of *Dear Friend*). Arriving as "blind and intuitive," it essentially defies reason.[12] It operates more like an affective force stirring from within—not unlike Williams's "structure of feeling" that we have suggested to first pertain to or affect the personal before finding its prevalence in the collective—which not only sticks to her but also overwhelms and undercuts her sense of existence, buoying her suicidal ideation. This is why, in order to explain her suicidal ideation, the best she could say is: "One never kills oneself from knowledge or understanding, but always out of feelings."[13] And yet, paradoxically, this feeling of negating emptiness is the only way existence makes sense for her. As she sees it, existing is not only about being capable of living life to the fullest but also being "capable of... diminishing our precarious selves."[14] And she understands that this desire for "nonexistence" is a deeply personal feeling.[15] As mentioned above, this is indeed rarely the perspective of the collective, wherein suicidal ideation is almost always negatively interrogated while "one's will to live... is never questioned."[16] Thus, no one can fully understand why she desires or even needs this feeling that defies common sense, one that deviates from what it means to be alive, to exist meaningfully, or to live with the gratitude of being in the world; no one will be able to comprehend how and why she inhabits this feeling. Conversely, no one, nothing, can convince her otherwise of this feeling either.

It is in negotiating this nihilistic yet irresistible feeling by oneself that, according to Li, the question of melodrama arises. For Berlant in her study of this genre, melodrama as we know it is a reflection of the universality of human suffering: "melodramatic conventions" are means to "locate the human in a universal capacity to suffer."[17] This aspect of melodrama applies to Li's version no less if we acknowledge that Li's melodrama of navigating suicidal ideation is actually *not* an uncommon human condition but a more prevalent situation affecting more people than we are willing to count. For Berlant, melodrama is moreover implicated in sentimentality, whereby the acting out of inner or private sufferings through indulgences in fantasies more or less enjoyed by the masses allows "the sentimental subject" to be "connected to others who share the same sense that the world is out of joint, without necessarily having the same view of the reasons or solutions."[18] Here, melodramatic sentimentality, or sentimental melodrama, becomes more than a personal affair. The personal is no longer "organized by the singular autobiography" but extends into the general domain, affirming an "intimate publics," which is "an achievement" in Berlant's eyes, since publics "magnetize optimism about living and being connected to strangers in a kind of nebulous *communitas*."[19] Melodrama in Li's terms, however, resists this slide toward the general or publics. Certainly, melodrama might involve drama or histrionics in one's response to the sense of failure, but these dramas or histrionics in Li's melodrama are not really intended as spectacles for an audience to gather and watch. I have cited the following lines from Li in the introduction, but let me quote them again, where Li sets melodrama in opposition to tragedy and comedy: "Tragedy and comedy involve an audience, so they must give—sharing themselves to elicit tears and laughter. Melodrama is not such a strategist. It meets no one's expectation but its internal need to feel."[20] In other words, melodrama, for Li, is very much an affective response that moves *away* from the social field and back toward the personal domain in order to attend to one's "structure of feeling"—that is, with what can be felt only by oneself.[21]

If it is not already evident, Li's melodrama, in trying to respond to one's desire to exit existence, or perhaps more precisely to the *failure* of that desire to pass into an act, does not actually offer any respite or relief. It leaves living on after that failure at an impasse. As Li says, in comparison to tragedy and comedy again, "If a tragedy makes us weep out of compassion and a comedy makes us laugh out of appreciation, a melodrama alienates and discomfits."[22] She continues: "When we cry, we cry under protest, suspicious of being manipulated; when we laugh, we laugh with the belief—doubtful—that we are beyond its absurdity."[23] In other words, melodrama neither has tragedy's cathartic function nor comedy's consolation of a return to order: in its tears, there is no purging of melancholic emotions or the "structure of feeling" that seemingly drives one toward suicidal ideation; in its laughter, there is no happy return to a bright, optimistic mode of existing. Instead, there are only frustrated tears because one is still fed, or made to accept, the narrative of the good life while no one else understands the refusal of such a narrative; there is only cynical laughter because one knows that living on is just the absurd prolonging of a senseless existence, if not a living out of the failure to "die at the right time," to cite Nietzsche once again.[24] Here, one could add that melodrama in Li is suspicious of sentimentality, especially if one understands it as Berlant does, that is, involving "fantasies of the good life" where "the social world" can become "an affective space where people ought to be legitimated because they have feelings and because there is an intelligence in what they feel that they *know* something about the world that, if it were listened to, could make things better."[25] The social world, as Li discerns, is not (yet) receptive or prepared to listen to those with feelings of inconsolable failure and/or suicidal ideation. For Li, then, melodrama is a reiteration of failure and not an "achievement" as Berlant would want it.

Leaving one indissolubly uneasy with one's sense of failure, leaving one irremediably out of sync with the world, it is not difficult to see how melodrama barely sustains any form of living on after failure, any form of existence that is traversed by failure's shared unshareability. It is thus not surprising if we struggle with the genre of melodrama, if not refuse it too. As Li recognizes, "In life we shun melodrama, as its audience, and more urgently, as participants," and this refrain from melodrama only widens the gulf of shared unshareability between oneself and the world.[26] To see this, we have to first understand why we avoid melodrama as its participants. We do that, according to Li, because we know how it can throw into disarray our ties with others, especially when melodrama replays the failures of our past relations with others. This threatens to make us lose confidence or conviction in any reconnection with others, as it either anticipates a shared unshareability to come by thinking that the past will repeat itself or betrays one that is already underlying between us and others. Melodrama can also remind us of our failure to die at the right time, and in this case, it renders any attempt to conjure a progress narrative of our life dubious. In this case, it also disrupts the order through which we try to keep our emotions in check, through which we do not expose our emotional or psychological vulnerabilities, our breakdowns, our inability to keep ourselves together, our lapse in rational control, and the subsequent precipitation into sentimental despair. Melodrama is like a siren song here, drawing us back to our sense of existential failure, which is also why, for those who fear facing one's sense of failure straight on, for those who fear what such an encounter could do to oneself, melodrama is to be kept at bay as much as possible.

It is this siren song that drives others away as well from melodrama, further exposing failure's shared unshareability as without suture. As suggested previously, the siren song might very much be personal music, but there is the risk that this music might flood the audience's own life soundtrack that sustains the order or sense of their existence. Perhaps this is why Li herself avoids others who seek an exit from existence. Li is indeed not the only one with suicidal thoughts in *Dear Friend*. Almost right at the beginning of the text, we read of the "acquaintance" to whom Li gives her only two minutes on the phone. The acquaintance jumped off a building two weeks later, and Li declined attending her memorial service. In this case, there seems to be a refusal on Li's part to have any share of another's melodrama. In other words, shared unshareability is not just the affect one feels about how one's sense of failure and desire to exit existence can never be shared with another; it is also one's cruel projection onto another who might just share a similar sense of failure and suicidal ideation, a projection that however demarcates a distance between one and the other, hence refusing or precluding any sharing. At the same time, though, one must also not ignore the fact that being melodrama's audience can be exhausting, especially when the melodrama seems drawn-out and its author stubborn not to heed the audience's counsel to dispel all negative thoughts, leaving the pessimistic horizon unmoved. This is perhaps why there also tends to be the endeavor by the audience to short-circuit and hijack melodrama, especially in the case of the melodrama of suicidal ideation where, according to Li, "the most private decision ... is often taken over by the public" such that "those who express strong feelings mistake themselves as the center of a story."[27] The pain of an existence traced always with "the violent wish that [one] had never been born"[28] or the wish "to stay invisible" from the rest of the world, therefore, can only be a "private matter."[29] After all, Li says, too, "one does not have the capacity to feel another person's feelings fully—a fact of life, democratic to all."[30] Unshareable is the feeling of an extinguishing nothingness or emptiness, the desire to exit from existence, and/or the failure to die at the right time. The only way to go on, and if one does go on, is solitarily.

Yet solitariness or "loneliness" exposes precisely "the inability to speak with another in one's private language" of one's failures through melodrama, if not the inadequacy or even failure of the genre itself in coping with the sense of personal failure and its shared unshareability.[31] Something more is needed, therefore, in order to negotiate the feelings to which melodrama seeks to attend.[32] For Li, it is writing, which is undoubtedly an even more private activity, and writing here means to write arduously, fanatically, with abandon, as if there were no tomorrow (and I would add that this genre of writing is quite different from the more diary-like writing for which Foucault advocates for his notion of a "care of the self," as seen in the preceding chapter). As Li says, "[The] tireless drive to write must have something to do with what cannot be told."[33] Or, as she recounts her career-switch, the "absoluteness of the abandonment" of herself into the world of creative writing was done "with such determination that it is a kind of suicide."[34] We see here a certain relation between the fervor for writing and an unspeakable death-wish, and I would argue that suicide in this case is more than a metaphor. The text seems to suggest that the acts of inscription granted by a writing career can possibly be steps toward actualizing suicidal ideation; the vocation might enable one to carve out a space wherein the idea can potentially pass into act. Admittedly, all this is not immediately evident but very much a speculation. Nevertheless, we could say that a certain rehearsal for this seems intimated through her thinking about the end of lives of her characters when a novel concludes. According to Li, such a thought is akin to a "secretive . . . suicidal thought lodged in the corner of one's mind."[35] Otherwise, Li would also say that writing in general is very much "[her] way of rehearsing death,"[36] a way by which she "could will [herself] into a nonentity."[37] Certainly, we might read, toward the end of *Dear Friend* that Li had "agreed to give up," upon leaving the hospital wherein she sought help for her suicidal depression, "the thought of disappearing from the world."[38] However, her writing betrays how this conviction is actually quite untenable. As Li acknowledges later, there is always that "difficult moment" when "the same pattern repeats itself"[39]—when the melodramatic siren song swells up from within to lure her yet again to drift toward nonexistence. The thought of exiting from existence is thus not really "an emergency exit," one taken emphatically at a decisive moment for a definitive departure but rather an exit through which—and through writing—one has already started to slip into, surreptitiously, imperceptibly (to oneself too), gradually, step by step, breath by breath, sigh after sigh, word after word, at each repeated "difficult moment" in life.[40]

Writing thus leaves one very much in the impasse no less than melodrama, to which writing seeks to supplement, barely offering any resolution or consolation. As Li puts it: "Uncharitably one writes in order to stop oneself from feeling too much; uncharitably one writes to become closer to that feeling self."[41] In other words, one might write in the endeavor to negotiate with the melodrama stirring from within, but that very same practice of writing only augments or intensifies that melodrama. At the level of the personal, writing only compounds the sense of failure since, if the "difficult moments" inflected with the desire to exit existence and the sense of failure from the inability to do so are essentially incommunicable, "any word is the wrong word when it is too close to the unspeakable."[42] Every other word, then, only adds to the existing sense of failure. At the level of the interpersonal, the writing of melodrama, if not melodrama as writing, only reiterates the near impossibility of empathy or fellow understanding. As Li says: "The inadequacy of writing is similar to that of connecting to another person. It is essential that a story allow its melodrama to meet the reader's, yet melodrama makes such encounters rare."[43] Put another way, and to riff on Li's words elsewhere in *Dear Friend*, what can be spoken with another actually cannot sustain the existence that one is still bearing; what cannot be spoken, or what is left unsaid, such as the lingering desire to disappear from the world, meanwhile, effectively undermines the relation one has with another.[44] What remains, again or always, is the sense of failure's shared unshareability.

Where Reasons End (2019)

If the one who embraces the sense of irredeemable failure feels that he or she has exclusive rights to failure's shared unshareability, this illusion can be quickly dashed when another, especially someone close, lays claim to it first. On a biographical note, the wresting of the exclusive sense of shared unshareability from Li would come from her elder son, who committed suicide in 2017, the same year *Dear Friend* was published. To come to terms with the unthinkability of how one could lose someone close to failure's shared unshareability, and worse, to its precipitation into suicide, it seems like the genre (in the classical sense) of memoir, as deployed in *Dear Friend*, is no longer adequate. Neither is the distance from sentimentality sustainable. Li thus turns to fiction in her next work, the novel *Where Reasons End*, published two years after her eldest son's death and which concerns a mother who lost her fourteen-year-old son Nikolai to suicide. Rather evidently "autofictional"—and Li has since acknowledged the autobiographical dimension of this novel[45]—it is also a work of mourning, a playing-out of a mother's imagined, or more precisely phantasmatic, conversation with her dead son.[46] This is melodrama as conventionally understood, no doubt, which sustains a mother's sentimental fantasy of her son existing in some immaterial form in a realm not entirely detached from this mortal world, of being able to still communicate with him.[47] But the novel is also a testimony of the fact that failure's shared unshareability does not solely rest with her, that her desire "to strike back at the body that lives in time and feels pain," according to Cusk again, is actually *not* "her own entitlement."[48]

Like Li, Nikolai barely betrays any sign of bearing a sense of existential failure. Nikolai's childhood reads nothing like failure. With clearly no lack of family love, well-liked by friends, and seemingly good at everything he does, it is beyond comprehension, at least from a mother's point of view, why Nikolai would wish, like Li, for nonexistence. Unless doing well, which can translate into the desire to overachieve if not seek perfection, is a tell-tale sign of a predisposition toward inhabiting an acute sense of failure. The flip side, if not curse, of perfectionism, however, is arguably the hypersensitivity toward failure.[49] Doing well is indeed insufficient for Nikolai; it is "different from being perfect."[50] Falling short of perfection only amounts to a failed existence. Reality, however, tends to render perfection impossible, making a life that seeks only perfection unforgiving,[51] making it fall into disappointment, despair, anguish, hopelessness, or "inconsolable bleakness."[52] Since nothing less than perfect is acceptable, existing as such is only to suffer "the weight of living," and Nikolai sees no other way but to take himself out of an unbearable, compromised, prosaic life.[53] To be sure, or at least according to the narrative, the need to be perfect in Nikolai is not driven by external pressure or influence, even though one could suspect systemic structures or ideologies of success to be already internalized or naturalized in him. His mother in fact also dissuades him from such a quest, reminding him that it is OK to be imperfect, that an imperfect life can still "mean something."[54]

Yet such consolation barely helps. It hardly lifts one up from the abyss of despair, from the anguishing sense of failure. It even makes things worse. As Nikolai tells his mother, the more she tries to talk him out of his obsession with perfection, "I suffer more because you want to do what the world does, to dim the bright and to blunt the sharp."[55] So, it is all Nikolai, to want to a have a life that is nothing but perfect. "Perfection is my only way of living" as he says.[56] This desire structures Nikolai's sense of existence; it constitutes his ontological structure. Not unlike the case of Li's desire for "nonexistence" in *Dear Friend*, no one, nothing, can talk him out of it either.

The perfectionist's curse aside, there is also the matter of time. Time does not forget failure. It remembers failure past, present, and future. It archives past failures and saturates present time with remembrances of them, in addition to whatever new failures that it indiscriminately receives at present. Time is never inhospitable to them, and it carries all these into the future, rendering failure effectively unforgettable—as unforgettable as time (not to mention giving failure an accumulative effect, too, as said in our introduction). Time might heal the hurt from failures, but it sure does not forget. As long as there is time—and there will always be time—existence will indelibly be punctuated or punctured by the sense of failure. To put it in a Barthesian way, time is the phenomenological support for the *punctum* of failure, providing the medium on which the sense of failure can leave its legible marks for us to read over and over again and by which failure's affects can circulate and henceforth be palpably felt by us. Or, to move closer to Li's rhetoric, time is melodrama's beat, sustaining melodrama in the pulsation of life, giving it a rhythm according to which it will swell up and overwhelm existence from time to time. To see time as such is also to discern the very punishing effect of time in its very unit; it is a way of *not* glossing time as a general flow that drowns out singular temporal moments that resonate with the sense of failure in its intensity. This dissection of time, or "time thus broken down," as Nikolai puts it, only "makes quicksand," and one sinks in quicksand, precipitating into the abyss of imperfect life.[57] Time, then, is effectively more unforgiving, way crueler than the self that chooses the relentless pursuit of perfection, and it is time, more than life itself, in fact, that Nikolai avows to "unfriend or unfollow" through suicide.[58]

The issue of time is important because it is not the first time in Li's writings that we read about suicide as the gesture or attempt to defeat time. Already in *Dear Friend*, Li has written that suicide might be the "courageous endeavor to kill time" literally, which is admittedly nothing short of hubris.[59] There is thus some sort of staging of something shared between Li and Nikolai: they share a common enemy in time, sharing the conviction in suicide as the way to counter time, to get out of a failed existence. Nikolai apparently recognizes this sharing, which is why when the mother in *Where Reasons End* tries to retroactively reason with Nikolai against suicide, telling him that "there are a million things worth living for," he is able to give the irrefutable response: "You don't even believe it yourself."[60] He rightly highlights the contradiction of her telling him about the positive or optimistic possibilities of life while she herself—privately—sees only negativity in life.[61] In a way, this exposes the mother's inability to reckon with the impossibility to reserve failure's shared unshareability and the subsequent desire for nonexistence for herself, her inability to reckon with the fact that these can find their sharing in Nikolai. But, of course, Nikolai, for his part, never did share his sense of a bleak or failed existence and his desire and decision to quit existence when he was alive either. Perhaps that is why, if there is indeed some sort of sharing, it remains unthinkable for the mother: she cannot understand how Nikolai can have similar dark, pessimistic thoughts. What is shared is effectively left unshareable, therefore, not just because Nikolai never communicated his inner thoughts but also because the mother denies that the sharing had been in place all the time. All this unshareability, to the mother, is what essentially defies rational thought or reason. Its recognition or revelation in another—especially a loved one, a mother's child or mother's pride—is "where reasons end."

When reason or reasoning fails, one is left only with the need to feel. And when one has trouble feeling, or when one finds it uncomfortable to be in touch with one's feelings, perhaps writing can fill that gap. As Nikolai says, "I always imagine writing is for people who don't want to feel or don't know how to."[62] Indeed, for the mother, writing is the means to deal with the sadness of shared unshareability: the "sadness that stays inside one," more profound than the "sadness that takes over like an erupted volcano," and this sadness that never leaves the self is undoubtedly melodrama in Li's sense.[63] But once again, writing remains imperfect in the face of the task at hand. Put harshly, writing fails; putting it kindly, it flails as genres do, to borrow Berlant's phrase again. With respect to this melodrama of internal infinite sadness, writing can only be "immoderate" and "imprecise."[64] Or, as the mother puts it simply to Nikolai, "Words fall short."[65] Nevertheless, it is her only way through which she approaches "the unspeakable."[66] We have already seen this term mobilized in *Dear Friend* to refer to the unavowable and inextinguishable sense of failure and the desire to quit existence that follows in the wake of such a sense of failure. In *Where Reasons End*, it might refer to something similar in Nikolai, something to which the mother no doubt wants to get closer in order to accept Nikolai's suicide. But it points more to her inconsolable sadness of losing Nikolai, the "wound that stays open always, always, and forever."[67] It points even more, I would say, to the forever shared unshareability between herself and Nikolai of all the sense of failed existence, the subsequent desire to quit life, and the infinite pessimism that follows after.

If there were to be any sharing of failure's shared unshareability between one and another, this possibility rests, as *Where Reasons End* recognizes, only after life or posthumously—that is, when one has passed and the other is still in this mortal world. This clearly does not offer any consolation, since one must admit that this sharing is, as said earlier, phantasmatic at bottom: it does not occur in any real terms but in the imagination, in the fictionalizing work (of mourning), in the sentimental fantasy, of the one who remains alive. Such a posthumous sharing is, again, conventional melodrama as we know it, and *Where Reasons End* as a whole can be regarded to belong to such a convention. Now, if such a melodrama fails to offer any real consolation, if such sentimentality disappoints, this disappointment, as Berlant has argued in *The Female Complaint*, is in fact what structures sentimental melodrama. In other words, it is because of this structural disappointment that more sentimental fantasies can be generated. In a similar vein, perhaps it is the continued act of writing—because it fails in its ways—that allows one to hold on to a sense of that shared unshareability, to assure one that at least there had been that shared unshareability, even though it was, or is, essentially, paradoxically unshared or unshareable. Writing, in other words, is the continued playing out of the melodrama (both in Li's sense and the conventional sense) of wanting to feel the real but impossible share of shared unshareability. To feel this melodrama, one needs writing; writing is the continued negotiation with this melodrama. In this regard, the reiteration of a posthumous sharing or recognition of shared unshareability in Li's subsequent novel *Must I Go* perhaps bespeaks Li's desire to sustain the melodrama concerning her struggle to come to terms with failure's shared unshareability in a child who has passed.

Must I Go (2020)

But what about one's own sense of failure and its attendant shared unshareability? As discussed previously, the "autofictional" form of *Where Reasons End* might have allowed one to approach the sense of shared unshareability in another, but the sentimentality afforded by such a form might also have her almost completely submit to the other, leaving little room for one's own. Yet, to reiterate, one's own sense of failure and its shared unshareability never goes away but always returns to discomfit the self, to remind the self how it barely leaves the domain of the personal despite or in spite of any attempt at a sharing of another's shared unshareability. As said, *Must I Go* is the continued endeavor to hold on to a lingering sense of shared unshareability with a departed child, but what also unravels is the resurfacing of one's own sense of shared unshareability and the need to re-attend to it or even reassert it. Perhaps this is why *Must I Go* takes greater distance from autofiction and returns to the form of melodrama with minimal sentimentality that we have seen in *Dear Friend*. The distancing from autofiction and the sentimentality it affords, as we will see, also brings us to the reckoning that, at the end of it all, what remains is only the shared unshareability of one's failures and nobody else's. It is possibly even the judgment that sentimental autofiction can never suture the chasm of shared unshareability between one and another.

Despite the remove from autofiction, there is, like in *Where Reasons End*, a loss of a child in *Must I Go*, except it is no longer that of a son. Rather, it concerns the death of a daughter, Lucy, who incidentally dies by suicide too but at a later age of twenty-seven. While there seems to be no reason, as his mother sees it, as to why Nikolai would take his own life, a disappointing life accentuated by a marriage that was breaking down is suggested to be a contributing factor to Lucy's death. Nevertheless, like in the case of Nikolai, the thought of death, apparently without reason too, has always accompanied Lucy since she was young. As Lilia, her mother and narrator of *Must I Go*, recalls, she had seen Lucy's self-harm "scars neatly lined up on her inner arm."[68] Unlike the mother in *Where Reasons End*, though, Lilia does not probe to find out the reasons for Lucy's actions. Lilia adopts a cooler disposition, instead, "only warn[ing] [Lucy] that she would look ugly in a summer dress."[69] At other times, she would even opt for an indifferent response. Lilia recounts again: "Lucy used to threaten me that she would kill herself.... I didn't allow her to provoke me so I ignored her. I thought the threat would become a joke between us one day."[70] Lilia clearly skirts the issue of Lucy's suicidal ideation, deflecting the need to address the latter, avoiding melodrama as we know it, seemingly hoping that it would somehow go away in the future as Lucy grows older. Unfortunately, that would *not* be the dénouement of Lilia's choice to not have a share in knowing what troubles Lucy's existence. Despite or in spite of Lilia's responses to Lucy's suicidal ideation, one must not assume that Lucy would communicate or even share her dark thoughts. As Lilia says, too, Lucy was "so good at pushing everyone away."[71] Lilia thus recognizes an irreducible shared unshareability with respect to Lucy's sense of failed existence: shared because there were already signs—the scars, the outbursts—made manifest to the world of Lucy's desire to exit existence; unshareable because, Lilia believes, Lucy will always leave certain things unsaid in her tendency to withdraw from the world. Nevertheless, what cannot be denied is that Lilia makes a conscious effort in bracketing Lucy's shared unshareability, while the mother in *Where Reasons End* is always regretful that she missed the signs of that in Nikolai. But what Lilia seems to also suggest is that no sentimentality would have bridged, or will ever bridge, that shared unshareability.

If Lilia did not want to have a share in Lucy's negativity when Lucy was alive, neither does she seem to accept the aforementioned shared unshareability after Lucy's death. This can be elicited from her consideration of life after Lucy died. According to her, "Every morning since Lucy's death, I wake up and say to myself: Here's another day that Lucy refused to live. Not a day she gave up. If she gave up something I could give it up too. But she refused flatly to have today, and tomorrow, and the next day, and the next day."[72] Here, she makes the distinction between quitting and rejecting life, a difference critical enough for her to say that she might accept or even partake in the shared unshareability if it were a matter of quitting existence on Lucy's part, perhaps because she might sympathize with Lucy's having not enough fortitude or will to live on. Lilia believes, however, that it was a case of rejection for Lucy, which can be more willful, and this is why she has "all the more reason . . . to live each day, to prove a point," which is to "refuse to accept [Lucy's] refusal."[73] Lilia's living on after Lucy's death, then, is a testimony of her resistance against accepting the trace of shared unshareability left by Lucy. This is why Lilia will say that in the wake of Lucy's death, "I haven't stopped arguing with Lucy for thirty-seven years. . . . everything in my life is a part of that long argument with Lucy."[74] In choosing argument here, which is some form of rationalizing, Lilia contra the mother in *Where Reasons End* refuses conventional melodrama and/or sentimentality, if we assume such melodrama and/or sentimentality to do away with "logical" reasoning.[75] She avoids dramatics or histrionics, adding: "I didn't cry. Crying is not my way. Arguing is."[76] Or, sharing in the disposition of "hardness" as practiced by Sidelle Ogden—lover of Roland Bouley, Lucy's biological father, who lost a son to a war and then a husband to illness and old age—Lilia will say, "I don't mope."[77] And she will not buy into the drama of hope or optimism that life will get better: she renounces the notion of a "silver lining," recognizing it to be "invented by people who can't accept that sometimes life is just bad, terrible, hopeless."[78] To life that dishes out tragedy to her, she responds by saying, "Dear life, I have no interest in being any part of your drama."[79] In other words, in going through the daily anguish of contesting life's drama and Lucy's decision, living on after Lucy's death is Lilia's melodrama in Li's terms—that is, tearlessly bearing (with) all that actually makes existence unbearable.

We have already seen in *Dear Friend* and *Where Reasons End* how, where melodrama is at stake or in question—where feelings needs to be felt—writing follows, regardless if it successfully articulates those feelings or not, if it soothes them or not. Now, if Lilia rejects conventional melodrama, she seems quite averse to writing too. At the beginning of *Must I Go*, we read of Lilia at her senior home where a memoir-writing class is being offered to the residents. While her friends there express enthusiasm for the class, she condescends to it, joining in only reluctantly with the following cynical thought: "Who wants to pull open that drawer called life for others to see?"[80] Her disdain for words or writing is only reaffirmed later when she considers words to be undesirable like weeds, and she would gladly be "a weed whacker" to see "all those useless words gone."[81] And yet, we cannot fail to point out the irony that Lilia herself is nevertheless committed to words or writing. If her way to cope with life is arguing, argument still needs words. Furthermore, we see Lilia engaged in the very act of writing in the second part of the novel, which is essentially about her reading Roland's diary entries while supplementing many of them with her own commentaries, so that both Iola and Katherine—Lucy's granddaughter and daughter, respectively—may understand better not only Lilia herself through her thoughts but also the life and thoughts of Lucy's father. To be sure, this irony is not lost on Lilia. Ever sharp in her observation of both the world and herself, she has no lack of self-reflexivity with regard to her endeavor. As she writes: "I see this is the danger of writing anything down. Happy people have no use for words. I've always been a happy person, but you see now that I've put these words down on the page I'm becoming a downer."[82]

But can we trust Lilia when she says that she has "always been a happy person"? Does she not actually share some of the negativity that is found in Lucy? Which is also to say that there is perhaps some shared unshareability between Lilia and Lucy that will only be unveiled through writing, which is also the writing of Lilia's melodrama of surviving Lucy's shared unshareability. Throughout the narrative of *Must I Go*, Lilia hardly comes across as one who is, or was, happy. After all, she would also acknowledge sharing similar traits with the unhappy lot that is Lucy and Roland: "Sensitive and selfish people: Roland was one. I was one. Lucy too. Pains in the neck."[83] All these traits translate no doubt into Lilia having had her fair share of histrionics, of melodrama as we know it. Which is to say, too, that if she finds herself incapable of feeling, finding her heart cold, that has *not* always been her mode of being. Rather, it comes after the death of Lucy. As Lilia says, Lucy's death brought about a "sudden emptiness" in her, one that is "worse than having your heart broken" because "if someone broke your heart, you could still gather the pieces and glue them back," but "Lucy's trick was to make that heart disappear."[84] It is the sense of an empty heart (perhaps not too foreign to the sense of emptiness in *Dear Friend*) that makes the need to feel even more urgent than before for Lilia, regardless if she acknowledges that or not. And this is why Lilia finds herself ineluctably committing to words or writing, acknowledging that "words are the most useless things that we cannot afford to lose."[85] Like in the case of Roland, then, who is reluctant to burn the correspondences between himself and Sidelle, telling the latter at her deathbed that "the living needs to hold on to things" in order to "live on," words are the only last things onto which Lilia can grasp in order for her to survive Lucy's death.[86] And like Nikolai's mother, Lilia needs writing to negotiate Lucy's shared unshareability surrounding her sense of a failed existence and her decision to exit it. But to come back to the question of happiness in Lilia's life: it is also through words that a certain undeniable unhappiness undercutting Lilia's sense of existence is betrayed. According to her: "Happy people should live as long as they want. It's the unhappy ones who should think twice before getting past forty or fifty."[87] Here, one suspects that Lilia is referring to herself no less with respect to "the unhappy ones," that she regrets living to her present age. This is also to say that like Lucy, there is a desire, too, albeit not explicitly articulated, to exit existence in her: better to be done with unhappiness at an earlier age, to exit existence at an earlier age if one is unhappy. Living beyond would be disastrous; a worse failure, perhaps. As Lilia says, by then "it's much worse. You become moldy and infect others. Sometimes it's more than dampness. It's humiliation."[88]

What also comes to be revealed through writing, then, is the shared unshareability between Lilia and Lucy regarding suicidal ideation: they both share it, but they do not communicate this sharing with each other in any timely fashion—that is, when both of them are alive. This is further affirmed when Lilia poses the following questions, which clearly take the side of Lucy's decision to reject living, hence bringing Lilia closer to Lucy's shared unshareability: "Is it so much of a tragedy if you live your life a little differently from most people? And choose to die in a different way from most people?"[89] Arguably, then, suicidal ideation is no stranger to Lilia either; she has her fair share of existential dread, of the failure to want to exist. This brings us to some of the final words of the novel, which also make up the novel's title: "Must I go." The phrase is Roland's, found in a diary entry recording the last days of his wife Hetty. Even though it is essentially a loveless marriage between Roland and Hetty, Roland still cannot bear to lose her to death (by old age). He thus writes, "Must you go, Hetty?"[90] But the self-absorbed or narcissistic Roland will quickly turn the question around to address his own mortality: "Must I go?"[91] At first glance, the question might reflect a fear of death in Roland, a refusal to depart from the world of the living. After all, there is the belief in Roland that he would be able to sidestep mortality and/or old age, as he sees himself different from the rest of his peers, believing himself to inhabit a different temporality from them. According to him, "In a sense I am not of my generation, and that gives me the illusion of always being young."[92] Lilia would also say of him, "He was the kind of man who wanted to live forever."[93] And yet, there would nevertheless be a number of diary entries that not only records Roland's sense of despair, hopelessness, and negativity toward life—brought about no doubt by his failure to be a successful novelist—but also his moment of wanting to quit life. In such a moment, he would be swarmed with a "dark mood,"[94] anguishing "enough for [him] to look around and see if there is a pistol lying by my hand."[95] This "dark mood" clearly was never shared by Roland with any of the women in his life: neither with Hetty nor Sidelle, nor with Lilia during the couple of encounters between them. Here lies, therefore, yet another shared unshareability— one furthermore intergenerational—touching on failed existence and the desire to exit this existence traversing Roland, Lucy, and Lilia. Given this "dark mood," perhaps one could read a preposition into Roland's phrase in order to expose what might have been unspeakable to Roland. That is to say, underlying, if not undercutting, the death-fearing "must I go" might just be the phrase "must I go *on*." In other words, the question that remains in Roland undeniably, irreducibly, irrepressibly, is: must he go on living?

As said, Roland's phrase is significant enough to stand as the title of the novel. It also resonates enough with Lilia such that she will want to provide a response, one that ends the entire narrative. Her response to Roland's phrase is this: "Yes, Roland, yes. We all must."[96] We all must go, indeed—we must all move toward death in our existence. But we do not necessarily proceed according to the supposed "natural" course of life. As noted previously,

Lilia advocates for and contemplates a different approach to death, one not so different from Lucy's, in fact. In this respect, our modified phrase "must I go on" applies as much to Lilia as to Roland, and I would argue that this question cuts through Lilia's narrative throughout the novel. Must she go on living after the death of Lucy, after her own failure to keep her alive?[97] How much more and longer must she go on writing to play out the lingering melodrama of shared unshareability between herself and a lost loved one? More pertinent to her own sense of existence, must she go on living after her own failure to die at the right time? For how long must she continue bearing with writing, so as to negotiate the melodrama of contesting life with her own desire to exit existence? Left nevertheless to write in order to try answering these questions, one's continued existence in time can only be the reaffirmation or even intensification of the impossibility to quell the melodrama of living on after failure. Each step into the future, as such, is but the restless flailing for an adequate form of writing to manage existence in failure's wake. And as Li bleakly reminds us in *Dear Friend*, "language," at the end of it all, "does little to help a mind survive time."[98] We can possibly "kill time" (this time by writing and not by suicide), but, ultimately, "language kills us."[99] In other words, writing is only *self*-defeating. Or else, it is the inscription of yet another failure, multiplying the sense of existential failure: the failure to answer the question: "Must I go on?"

Living On with Co-Ontological "Crisis Ordinariness"

What does living on mean, then, after reckoning with failure's shared unshareability, after recognizing that the melodrama deployed to cope with it leaves one nevertheless out of sync with one's sense of existence, after realizing that this shared unshareability can be found in a loved one too and that any sharing of it can be possible only posthumously or phantasmatically through the supplementary act of writing yet only to discover for oneself that writing widens, if not deepens, the existential abyss that is shared unshareability? In a sense, one could say that such a living on is living out what Berlant has also called "crisis ordinariness." Through this term, Berlant wants to underscore that crisis and/or trauma is not, or should not be, registered only at a larger, historical, or even "evental" scale, since it also oftentimes strikes lastingly with even greater negative effects at the level of the personal in one's ordinary, everyday life or situation and so must be recognized there too. In Berlant's words, "Crisis is not exceptional to history or consciousness but a process embedded in the ordinary."[100] According to Berlant, too, through such crisis ordinariness there will be those who are "figuring out how to stay attached to life from within it, and to protect what optimism they have for that, at least," and such "affective rhythms of survival" find their ways in personal "stories about navigating what's overwhelming."[101] In a way, then, the literary is a potential site where the explication of crisis ordinariness and the genres flailing to manage it can be found, and we have indeed looked at Li's writings to see how the personal sense of failure and/or the sense of personal failure, including the shared unshareability of this sense, can become crisis ordinariness that sees to melodrama and writing as ways to negotiate it. To be precise, crisis ordinariness for Berlant is very much untethered from "systemic failures" that entail "racial, gendered, sexual, economic, and nation-based subordination"—that is to say, "structural contingency" that "will create manifest crisis situations in ordinary existence for more kinds of people."[102] Such a crisis ordinariness can no doubt be found in Moshfegh's *My Year of Rest and Relaxation*, Cusk's *Outline* trilogy, and Sedgwick's *A Dialogue on Love*. In Li's (and Levé's) works, though, crisis ordinariness disseminates more from an ontological affective structure of failure, one that is further intensified by the tragic, posthumous discovery of this feeling in another, the *co-ontological* fact of this feeling. Li's "crisis ordinariness" is perhaps more ordinary than "systemic crisis," therefore, but it is definitely no less traumatic.[103] Li's works have also shown that living through crisis ordinariness does not necessarily open up to any optimistic horizon: every other day lived after failure in Li's works only awaits an exit from existence, waiting for existence to take one out of existence; it is hardly about hanging on to existence or being relentlessly attached to some optimism of a "good life" to come. Such a living on can thus be said, one final time in this book, to be also crueler than Berlant's "cruel optimism."

—

Perhaps living on in Li's works is more like what Derrida has said about the very phrase "living on": not so much "'life after life' or life after death, more life or more than life" but "the state of suspension in which *it's* [life, that is] over—*and* over again, and you'll never have done with that suspension itself."[104] In other words, it is more a feeling of being already dead, even though one is still living, except such a mode of existing is only in Camus's sense of absurdly going on with life only because life goes on. Derrida will continue to say: "Living on is not the opposite of living, just as it is not identical with living. The relationship is different, different from being identical, from the difference of distinctions—undecided, or in a very rigorous sense, 'vague.'"¹⁰⁵ It is a matter of "lifedeath" (*lavielamort*), as he would put it elsewhere, which is to say, inhabiting a life-death continuum in which life and death are not distinct from each other and yet not the same with each other either; in this "vague" continuum, life is inflected with aspects of death as much as aspects of life spill over into death.¹⁰⁶ Put another way, living on as lifedeath is where living feels like death as much as death might seem to suggest another form of living. Here, according to Derrida, the one who lives on "is also phantom revenance (the one who lives on is always a ghost)," which we can no doubt discern in Li in *Dear Friend* after her failure to "die at the right time" and amid her melodrama touching on this failure's shared unshareability, in the mother in *Where Reasons End* as she trucks with the dead through the phantasmatic conversation on failure's shared unshareability with Nikolai, and in Lilia in *Must I Go* as she spends the rest of her life arguing—an argument predicated no less on failure's shared unshareability again—with a long-dead Lucy and, as intimated prior, wondering if she must go on as such or even go on living.¹⁰⁷

Otherwise, we may recall Cusk from the previous chapter and say that Derrida's lifedeath may also find its resonance with her notion of aftermath. As Cusk had learned from her history teacher, "the etymology of the word 'aftermath' is 'second mowing,' a second crop of grass that is sown and reaped after the harvest is in."¹⁰⁸ But what her history teacher wanted to emphasize was *not* the life that is made available after the clearing of a previous one. That is what every existing "civilization, order, meaning, belief"—or what can be considered the social, as suggested in our discussion on Cusk in relation to Barthes's Neutral—has come to be: "These were not sunlit peaks to be reached by a steady climb. They were built and then they fell, were built and fell again or were destroyed."¹⁰⁹ Put another way, the life of the social is predicated on the death of the one that came before; and this death no doubt continues to haunt that existing life. To interrupt the circuit or continuum of violence of the lifedeath of the social, Cusk's history teacher would profess to prefer the "darkness and disorganization" of aftermath before civilized life sets in, where she also sees, on a positive or optimistic note, the potentiality for creation and "not mere negation, mere absence": "Better ... to live ... the disorganized life and feel the dark stirrings of creativity, than to dwell in civilized unity, racked by the impulse to destroy."¹¹⁰

Be it lifedeath or ordinary co-ontological crisis ordinariness, it is necessary that we do not deny, negate, or invalidate the modes of being and the accompanying genres of those who acknowledge and/or immerse themselves in the entanglement of existence and failure, those who accept and inhabit the shared unshareability of such an existence. These modes and genres constitute no less means to live in the present, even though they harbor the desire to be done with existence, or even though their existing is an expression of that desire. They should be recognized as such, in fact, more so especially because they resist or refute ideologies of success and their itinerant narratives of grit, resilience, and progress; they suggest and legitimize other existing forms of living that do not conform or accede to the neoliberal capitalist "good life." And they do not require of others any action on their part. They just need a space for them to be articulated, and the best others can do is to listen on the side, silently and/or inconspicuously. Such a listening cannot be a tuning out of another: it should *not* be one of indifference or one that hastily seeks to shut down the discourses and/or genres emerging in that space like Lilia did to Lucy in *Must I Go*. Neither should this listening entail some kind of presumptuous fine-tuning, which either endeavors to reinterpellate the other to normative or "normal" ways of living, as the mother attempts to do so with Nikolai in *Where Reasons End*, or co-opts the other into some collective reparative project. This listening is an *attunement*—a *Gestimmtsein*, as Heidegger would call it, as mentioned in our introduction, or, in Nancy's terms, *être-à-l'écoute* (being-listening)—that is an affective inclination toward the other without any interference or intervention of action or words, an inclination through which the other can sense an affective attention to them, an inclination that is inflected with the knowledge and respect of the shared unshareability between one and the other.

CONCLUSION

POSTSCRIPTING IN KATE ZAMBRENO AND AFTERTHOUGHTS ON FORM AND METHOD

We ended the preceding chapter with the idea of living on after failure as a mode of "lifedeath" or "crisis ordinariness" without optimism. We have also said that in response to such a living on, we must not be negligent or, worse, dismissive of the genres—discursive or otherwise—that are flailing as a consequence of the discomfit one feels with the incontrovertible sense of failure. We must not tune these genres out; neither must we seek to "fine-tune" them, which would only imply a negation, invalidation, or delegitimization of their existences and their modes of living on with or after failure. In a way, we must allow or accord them space for their expression, if not acting out. This would be the least but perhaps best care that we can give to those who feel the ineluctable entanglement of failure and existence. All this is also to say that despite or in spite of what we have called failure's shared unshareability, the sense of failure, when "exscribed," to recall Nancy's term that we have borrowed earlier, too, still seeks some kind of response from others, albeit a response that requires no explicit gesture or act—that is, a response where nothing needs to be actually said or done. To repeat, the exscription of failure cries out only to ask to be heard or read (without intervention). The exscription of failure, then, is also an address to others. In this respect,

I want to return to a suggestion made in the introduction and further consider failure as, or in the order of, a *postscript*.

A postscript, as its prefix "post"—indicative of a missive sent out to the world—would suggest, is undoubtedly a form of address. Certainly, a postscript might be a text that is added to the main one after the latter is written, arriving like an afterthought; but it also demands to be read, or at times responded to, as much as the main text. As such, it is also possible that a postscript does not necessarily merely add to what has been said in the main text: it can bear a surprise element, giving a twist to the main text, altering our perspectives on the latter, taking us toward directions other than the main text's principal idea. The postscript can thus be as violent a supplement as a preface, as how Derrida has read the Hegelian preface of *The Phenomenology of Spirit*: a text that can threaten to replace the main one. Or else, as we have suggested in our reading of Sedgwick's *A Dialogue on Love*, it can act like a dark or pessimistic supplement to her principal theoretical work, displacing the latter's project of fostering a hopeful and positive "reparative reading." Regardless of the postscript becoming a "violent supplement" or not, we could also say at this point that the postscript is a mark of failure: either the failure of the main text to succinctly or effectively say what it wants or has to say within the given time and space or the failure of what needs to be said to be included or featured in the main text, relegated only to an addendum.

Failure is very much like an addendum. The sense of failure, or even more failures, can certainly pile on a first failure. This is similar to a postscript, since things do not necessarily end with one postscript: another post-postscript can be added, and so on and so forth, ad infinitum. Both failure and the postscript can thus have an unending and accumulative effect, and this can add to the sense of failure effectively having no closure ever in our lives, as I have tried to suggest throughout our readings of contemporary literary texts, hence reinforcing the idea of failure as an irreducible structure that stays with us throughout our lives.[1] To be precise, though, failure does not add or attach itself to its object (or "victim") quite like a postscript. Sure, the sense of failure, like a postscript, can come after the fact: it typically needs a certain duration before consciousness recognizes that a certain action has been wanting or another compensating action needed, and it is this consciousness that oftentimes gives rise to a sense of failure. However, not quite like the postscript, which we can intend or hope to add at a later time through a consideration of the economy of the existing discursive space, failure is hardly the intended or belatedly desired addition; it is never part of the original plan. After all, hardly anyone would deliberately set out to fail or to have failure as part of one's goal. Failure is more than an addendum, therefore; perhaps it is the more veritable "violent supplement," as it alters original plans or outlooks, making one lose confidence, determination, commitment, or even basic interest. Put another way, failure is not the postscript that one has ever intended or desired to write. The sense of failure, as this book has demonstrated, nevertheless writes itself out, many times over, too, exscribing itself in the discourses and gestures of the body whose existence it traverses. To follow Li's rhetoric, the internal or private melodrama of personal failure never ceases, never lets up in terms of discomfiting the self; it never finds its resolution, never quietens down.

Almost unfailingly, then, the sense of failure *postscripts* itself onto the sense of existence, pushing the latter, at times, as seen especially in the chapter on Sedgwick's *A Dialogue on Love* and Levé's *Suicide*, toward a negative ek-sistence, where existence wants a literal out of existence. And to recall what Sedgwick suggested in *A Dialogue on Love*, a discourse on a care of the self of such an ek-sistence would only extend the "thread of the labyrinth," further entangling or knotting up the desire to exit existence with the sense of existence, rather than relieving the latter of the former. It potentially leads existence toward darker ends. This is where—and we do not forget the question of "lifedeath" here—we can think the postscript to be some form of posthumous writing, where the *post-* now signals the sense of an "afterlife." A postscript, in this case, would be the haunting or haunted writing of the one who, because flooded by the sense of failure, feels as if already dead. This is arguably the case with almost every text discussed in this book. They no doubt take on the senses of a postscript as outlined earlier: like an afterthought, which compounds the sense of failure in existence, which alters the sense of existence. But we can also elicit some spectral affectivity from the texts' respective narrators: the desire to sleep and hence perchance to disappear from the world in the narrator in Moshfegh's *My Year of Rest and Relaxation*; the narrator's aimless drifting as if toward ek-sistence in the sea of Athens or even her almost soulless peregrinations in general in Cusk's *Outline* trilogy; the claim to a ghostly trace in Sedgwick's *A Dialogue on Love*; the foreshadowing of the narrator's ek-sistence by assuming the dead friend's point of view in Levé's *Suicide*; the narrator's sense of nihilistic nothingness in Li's *Dear Friend* and the narrator's trucking with the dead in *Where Reasons End*.

But perhaps there is no singular body of works that takes on all the senses of *postscripting* so consistently and/or persistently as Kate Zambreno's. The text that would explicitly announce her works as postscripting is arguably *Appendix Project* (2019). This text is a collection of talks by Zambreno, which also includes a few written essays, but it is slightly more than that, too, given that it is consciously and carefully edited such that it also includes—as a postscript does—supplementary afterthoughts on the talks. On one level, it can be, not unlike Sedgwick's *A Dialouge on Love*, self-indulgent or even narcissistic, since the talks and/or essays all pertain to her writing processes or experiences with regard to her earlier *Book of Mutter* (2017), a work of mourning that allows Zambreno to work through her grief over her deceased mother. On another level, it allows Zambreno to register the authorial regrets for what she had failed to include and the elements she felt compelled to remove in the earlier work. In her own words, *Appendix Project* is where she finds herself "circling back on [her] failure and errata."[2] And this "circling back" serves to reinforce her sense that a book, if not literature in general, is no less a failure essentially, insofar as a work "feels [like] a shadow of what . . . could have [been] written."[3] This sense is only reaffirmed when a book seems to need an appendix, which is as much a mark of failure, since the appendix can be "seen as unnecessary or excessive to the *body* of a text,"[4] which is to say, a redundant or superfluous nonessential addition. Put otherwise, the book would not need an appendix if it had been precise, if it were successful at being concise. This sense of failure notwithstanding, *Appendix Project* can still take on the contour of a care of the self that, toward the end of the text, recalls the Foucauldian project of recording everyday routines and ordinary thoughts. As Zambreno recognizes there, "To write of grief, which is to write of solitude, is to write the banal details of a life."[5] But we keep in mind that Foucault in *The Hermeneutics of the Subject* lectures had also said that the banality of life includes meditations on death. The deaths with which *Appendix Project* is preoccupied are those of Zambreno's mother, Barthes's mother, and Barthes's own. Nevertheless, we can also elicit from the text Zambreno's inscription of her proximity with, if not approach toward, death.

Zambreno's taste for a negative ek-sistence is rather evident right in the first appendix (A), where she mentions On Kawara's series of telegrams catalogued under the title "I AM ALIVE," which began in 1969 and which includes the three telegrams that respectively announce: "I AM NOT GOING TO COMMIT SUICIDE DON'T WORRY," "I AM NOT GOING TO COMMIT SUICIDE WORRY," and "I AM GOING TO SLEEP FORGET IT."[6] This is not a mere passive observation on Zambreno's part, for she will, toward the end of this appendix, somewhat assume On Kawara's voice or standpoint and write, paraphrasing On Kawara, "I do not know how I will die. . . . But as I write this, and hopefully you hear this, I am still alive."[7] I think it not difficult to sense that the declarations "I am alive" (both On Kawara's and Zambreno's) and "I am not going to commit suicide" betray a desire for death, subtending the discourse like a posthumous postscript discussed previously. This suspicion can be confirmed by Zambreno's fascination with things spectral. For example, when she looks at photographs of her half-sister, she writes of her as "special, singular, then fading away, in the background, when there are new babies. She disappears from the second album, becomes the ghost. I don't know why I have such a need to catalogue this, to archive it into language. I doubt that it is interesting to others, except perhaps the feeling underneath it."[8] As I would read it, Zambreno seems to aspire to the "fading away," the disappearance, or the becoming-specter of her half-sister. In other words, "the feeling" she feels "underneath" the images of her half-sister is her inclination toward a negative ek-sistence. The taste for the posthumous postscript becomes undeniable, I believe, when Zambreno writes that writing is like "following after ghosts," and as a writer, she says that she is "the ghost, hovering over, . . . attempting to come closer" to other ghosts.[9] Otherwise, she feels akin to a spectral being in her insomniac state: "when . . . extremely sleep deprived," she is "convinced that [she is] a ghost."[10] In yet another context, as she reflects on mothering her infant daughter while mourning for her mother, she wonders if she is "closer to life, and thus closer to death."[11]

Yet, we should not ignore the fact that Zambreno has also written in *Appendix Project* that "writing for [her] is a form of resilience."[12] However, as I would argue, her discourse of resilience ironically sustains an intimate proximity with ek-sistence, which we can elicit from her reflection on the anatomical appendix. When this appendix fails, it has to be removed. What remains, then, is only "impending death," and life, no matter how resilient, must recognize the "vestigial remnants" of existence, which only have death in sight.[13] This is to say that if *Appendix Project*, as Zambreno claims, is a literary or aesthetic extension of the thought of such an organ failure, then it must acknowledge no less the deathly horizon. It cannot forget or erase the trace of, or even desire for, negative ek-sistence, which has, in fact, been announced in *Book of Mutter*. There, Zambreno recalls in her childhood, "[writing] little suicide notes and [sticking] them in [her] schoolgirl desk," and she will furthermore acknowledge, "I have a vague desire to die."[14] This desire, which can also be said to be an inclination toward a spectral existence, never ceases to postscript itself in Zambreno's later works, including *To Write as if Already Dead*. In the latter, Zambreno was asked by Columbia University Press to write "a short book, a study, about a novel of [her] choice," and she seeks to focus her attention on Hervé Guibert's *To the Friend Who Did Not Save My Life*.¹⁵ Like in Zambreno's earlier *Screen Tests*, where she highlights Barbara Loden as a figure of failure—a washed-out actress and a failed film director because of the lack of commercial success of *Wanda*–, we see Zambreno doing something similar to Guibert. In *To Write as if Already Dead*, Guibert, for the large part, comes across as one whose mortality was failing because of AIDS. We are also reminded how he would attempt suicide but failed, only to die of AIDS two weeks later. Zambreno would also underscore Guibert's failure to meet his writing deadlines as well as "the failure of Guibert's novel . . .—the rushed, passionate, desperate, furious character of it."¹⁶ The interests in Loden and Guibert reflect Zambreno's gravitation toward figures of failure, but Loden and Guibert are also no doubt foils to her own sense of failure, her own sense of failed existence.¹⁷ Thus, instead of a focused study on Guibert's novel, the final published text of *To Write as if Already Dead* is, aside from some notes on Guibert and his works, a gathering of reflections on the failure of her will to begin writing the study and her subsequent failures to meet her own deadlines, on the conditions surrounding those failures, on the state of writing and the publishing world, and on her friendships—including failed ones—with other female writers.

We will therefore read in *To Write as if Already Dead* her need to care for her first daughter while expecting her second, leaving her hard-pressed to find quiet time to write; her feeling of sickness—"headaches, vomiting, diarrhea, the excruciating shoulder blade and rib pain on the left side, along with a painful left breast"—while no doctor would endorse a mammogram screening because of her pregnancy, hence making her feel uncared for, left aside by the "alienation of medical bureaucracy";¹⁸ the arrival of the COVID-19 pandemic and the stress and anxiety she feels of possible fatal infection and contamination by others; her sense of economic precarity as she has yet to find a tenured university position, with her health insurance possibly expiring by the time she gives birth; her sense of dejection as her preceding novel (presumably *Drifts*) is rejected by a desired press—and "everywhere," according to her—because of the editor's irritation at "autofiction" while another "autofictional" work by a (presumably white) male writer gets published by the same press; her disgust and disenchantment with the publishing industry, which is more keen to put out "polished turds" and is wont to "fatigue and sicken" her instead of supporting or loving her;¹⁹ and her self-disappointment at not being the humble, good reader to her friend Alex Suzuki but, from a narcissistic "vantage point of having published seven books, a number that feels excessive," goads Suzuki to publish more than blogs, hence making herself feel "like a failure as a participant in the greater project of literature," which she imagines to involve critical dialogues between writers who assume equally the role of a reader of their fellow writer's works.[20] In light of these, Zambreno would admit to "want only to describe my exhausted body at work, writing in a room, contemplating the exhaustion and illness of another body, writing in a room."[21] Given this need to inscribe the exhausted body, which is also largely a body in physical and emotional pain, in addition to the general mundanity of the thoughts and events written down (or out, as in an exscription), *To Write as if Already Dead* is a practice no less of a Foucauldian discourse on a care of the self.[22]

Yet, like Sedgwick's *A Dialogue on Love* and Levé's *Suicide*, Zambreno's *To Write as if Already Dead* as a discourse on a care of the self bears a dark, pessimistic tinge, tracing no less a trajectory of negative ek-sistence. This is arguably undeniable if one considers how death is a leitmotif throughout the text.[23] Not only is there Guibert's death in the background, but when it comes to her pregnancy, too, she cannot avoid—just as in *Appendix Project* where she was writing while pregnant with her first child—thoughts of death. In her own words: "When I am approaching labor, as I am now, I think of death the entire time. Partially because birth feels so close to death. Not only because of the risk of maternal mortality. My body is slowing down, heavy, I can only eat small meals, just like my mother when she was dying."[24] And when speaking of the rejection of her novel by presses, she accompanies that discourse with the statement, "I am already dead."[25] Then there is also the question of writing, which, following other writers that came before, she would associate with dying. This explains the title of the text itself, which a friend of hers says, without remembering the source, is a quote from Marguerite Duras. Zambreno will also quote Kafka, saying, "I need solitude for my writing, not 'like a hermit'—that wouldn't be enough—but like a dead man."[26] And when she thinks of such solitary times to write—for example, in the wee hours of the morning—she revels in "the beauty of *not existing* in those early hours, except for the sound of the fans and the occasional car on the street."[27] But what seals *To Write as if Already Dead* as a posthumous postscript is when Zambreno cites again the same three telegrams of On Kawara that she did in *Appendix Project*.[28] There is an irresistible pessimistic trajectory underlying, if not guiding, this text, therefore. Otherwise, an outlook with a contrary perspective is only incredulous. Toward the end of *To Write as if Already Dead*, Zambreno writes of "having this fantasy that turns out to come true," which consists of the end of the pandemic, her being "free and unencumbered" and able to travel to Elba and stay in a villa near where Guibert used to live, her being able to leave household chores to the care of someone else, being able to "write the Guibert study now."[29] But she will add—and we will know here that the text, this posthumous postscript, if not a postscript to a missent or undelivered postcard, has always been addressed to someone—in a tone typically adopted by someone having trouble convincing others: "I don't know why you don't believe me, but this really did happen. It did. I wrote you a postcard—did it not arrive?"[30]

It is no doubt tempting to bring in a critical reflection of Derrida's reading of a postcard at this point, but this is certainly not the place to do so.[31] Let it be said very simply, then, that for Derrida, the idea of a postcard bears, first, a similar shared unshareability that we have elicited from failure. According to Derrida, the "postal principle" consists in the "distancing" (*l'éloignement*) between the sender and the addressee: without this distance, there would be no posting, no desire or necessity to send out a word.[32] Once the word is sent out on a postcard, everything, on the one hand, can be read by whoever handles the postcard as it travels from the sender to the addressee. On the other hand, it is also possible that nothing can be deciphered because of a secret coded within the language of the message, a shibboleth that can only be decoded by the addressee. And yet, as Derrida recognizes, it is also possible that both the sender and the addressee forget what the secret was or how to decode that secret, hence leaving the message no less incomprehensible to the addressee. It is in this regard that Derrida will say that the post "begins with a destination without address," that "the direction is not locatable at the end of it all" or that simply "there is no destination."[33] But because the successful sending of a postcard would supposedly confirm both the living signature of the sender and the vitality of the addressee there to receive it and read the words addressed to them, the always possible nonarrival of the postcard, on the contrary, as Derrida further argues, would presuppose and imagine or speculate that both the sender and the addressee are or can be dead. Yet, paradoxically, they can be kept alive (posthumously), say, through memory or imagination, when it gets read by others. It is critical, therefore, that a postcard is also addressed to an unknown other at the same time. This incalculable destiny, if not mischance, of the postcard is what gives it an apocalyptic, catastrophic, and tragic—all Derrida's terms—dimension. And to add to this pessimistic or even posthumous contour, death is around the corner in Derrida's discourse. He would say, "I write for dead addressees, not those to come but already dead at the moment when I arrive at the end of a phrase."[34] Or, "If now I am sending you always the same card, it is because I would very well like to die, to finally enclose myself in a single place, be it a bordered [*bordé*] place, a single word, a single name."[35] And he would hint at negative ek-sistence: when challenged by an obnoxious, provocative Oxford student as to why he had not committed suicide, which would only be to follow through his theory of the trace that marks its author as already dead, he would respond by asking in return what proves that he has not done it "and more than once."[36]

But we are losing our way; we risk having taken a detour away from our designated end. Let us return to the postscript, therefore. A postscript—because it is always adding itself onto a space wherein there is actually no space or time for it, because it can do so multiple times, because it can never completely say what it wants to say adequately or in any timely fashion, even assuming a posthumous dimension in the attempt to compensate for that untimeliness—can be said to be flailing—that is, always flailing like a genre seeking a form. If failure is of the order of a postscript, then it could be considered a genre without form as well. Correspondingly, any writing of failure, as long as it stays with failure's negativity and not try to sublimate it into something of its opposite, would likewise be a flailing genre always in search of a form. In many ways, I have already suggested this in our discussions of the literary texts that engage with failure. They never rest with one genre (in the classical sense). Certainly, most of the writers discussed here adopt the genre of the novel, as in Moshfegh's *My Year of Rest and Relaxation* and Cusk's *Outline* trilogy. Li and Zambreno have experimented with this genre, too, as in Li's *Must I Go*, or else with the novel in a more "autofictional" register, as in Li's *Where Reasons End* and Zambreno's *Drifts*. But they have also felt the need to turn to other hybrid forms that include the memoir dimension and/or essay form, as in Li's *Dear Friend* or Zambreno's *Appendix Project*, *Screen Tests*, and *To Write as if Already Dead*, and perhaps we could include Sedgwick's *A Dialogue on Love* and Levé's *Suicide* and *Autoportrait* in this mix. The multiplicity of forms or genres of writing and the multiple times that failure needs to be reiterated in various ways also mean that failure never really gets written in the way it would want. Failure even fails in this aspect. (I believe this is also what Jones intimates in his reading of Melville's composition of *Pierre*, which he takes to be an endeavor "to find literary form to express an essential condition of human fallibility" but ultimately remains a testament to how "form shares in failure quite literally."[37]) It is on this note of failure failing form and/or form failing failure that I will now like to conclude by reflecting on the question of form in relation to the composition of this very present book. To do so, we will have to return (like a postscript) to a consideration of the method employed in this book.

Whither Methodology and Form?

I have intimated in the introduction that, in my attempt to think failure qua failure, the methodology deployed is foremost a "deconstructive" one, drawing particularly from "deconstruction," in Derrida's terms. It is one that encourages an experience of an impasse from which we do *not* try to get out but in which we remain in order to let unfold all the thoughts that come with, and to, this very experience. Such an experience of the impasse is also the refusal to allow thought to be governed by a binary polemic, especially the failure/success binary. It particularly refuses the quick movement toward the supposedly "better" end, which, in the failure/success case, is presumably the "success" pole. Staying in, or with, the impasse, I believe, is how we tarry with failure, how we dwell in it, wallow in it. This is not to say, however, that the "deconstructive" approach is flawless with regard to thinking about failure. Even Derrida supplements failure with a progress or success narrative when, in what appears to be a riff on Beckett, he tells us that we "must fail *well*," and this in the context of mourning a friend, where he argues that the failure to remember the friend in any complete manner, or to have faulty memories about him or her, is but the opportunity for us to keep recalling the friend by rectifying our memory of them.[38] In other words, a "deconstructive" line of thinking, even though seeking to embrace failure, can also inadvertently give the latter some positive or success horizon.[39] Yet, the principal problem with "deconstruction" in relation to failure is that it seems to bracket negative affects: indeed, one hardly finds the elucidation of shame, depression, anxiety, pessimism, and other affects that accompany failure as a foreground in "deconstruction," and I suspect this is how it fails to stay in the impasse of failure. My sense, then, is that the "deconstructive" approach in itself is insufficient in the tarrying with failure. (This is also not to forget, as I have stated in a note in the introduction, that Blanchot is not in favor of thinking about failure, fearing that it brings us back to a binary logic that makes us yearn for success.)

This accounts for this book's concomitant following, to a certain extent, of the "affective turn" in literary studies as put in place in the field since Sedgwick. There is no doubt that it was Sedgwick who has taught a generation of contemporary feminist and queer theorists, including Berlant, Edelman, Love, Muñoz, Cvetkovich, and Halberstam, a mode of reading that is not so caught up with exhibiting our ingenious close reading "talents," for this would only breed a "paranoid reading" all too anxious to generate a "strong theory" that disallows both unexpected "bad surprises" that undermine our hypotheses *and* "good surprises" that exceed the limits of what we might have considered critical reasoning or critique as taught to us by a "suspicious hermeneutics." Instead, we should adopt a "depressive position" through which affects, especially negative ones, in texts and in readers, can resound and be treated differently other than being repressed or suppressed. In a way, one could argue that failure studies have elicited the "good surprises" from the sense of failure; they present a "reparative reading" of failure, recuperating failure's negative affects and giving them a positive spin. However, this is largely done without first giving real, sustained, rigorous thought to failure. In other words, we have in fact not yet attended to the negative affects in thinking, understanding, and elucidating *failure as failure*; we have not let go of our affective and hermeneutical defenses and allow possible or even imminent "bad surprises" such as negativity without restitution or salvation to take over, to lead us in directions beyond our determinations. It is in this regard that I suspect failure studies to perform its own "paranoid reading" by never quite allowing failure and its negative affects to reach their ends (say, the rabbit hole), always already precluding or disavowing the "bad surprises" toward which they can lead. This is where I resist the too-reparative horizon of failure studies and insist on the structural impasse that "deconstruction" has taught us, if we are to see *failure as failure* all the way through, along with all its itinerant affects. In this respect, I would like to consider this book a putting into practice of Silvan Tomkins's axiom that "affect theory must be effective to be weak."[40] As Tomkins reminds us, "effective" here involves precisely, directly engaging with, or diving into, the very thing that one fears (e.g., failure). It does *not* mean that we can be *successful* in overcoming failure. Being "effective" can in fact mean that we fail, too, if not fail worse (or better, as Beckett would want it), but the point is not to avoid the thing we fear. And we will not take any "effective" experience of failure to be *the* experience of failure, which is what "weak" entails, according to Tomkins's phrase. Thus, if we seek a "weak theory" of failure, it is important that we elicit, as we have done, specific genres—classical or otherwise—from each unique experience of failure and elucidate how these genres variously negotiate with the question of living on with/after failure. To this I would also add that we do not forget our own "weak thought" of failure, which recognizes failure as "inoperative," negativity, impasse, if not that which breaks down or breaks apart.

In general, the book's methodology can be said to be one in which certain aspects of "deconstruction" are in dialogue with those of the "affective turn" in contemporary feminist and queer theory, one that I would say implicates itself in an "affective structural impasse." Yet the book, as a whole, is no less a questioning of methodology with regard to failure: it is flailing for a methodology, to borrow, one last time, Berlant's rhetoric. It is itself a question as to how there can be any effective, if not "successful," thinking and writing about failure within an academic framework—that is, outside of the fiction genre. As I would put it, any writing of failure is always in search of a methodology. Given the book's proposition to resist any success narrative in relation to failure, it would even seem a contradiction to have something like a book, or something with a recognizable structure of an academic book, with more or less a narrative that has a supposed beginning, middle, and end; an overarching argument; transition between chapters, and so forth. Form is undoubtedly at stake here, therefore. I remind readers that this book has so far dealt with genres as Berlant understands them, with discursive and nondiscursive expressions that are not fully constructed forms yet can be suggestive of forms in the making. In short, this book takes form and genre to be different, and the questions at hand related to form are: Is there a form "proper" to the academic writing of failure? What or which form should an academic book on failure take? To be truthful to the claim of this book, to dwell with and/or in failure, should the book in itself *not* succeed? To have such an object as this very book itself seems but a mark of "success" in certain regards. But what are the alternatives? Do we have to think anew Flaubert's dream of a "book on nothing" (*un livre sur rien*), which would now go beyond his ambition of a book saturated with received ideas such that it would paradoxically be evacuated of them, this time either filled with received ideas of failure or, perhaps more radically, literally nothing or no words within the pages? Or do we have to revisit Derrida's idea of the "end of the book" and, again in more radical terms than rethinking writing as nonrepresentational but inscribing its own trace that secures its quasi-immortality beyond its own spatiotemporal context, imagine a mode of writing that undoes the very latter operation, if not thoroughly breaks down in itself such that neither a trace of writing nor a book remains? We could put these Flaubertian and Derridean challenges in more banal ways: Should we have instead a pseudobook that only contains multitudes of senseless, disorganized, incoherent discourses just to assume the semblance of a failure of a book or a narrative?[41] Or to have nothing to show, like the juvenile example of submitting a blank answer sheet in response to an assignment on what courage is? While this book is not equipped to address or meet the Flaubertian and Derridean challenges, I find the latter mundane options too easy, a cop-out, a superficial struggle with failure, nowhere near a critical engagement with the question of form and/or methodology in thinking and writing about failure and its affects.

In its very limited and cursory ways, my query into the relation between form and failure extends or even problematizes some recent reinvestments in forms in literary studies. It echoes Eugenie Brinkema's call for the thinking of "affect as a problematic of structure, form, and aesthetics," not forgetting our consideration in this book of failure as some kind of affect.[42] It also responds to Anna Kornbluh's celebration—professedly inspired by Caroline Levine's book on the very topic—of forms that see to the building of new sociopolitical formations, especially those that counter reactionary, divisive, and therefore destructive ones. They look instead toward new ways of making sense of life, especially those that register the ongoing mutations that involve "composed relations, institutions, states" with which life is entangled, those that bring to surface what "make relations possible" and how these "relations in turn enable other forms."[43] It is in this light that Kornbluh sees in forms "new opportunities for engaging with aesthetic productions as sites . . . for mediating social building, for building in criticism projects for social composition."[44] This no doubt aligns with Cvetkovich's, Halberstam's, and even Berlant's aspirations for a communitarian horizon through the sublimation of failure via aesthetic projects. Yet, through readings of Li, Cusk, and Levé, from whose works I have also elicited failure's shared unshareability, my reluctance toward a communitarian aspiration has already been declared. And alongside the all-out negativity that I have underscored with failure's shared unshareability, my trajectory might even be more destitute than Agamben's "destituent potential," which Kornbluh notes to be "the flow of vitality without constitution, structure, order, or form" and to which she opposes, for mine does not even suggest any vital current.[45] Nevertheless, and paradoxically perhaps, what I have been seeking in or through this book is to afford a discursive and affective space to those who desire to wallow alone in their sense of failure.[46] Put another way, this book is no less invested in a form that could accommodate forms of existence that deviate from forms of life that have been regarded as "normal" or those that have been normalized as normative—that is, those that are productive, high-functioning or -performing, hopeful, and optimistic.[47] In Levine's terms, this book would be the case where "forms will often fail to impose their order when they run up against other forms that disrupt their logic and frustrate their organizing ends, producing aleatory and sometimes contradictory effects."⁴⁸ In other words, the form of an academic book falters when it confronts forms of failure in real life. In any case, if I am resistant against form, what I push back against, more specifically, is any common form or a singular form that claims to be able to capture all the individual senses of failure.⁴⁹

In all, the real challenge, as I see it, is to elucidate what I have called in this book the *affective structure* of failure or failure's *affective structural impasse*, while at the same time acknowledging the inadequacy of encapsulating this very endeavor within a form of an academic book, hence always on the lookout for more corresponding forms (or rather, those that fail like failure does). To reiterate, the (academic) writing of failure can only always be in search of a methodology. Put yet another way, this book, despite itself, seeks a methodology and/or form that would allow failure and its affects to disturb, trouble, haunt, and hopefully undo the book's narrative and/or structure. But this will have to be left to the "to come" of things, without any expectation and/or anticipation for its materialization, left to the indifferent hopelessness of an *optimism without optimism*. It is in this respect that I agree with Kornbluh that there can be "value [to] what forms build," provided that they do not conveniently, lazily, and uncritically refer to, or repeat, past or existing modes of doing, representing, and thinking about things.⁵⁰ Following Juan-Manuel Garrido, who draws much from Nancy's thought, I would also say that form is always forming, in formation.⁵¹ Otherwise, one could also defer to Levine to think of form to "mean all shapes and configurations, all ordering principles, all patterns of repetition and difference," even though they might not be whole, even though their rhythms break down, even though no order is attained at the end of the work.⁵² Or to follow Brinkema in *Life-Destroying Diagrams*, where she would also say that as long as the form of an all-out apocalyptic failure remains to be attained, an existing form of failure—insufficient in relation to the former absolute failure—can gesture toward other yet unthought-of "excess, noise, residue, disturbance to completion," which are expressions of failures no less and which also only affirm that "there can be a failure of a failure"—that is, other yet-to-be-articulated forms or genres of failure in the wake of existing ones.⁵³ This book, in other words, in its present form, arguably fails at its proposed methodology, perhaps its own argument even, failing the very thing it preaches. (As Bradatan would say, too, "Any study of failure is a study in failure."⁵⁴) Yet, perhaps it is also as such that it stands as a (true) failure, and this is why I have kept it to the conventional academic book form so as to be always reminded of its failure of form.⁵⁵ Anything that is not failure in its absoluteness—that is, failure that leaves nothing to be saved at all—is, to quote Brinkema again, "failure full stop."⁵⁶ And as Eugene Thacker has said in the preface to his *Infinite Resignation*, the fact that something gets written where silence should have been the order of things is but "the writer's failure." So, let the fact of the presence of a material book and the semblance of a book form be but the failure only of its author.

NOTES

INTRODUCTION

1. Bradatan, *In Praise of Failure*, 10.
2. I note that Renyi Hong has also used the phrase "affective structure" in a different context to understand how some of us have become so passionate about work. See Hong, *Passionate Work*.
3. Some notes on these failures are in order: It is by now generally accepted that 9/11 was a response to problematic US foreign policies and a result of internal security lapses. The 2008 Great Recession has now laid to rest the myth of financial institutions as being "too big to fail," with financial analysts arguing against the defense of this phrase and companies associated with it since. The #metoo movement rightly called out the masculine gender for failing mankind in abusing positions of power and authority to sexually harass women in workplaces.

    In 2020, with the death of George Floyd under police custody—a result a police officer pressing his knee against Floyd's throat during the arrest, which was then followed with mass protests across many US major cities—even the former president George W. Bush, responsible for the "war on terror," has called the country's systemic racism a "tragic failure." The historian Elizabeth Hinton recognizes it, more critically, as a "failure of generations of leadership" ("George Floyd's Death Is a Failure of Generations of Leadership," *New York Times*, June 3, 2020). With regard to COVID-19, the *New York Times* editorial board has called the response of the US health-care system to the pandemic an "epic failure" (editorial, March 20, 2020). By 2021, the World Health Organization also acknowledged the early responses to the pandemic as a global series of failures. It is not always policy failures when it comes to tragic school shootings. It can be the "abject failure" of an individual, as the head of the Texas State Police has recognized in the Uvalde elementary school shooting in 2022, where the on-site police commander delayed for almost an hour any action against the shooter (J. David Goodman, "Head of State Police Calls Response to Uvalde Shooting an 'Abject Failure,'" *New York Times*, June 21, 2022). In addition to these failures, we should also not forget how higher education has been at a new low in this present century: funding crises for humanities research and teaching that have led to the reduction in size, if not closure, of humanities departments in several UK and US universities; the drastic lack of tenure-track humanities jobs while even more graduates enter the job market, a hopelessly depressing situation that gave rise to the phenomenon of "quit lit" by many of the disenchanted graduates; its "structural failure" in protecting victims of campus sexual assault and duly punishing perpetrators, the reckoning of which coming belatedly only thanks to #metoo.

4   Cardona's *Global Failure and World Literature* apparently goes the other way.

5   This field is by no means even or cohesive. In any case, for a sample of this expanding literature, here are just some titles: Feltham, *Failure*; Feltham, *Anatomy of Failure*; Firestein, *Failure*; Sandage, *Born Losers*; Appadurai and Alexander, *Failure*; Dekker, *Drift into Failure*; Lukianoff and Haidt, *The Coddling of the American Mind*; Halberstam, *The Queer Art of Failure*; Jones, *Failure and the American Writer*; Lee, *Failures of Feeling*; Franta, *Systems Failure*; Graham, *Failing Gloriously and Other Essays*; Bradatan, *In Praise of Failure*; Bey, *Cistem Failure*; Kendi, *How to Be an Antiracist*; Harney and Moten, *All Incomplete*; Setiya, *Life Is Hard*. Even more recently, there is the *Routledge International Handbook of Failure*, where the editors signal toward a "critical failure studies."

6   Other writers whose selected works also register a contemporary sense of failure would include Jennifer Egan (especially *A Visit by the Goon Squad*), Sigrid Nunez (*What Are You Going Through*), Jesse Ball (*A Cure for Suicide*), Raven Leilani (*Luster*), Catherine Cusset (*L'autre qu'on adorait*), Pauline Klein (*La figurante*), and Michel Houellebecq (*Sérotonine*). Unfortunately, I do not have the space in this current work to discuss these works. Also, I am certainly citing authors from contemporary Anglo-American and French literature, fields with which I am familiar. I have no doubt, nevertheless, that certain works of contemporary German, Spanish, Italian, Chinese, or Korean literature engage with such a sense too. I leave it to experts in these fields to continue further the work of eliciting the question of failure in contemporary literary works of other languages.

7   See her eponymous essay, "Genre Flailing," and Berlant's thinking of genre as such can be found from *The Female Complaint* to *Cruel Optimism*.

8   As will be evident, my turn to the personal has nothing to do with the "self-help" counseling manner that is found in Setiya's *Life Is Hard*, not to mention that his aim is for us to get out of failure, "to loosen the hold of failure" (96) on us.

9   Levé's unpublished texts, collected and published as *Inédits*, arrived after the chapter on Levé was completed, hence the omission of any discussion of this text in this present work.

10 I do acknowledge that there will be those who perversely consider some of the phenomena mentioned in the list to be successes rather than failure (and this no doubt feeds into the discussion of the perspectival treatment of failure later in this introduction). However, a critical account of how these phenomena can essentially be failures lies beyond the expertise and scope of this book.

11 Other than "Worstward Ho!," from which the phrase cited comes, Beckett's other works such as *Waiting for Godot* and *Endgame* have also been understood to capture the twentieth-century zeitgeist of profound failure. Other modernist writers known to inscribe the pathos of failure in their works include T. S. Eliot, Virginia Woolf, James Joyce, Osamu Dazai, and Thomas Bernhard. We should also not forget *Stoner* by John Williams, which has now been acknowledged to be the best but most unknown novel on failure in the twentieth century. Gavin Jones in *Failure and the American Writer* will argue that before the twentieth century, failure was already foundational in nineteenth-century American writers, projected in the literary forms of that time. As he notes, too, for Henry Adams, one of his studied authors, "the nineteenth-century was a failed century" (158).

12 I do admit that the overall program of the Museum of Failure does not sound as pessimistic as I put it here. To the contrary, it looks forward to a positive or optimistic horizon through the learning of past failures. This move, however, is an aspect of current ways of treating failure that I critique, as will be seen later.

13 It is indeed highly doubtful that much, if not any, critical thought belies each enunciation of "epic fail." I add here that Eugenie Brinkema, while contemplating insufficient violence in the film *Cabin in the Woods* to bring about an inevitable general or more comprehensive or even absolute violence, hence only deferring the latter, reads this insufficient violence as suggestive of how "a twenty-first-century rereading of the twentieth century ends less in a will to formalization than with a will-less *whatever*." Brinkema, *Life-Destroying Diagrams*, 163. To me, such a statement resonates with the contrast between Beckett's formalized phrasing of twentieth-century failure and the "whatever" dimension of "epic fail" in the twenty-first century. I return to a consideration of failure and the form of writing in this book's conclusion.

14 Or, as Stewart has observed, the ordinary itself "falters, fails" too. Stewart, *Ordinary Affects*, 29. She would also say that it is in failure that the ordinary would be found (93).

15 See Beckett, "Three Dialogues." Speaking of the artist Bram Van Velde there, Beckett would say that Van Velde is "the first to admit that to be an artist is to fail, as no other dare fail, that failure is his world" and that from Van Velde one must learn of the "fidelity to failure." Beckett, *Proust*

and Three Dialogues, 125. Jones in *Failure and the American Writer* has likewise noted this take on failure by Beckett. As noted earlier, he will also argue that such an approach to failure was already nascent in nineteenth-century American writers such as Henry Adams, Edgar Allan Poe, and Herman Melville, where failure in their works is an expression of "a personal condition of white masculinity in crisis" (11).

16 It is beyond the scope of this book to critically think about the humor that belies "epic fail." Let me note, however, that the subject of enunciation scoffs or laughs at the failure but does not in any explicit fashion stand apart from it in order to critique it. In this regard, one might see in the enunciations of "epic fail" what Berlant has called "cruel optimism"—that is, a kind of optimistic attachment to an object that is actually doing more harm to oneself, a willing blind faith, or, in other words, in the supposed good promised by the object, instead of a critical distancing from it. "Epic fail" indeed largely does not renounce the failed object and/or the structure that is producing the failed object. Despite one's pronouncement of "epic fail," one still believes in the "good life" that the structure promises, "epic fails" included.

17 Jones, *Failure and the American Writer*, 161. Jones will also continue to say, in the context of the literary period in which he is interested, that such a rhetoric concerning failure "misses the peculiar shape failure takes in nineteenth-century texts."

18 For such a critique of "high theory" of those decades, see especially Terada, *Feeling in Theory*.

19 To be sure, I am *not* saying that affects are personal or derivative from the interiority of an individual or subject. As I will state later, following recent affect theory, affects arise from the circulation of internal and external forces. Brian Massumi calls this the "transindividual" dimension of affects and Jonathan Flatley calls this affects' "relational" quality. Massumi, *Politics of Affects*; Flatley, *Affective Mapping*.

20 Judith Butler has suggested that individual failures can be a result of failures at those macro levels: "No one person suffers a lack of shelter without there being a social failure to organize shelter in such a way that it is accessible to each and every person. And no one person suffers unemployment without there being a system or a political economy that fails to safeguard against that possibility. This means that in some of our most vulnerable experiences of social and economic deprivation, what is revealed is not only our precariousness as individual persons—thought that may well be revealed—but also the failures and inequalities of socioeconomic and political institutions. In our individual vulnerability to a precarity that is socially induced, each 'I' potentially sees how its unique sense of anxiety and failure has been implicated all along in a broader social world." Butler, *Notes Toward a Performative Theory of Assembly*, 21.

21 See Brennan, *The Transmission of Affect*; Ahmed "Affective Economies"; Flatley, *Affective Mapping*; Ngai, *Ugly Feelings* (the phrase "suspended agency" is found on page 1 of this text).
22 Williams, "Structures of Feeling," 130.
23 Williams, "Structures of Feeling," 128.
24 Williams, "Structures of Feeling," 130.
25 Williams, "Structures of Feeling," 133–34.
26 Williams, "Structures of Feeling," 134.
27 Williams, "Structures of Feeling," 134.
28 Williams, "Structures of Feeling," 128.
29 As Williams tells us, too, a "structure of feeling" arising in the personal can have "particular linkages, particular emphases and suppressions" (134) with past and/or existing fixed social forms. The sense of failure as a "structure of feeling" of our times, therefore, can indeed be a modulation of how the twentieth century has grasped failure, if not an ongoing process with how mankind deals with failure. We have suggested this in our discussion of how the sense of failure can be accumulative, except our inscription of it today may be more democratic, less stylized, and without the privileging of larger, geopolitical failures. Otherwise, the "structure of feeling" of failure in the personal can come from without, too, although this external source is not (yet) made explicit or manifest but only exists as a trace of something in the air. And this is why the sense of failure that comes from the outside is not necessarily attributable to institutions and their norms.
30 With respect to recent affect theory, this would be, again, the "transindividual" (Massumi) or "relational" (Flatley) aspect of a "structure of feeling." Also, it is when a "structure of feeling" finds its reverberation outside the individual, when it constitutes the resonance buzzing between the individual and the larger community, that it can signal the mark of a zeitgeist, or how, according to Williams, it "gives the sense of a generation or of a period" (131). It is given the literary works that interest us, the millennial-speak "epic fail," as well as the real-life phenomena of failures and the growing field of failure studies, that I have made the claim that the sense of failure constitutes very much the zeitgeist of our present century.
31 Williams, "Structures of Feeling," 128, 132. These aspects furthermore loosen a "structure of feeling" from the other traditional opposition of "feeling against thought"; instead, they allow a "structure of feeling" to embrace "thought as felt and feeling as thought"—that is, a "practical consciousness of a present kind, in a living an interrelating continuity" (132). As suggested earlier, this is indeed how we are understanding failure as an *affective structure* and not solely as structure.
32 Williams, "Structures of Feeling," 130.

33. Williams, "Structures of Feeling," 132.
34. See Ahmed, "Affective Economies." In following Ahmed's piece, one could perhaps also speak of a *subject* of failure. Of course, the *subject* in question in Ahmed's piece is one who disseminates a certain affect among their community, an affect generated from the passage of another who is different from them and from that community. In the example given by Ahmed, this affect is a negative one, such as dread. When the subject is successful in circulating that affect among their community, there results in the explicit hatred for that other. Like Ahmed, I critique such a subject. Moreover, I would also resist thinking the category of the subject amid the affect of failure; in relation to failure, I would argue for the *reject* as the more apt figure of thought. For this figure of thought, see Goh, *Reject*.
35. Williams, "Structures of Feeling," 129, 132.
36. Williams, "Structures of Feeling," 130.
37. Williams, "Structures of Feeling," 133, 134.
38. Bradatan, *In Praise of Failure*, 5.
39. Jones, *Failure and the American Writer*, 155.
40. See Firestein, *Failure*.
41. Bradatan, *In Praise of Failure*, 4.
42. Bradatan, *In Praise of Failure*, 3, 4, 10, 236.
43. Bradatan, *In Praise of Failure*, 10. I thought this statement of Bradatan's rather ironic given that earlier he would condemn business-management or entrepreneurship talk of failure as "a stepping stone to success" nothing but "self-deception by another name" (5). All this is to say that Bradatan does not stay with failure. In fact, that is clearly not his intention. As he says of his book, it is "not about failure for its own sake" (5).
44. Halberstam, *The Queer Art of Failure*, 23.
45. Halberstam, *The Queer Art of Failure*, 88.
46. See Carr, "In Support of Failure." In this essay, Carr also says, "My interest is not in rescuing failure, uplifting it, pulling from it happy, success-oriented resolutions or morals. Instead, I want to think about what could happen if we risk dwelling in the shameful muck and mire of our failure; if we give ourselves permission to experience failure on its own terms, not as something that exists only in opposition to something else but something that is *present*." As will be seen, or if it is not already evident, my rhetoric veers very close to Carr's. However, as I will point out in later notes, Carr does not necessarily stay with failure. The abandonment of failure's negativity for something more positive becomes undeniable in Carr's later essay, "Failure Is Not an Option," where she proclaims that "the virtue of failure should be...celebrated" (78), or that "failure should be welcomed, if not actively sought out, signaling as it does both the presence of creative, risky thinking and an opportunity to explore a new direction" (76).

47 As Marin says sarcastically, "We would like to see [in failure] the opportunity of a new life, a blank page, to endow a failure with a retrospective value in transforming it into knowledge, a richness, an experience. There would be virtues in failure. Really?" And she continues: "The large part of failures teaches us nothing. Worse, we often get stuck in the stammering [bégaiement] of the same failures, as if they were inevitable, and all this in a paradoxical jouissance of their almost reassuring repetition." Marin, *Rupture(s)*, 20 (my translation).

48 See Blanchot, *Le pas au-delà*; Blanchot, *L'écriture du désastre*; Nancy, *La communauté désœuvrée*.

49 Agamben, "On Potentiality," in *Potentialities*, 179. See also Agamben, *The Use of Bodies*, particularly the chapter "Work and Inoperativity." On another note, I stress a *thorough* "inoperativity" for our purposes to mark a slight deviation from Blanchot, Nancy, and Agamben. This is because, in Blanchot's case, the elucidation of *désœuvrement* does not signal the end of all literary or aesthetic work nor call for any moratorium on the latter. Instead, writing must continue in order to constantly remind us of the *désœuvrement*, which can also be a "disaster," that is always working from within. This is also not to mention that Blanchot is not inclined toward failure. For him, to do so "would be to be nostalgic of success." Blanchot, *L'écriture du désastre*, 25 (my translation). With respect to Nancy, the renunciation of any communitarian project, likewise, is not a call for the end of community. Instead, it reaffirms how community takes shape in its own terms, according to the desires of every entity that is coming and going according to their desires, hence constituting this community in its evolution *and* devolution. In Agamben's reclamation of *inoperosità* for human ontology, which, according to him, is also borne by "bare life" or *zoè*—which is to say, life as mere existing before it takes on any political, legal, social, and professional form and which renders it available for abandonment, banishment, or exile by a sovereign power—this is also done with a view of a "coming politics" that embraces *zoè* rather than setting it apart from political life or *bios*. Agamben, *The Use of Bodies*, 213. If it is not evident already, I am seeking to stay with "inoperativity" before it progresses to take on any affirmative and/or political value.

50 Ahmed, *What's the Use?*, 2.

51 Halberstam, *The Queer Art of Failure*, 92 (my italics).

52 Edelman, *Bad Education*, xvi. Edelman counts sex, queerness, Blackness, trans, and women as the "nothing" of "bad education," which are "not meant to appear" within the world dominated by white heteronormative morality but which nonetheless exert pressure on such a world. Following the works of Halberstam, Bey, and the Afropessimists Frank B. Wilderson III and Calvin Warren (especially his *Ontological Terror*), I would agree that this group of "nothing" is also associated with failure. I suspect,

though, my sense of *nothing* includes, on the one hand, more than that group to account for certain non-Blacks, non-whites, non-queers, non-trans, non-women, non-deviant-sex to be failed "nothings" that do not add up to normalized meaningful life, and on the other, a sense less than what Edelman would like the term to signify as I lean toward a *literal* "nothing."

I note too that Edelman associates the notion of incompleteness to his "nothing," which is, in Edelman's words, the "nothing" that is "fracturing the ontological consistence of what 'is.'" Edelman, *Bad Education*, xvi. As will be indicated in this introduction and the following chapter, Harney and Moten also mobilize this idea of the incomplete to celebrate the failure embodied by those who threaten to break the flow of the white, racist, capitalist order.

My learning *nothing* also runs counter, once again, to Halberstam's positive perspective on his project "about failing well, failing often, and *learning.*" Halberstam, *The Queer Art of Failure*, 24 (my emphasis). I discuss a little the problematics of the rhetoric of "failing well" in another note in the conclusion.

53   Jones, *Failure and the American Writer*, 157 (my emphasis).
54   Jones, *Failure and the American Writer*, 38.
55   Jones, *Failure and the American Writer*, 57.
56   Jones, *Failure and the American Writer*, 37, 16.
57   Jones, *Failure and the American Writer*, 12, 38. For failure as a source of alternative epistemologies and literary identity, see Ochoa, *The Uses of Failure in Mexican Literature and Identity*.
58   Jones, *Failure and the American Writer*, 159. A similar move of subjecting failure to a literary use is arguably found in Cardona, *Global Failure and World Literature*.
59   Jones, *Failure and the American Writer*, 43.
60   Jones, *Failure and the American Writer*, 51.
61   Jones, *Failure and the American Writer*, 39.
62   As Stefano Harney and Fred Moten remind us, "Resilience is the name for the violent destruction of things that won't give, won't return to form, won't bend when access is demanded, won't be flexible and *compli*-ant. Stopping when you are told to stop and moving along when you are told to move along demonstrates resilience and composure; but broken, breaking, dissed assembly demonstrates itself openly, secretly, dissembling in captured but inaccessible glance, for us, to us, as incomplete and much more than complete." Harney and Moten, *All Incomplete*, 44.
63   As many cultural theorists or cultural studies scholars have pointed out, we are dealing with failures of workplace cultures and work ideologies here. I will refer to their scholarship in the next chapter.

64 See also Appadurai and Alexander, *Failure*. They identify a "regime of failure"—that is, the apparatus formed by "a certain epistemology, political economy, and dominant technology" that determines, judges, and naturalizes what failure is, usually a human shortcoming set in opposition to the "success" of technology (2).

65 Such an entrepreneurship of failure constitutes what Bradatan considers "a mockery of failure by trying—without irony—to rebrand it and sell it as nothing less than a stepping stone to success." Bradatan, *In Praise of Failure*, 4.

On another note, I suspect Carr unwittingly or unconsciously falls into the trap of Silicon Valley–speak or ideology when she says, "To find a way to make [failure] work for me," "to make failure something I do, to make it my business." Carr, "In Support of Failure."

66 Harney and Moten, *All Incomplete*, 43.

67 Harney and Moten, *All Incomplete*, 64.

68 Harney and Moten, *All Incomplete*, 19, 44.

69 Harney and Moten, *All Incomplete*, 44.

70 See Dalke, quoted in Carr and Micciche, *Failure Pedagogies*

71 In his reading of Melville's *Pierre*, Jones has also noted that "perfectionist premises are primed to fail." Jones, *Failure and the American Writer*, 47.

72 Cusk, *Outline*, 41.

73 Deleuze, *The Logic of Sense*, 41. See also the section on "The Empty Square" in Deleuze, "How Do We Recognize Structuralism?"

74 See Cusset, *L'autre qu'on adorait*, 244, 252.

75 My thinking of failure as ontological here stands in contrast to that of Scott Sandage's, who argues that failure is a historical determination through the creation of the credit system, which rendered defaulters "losers" or "failures." It also differs from Colin Feltham's thinking of failure as a sociological phenomenon, driven by social groups that desire to make a clear divide from those who perform badly in school, those who traffic in vice, those who are poor, and those who cannot find jobs.

76 Jones, *Failure and the American Writer*, 16. Later, he would also say, "Failure has its own plot, based on fundamental contradictions deep within our moral and existential beings" (58).

77 See the chapter on Herman Melville on the relation between failing and the image of falling. Jones, *Failure and the American Writer*. John Ochoa has also reminded us that failure is "etymologically related to a fall," given that "the Latin *cadere* means both 'to fail' and 'to fall.'" Ochoa, *The Uses of Failure in Mexican Literature and Identity*, 5.

78 The sense of "after" in the title of this present work should be read in a similar vein. In other words, we are not speaking about the question of living on when failure is a thing of the past, when there is no more failure,

where life is assumed to be better. Rather, and to reiterate, it is more the case where failure is recognized to be ineluctably part of existence, where life is living on inextricably with failure.

79   See Ngai, *Ugly Feelings*, 4. The quintessential "neutral kernel" of failure's "structure of feeling" could also explain the experience of emptiness at the heart of failure.

80   I am following Werner Hamacher in his understanding of pleroma here, which signifies that which is supposedly filled up or sealed tight against spilling over yet nevertheless finds its contents escaping. In Hamacher's words: "What is supposed to be closed, once and for all, can never cease to close." Hamacher, *Pleroma*, 1.

81   It is in Seminar 20 where Lacan will say that jouissance "exactly implies the acceptation of death." Lacan, *L'éthique de la psychanalyse*, 222 (my translation). And in Seminar 19, in the session "The Desire to Sleep," which will be relevant to our next chapter, Lacan will also make clear that jouissance is not simply or all "enjoyment" but also bears some form of pain, since jouissance is when "one knocks oneself," when "one hurts oneself." (*quand il se cogne, qu'il se fait mal*) Lacan, *Ou pire*, 217 (my translation).

Néstor Braunstein provides a very clear explanation of Lacanian jouissance. Like how we have noted previously, Braunstein also underscores that there is pain involved in jouissance, in addition to jouissance being intimately associated with a death drive. See Braunstein, "Desire and Jouissance in the Teachings of Lacan." Useful for our thinking of failure, Braunstein also notes that jouissance "does not point to anything, nor does it serve any purpose whatsoever; it is an unpredictable experience" (106). He furthermore highlights its sacrificial aspect, which is not too foreign to the Georges Bataille's notion of unproductive expenditure in *La part maudite*, and which we will make mention later. According to Braunstein, there is "the malefic jouissance of stripping the other of the goods he holds dear" (106), and one can think of the dear goods of success that our contemporary cultures or societies cherish and from which our thinking of failure as jouissance is trying to untether ourselves.

And to reiterate the absence of an optimistic ending to jouissance, Lacan will say that jouissance is always on a repetitive loop with desire, if not chasing after desire. But desire, for Lacan, is always a lack, and so there is always a lost or impossible object for jouissance too. See also Braunstein, "Desire and Jouissance in the Teachings of Lacan," 106. Here, it is also perhaps appropriate to cite once more a line from Marin that I have done so in an earlier note: "We often get stuck in the stammering of the same failures, as if they were inevitable, and all this in a paradoxical jouissance of their almost reassuring repetition." Marin, *Rupture(s)*, 20.

82 Li, *Must I Go*, 164. Here, I am also resisting the perspective on failure by failure studies, such as Setiya, where he proclaims that "failure is a many-splendored thing." Setiya, *Life Is Hard*, 91.

83 Or, according to Marin: "Failure [*l'échec*] is often nothing other than itself: destitute [*pauvre*], disappointing, a pure dud [*raté*]." Marin, *Rupture(s)*, 20.

84 See Berlant and Edelman, *Sex, or the Unbearable*, xii.

85 And perhaps those who live in the negativity of the impasse of failure would be inhabiting "transitional forms that slow and extend ways to live inconveniently with each other." Berlant, *On the Inconvenience of Other People*, xi.

86 Berlant and Edelman, *Sex, or the Unbearable*, 120. Not unlike how we are thinking about failure as structure here, Edelman in this text also thinks of negativity in structural terms. According to him, "Negativity is unchanging *as structure* because negativity *structures change*" (121). In relation to failure, I would insist that the change that is ongoing in failure as negativity is *not* one for the better. The change does not bring about the overcoming of failure but the difference in the experience, sense, or feeling of failure from one moment to the next.

87 For a far more nuanced reading of the paranoid and depressive positions in Sedgwick, moreover with reference to failure, see the section "What Survives" in Berlant and Edelman, *Sex, or the Unbearable*.

88 Berlant and Edelman, *Sex, or the Unbearable*, 55. I provide another take on Sedgwick's *A Dialogue on Love* in one of the chapters in this book.

89 Agamben, "On Potentiality," 181, 182.

90 Shall we say that staying with the impasse and negativity of failure is the experience of the Real in Lacanian terms? For Lacan, in a 1975 lecture given at MIT, the Real is where one knocks oneself, and it is not difficult to see how the existential condition of failed experience is one that is full of knocks. Lacan also considers the Real as the impossible, and perhaps we can say that the Real of the impasse and negativity of failure is impossible only because we always tend to deny failure, because we always seek to construct the Imaginary of a life of successes.

91 Jones has also said, again in his reading of Melville's *Pierre*, "Failure . . . is *both* inborn *and* institutionally imposed, with no exit offered from its recursive loop." Jones, *Failure and the American Writer*, 58. In a more contemporary context, one that pertains in addition to race, Mimi Khúc has written, in a way that resonates with mine, of failure as "all-encompassing, endless, forever," which constitutes "a kind of crip time," rendering one to be in "an endless suspension in failure, even as everyday you are trying to 'do' your way out. There is no way out." Khúc, *dear elia*, 9. Khúc's book appeared after the completion of my manuscript, and as

such, I regret to say that I can only engage with her book more deeply in another occasion.

92   This recalls perhaps Edelman's notion of (queer) negativity, which involves the "willingness to insist intransitively—to insist that the future stop here." Edelman, *No Future*, 31. No doubt, the thinking and experiencing of the impasse of failure bears no less the sense of "no future." Not surprisingly, too, "no future" is also a phrase one finds in Beckett, "Worstward Ho!," 83.

93   As a preview of that chapter, I will just say that, in articulating failure's shared unshareability, I am resisting the communitarian contour that one might tend to give to the thinking of failure, something that can be found in recent affect theories that engage with failure. I note here too that my rhetoric echoes that of Elaine Scarry in her study of pain. Scarry was addressing pain caused by war and other physical violence, which leave visible wounds on the body. If there is pain associated with the sense of failure, this pain is neither locatable in the body nor does it leave an explicit, physical scar on the body. Nevertheless, this pain can be felt viscerally, no less, and sometimes worse, precisely because of its nonlocalized or nonlocatable quality. See Scarry, *The Body in Pain*.

94   See the discussion on "infrastructuralism" in Berlant, *On the Inconvenience of Other People*. My more literal reading of "infra," which is to say, something that pertains to the internal, something deep within the personal, also resonates with Stephen Marche's reflections on failure as the quintessential condition of writers. I believe this is suggested when he writes, "Failure is the body of a writer's life. Success is only ever an attire." Marche, *On Writing and Failure*, 7.

95   Berlant, *Cruel Optimism*, 4. Or, as she says further: "In the impasse . . ., being treads water; mainly, it does not drown. Even those whom you would think of as defeated are living beings figuring out how to stay attached to life from within it, and to protect what optimism they have for that, at least" (10). On another note, I agree with Berlant's thinking of the impasse in her dialogue with Lee Edelman: "The impasse not yet or perhaps never caught up in the drama of repair is neither life existentially nor life post-traumatically but existence, revealed in the stunned encounter: with the contingencies of structuring fantasy; in what one loves in one's own incoherence; and in the bruise of significant contact, with people and with words." Berlant and Edelman, *Sex, or the Unbearable*, 41.

96   Berlant, *Cruel Optimism*, 4–5.

97   Derrida, *Aporias*, 12.

98   If not lostness, there is surely a sense of loss too. According to Edelman, "Loss is not merely an emptiness but something more dimensional, something that fills the vacated space that's left by what used to be there." Berlant and Edelman, *Sex, or the Unbearable*, 47. Here, I would argue that

such a sense of loss effectively belies the sense of structure according to Deleuze as mentioned earlier—that is to say, structure as the noncoincidence of an occupant at a loss of place and the empty place without an occupant in sight. And loss inherent to the structure of failure, I would add, is one that is without knowledge of the object of loss. In that sense, it is like melancholia, according to Mark Fisher, which is sadness that does not have an object for which it grieves. There is, once again, as I have remarked in another note previously, emptiness.

99 Derrida, *Aporias*, 12.

100 Derrida, *Aporias*, 13.

101 I am clearly referring to Gianni Vattimo's "weak thought" here. However, while I am sympathetic to his taking into account of Being's "faded transmission," its "taking leave of" existence or "passing away," its "waning," its "fullness of its decline" or its "fully living its weakness" (Vattimo, *Weak Thought*, 45, 46, 47, 48, 50), I do suggest going further by suspending, interrupting, or even leaving aside dialectics, which Vattimo will say that his "weak thought" "has not entirely left... behind" (39).

102 Berlant, *Sex, or the Unbearable*, 56. And Edelman would add, "Drama, like negativity, may be harder to escape than we think" (50). Bradatan has also written that in failure, "we are out of sync." Edelman, *In Praise of Failure*, 4.

On another note, I added a hyphen in "dis-placement" in my reiteration of Deleuze's understanding of structure because place would seem to lose its function as place, or even status of place, as long as it finds no one to occupy it.

On yet another note, but staying with the question of mess and failure, there is Jean-Paul Sartre on Jean Genet (Sartre, *Saint Genet*). Sartre is indeed interested in the failures of writers such as Baudelaire (in *Baudelaire*) and Flaubert (in *L'idiot de la famille*). To his treatment of failure in Baudelaire, Maurice Blanchot will have a response. See Blanchot, *La part du feu*. As already mentioned, this present work will be more interested in twenty-first-century writings and so will leave out any discussion of these works. Nevertheless, I am indebted to Elissa Marder for pointing out to me this trajectory that starts from Baudelaire to Sartre and to Blanchot.

Meanwhile, Halberstam has also written that the "queer art of failure" "promises... to fail, to *make a mess* [my italics], to fuck shit up, to be loud, unruly, impolite, to breed resentment, to bash back, to speak up and out, to disrupt, assassinate, shock, and annihilate." Halberstam, *The Queer Art of Failure*, 110. We are clearly following a more passive, resigned attitude with regard to failure. As suggested, too, our sense of negativity is very close to Edelman's. Halberstam, as evident, wants instead to glean some form of political use from negativity. For him, "negativity might well constitute an antipolitics, but it should not register as apolitical" (108).

103   Li, *Dear Friend, from My Life I Write to You in Your Life*, 52.

104   The more positive outlook of Berlant's "cruel optimism" can be elicited from her take on optimism as "an orientation toward the pleasure that is bound up in the activity of world-making, which may be hooked on futures or not." She goes on: "Even when it turns out to involve a cruel relation, it would be wrong to see optimism's negativity as a symptom of an error, a perversion, damage, or a dark truth: optimism is, instead, a scene of negotiated sustenance that makes life bearable as it presents itself ambivalently, unevenly, incoherently." Berlant, *Cruel Optimism*, 14.

105   See Thacker, *Infinite Resignation*.

106   Halberstam, *The Queer Art of Failure*, 186, 187. With respect to Halberstam's optimism, or what he would also call "a new kind of optimism" (5), we should be precise to say that this does not imply an uncritical positivity. As he states, this is "not an optimism that relies on positive thinking as an explanatory engine for social order, nor one that insists upon the bright side at all costs; rather this is a little ray of sunshine that produces shade and light in equal measure and knows that the meaning of one always depends upon the meaning of the other" (5). Pessimists as we are, we cannot see that "little ray of sunshine." We are unable to be in tune with the positive mood and tone that Halberstam brings to the thinking of failure, we cannot envision the "wondrous anarchy" (187), to borrow Halberstam's phrase, of failure to the existing order of things.

107   On the impasse and getting stuck and their relation to depression, see Cvetkovich, *Depression*, 20–21. See also Critchley's *Notes on Suicide*, which encourages the composition of suicidal thoughts free from moral, religious, and even philosophical judgment, hence paving the way forward from Camus's *Myth of Sisyphus*, which rejects suicide as worthy of philosophical praise. But here, I am closer to Bradatan when he writes, following the psychiatrist Thomas Szasz, that "talking sympathetically about suicide . . . is not an apology for suicide. It's an attempt to understand, from within, one of the most difficult decisions a human being has ever had to make. If we can't do more to help these people, at the very least we owe them this understanding." Bradatan, *In Praise of Failure*, 187. In my view, this understanding can take on the form of giving them the discursive and affective space to stay with the negativity of the impasse.

108   See Hamacher, "Other Pains."

109   Heidegger, of course, has been seen as some sort of failure in philosophical circles, because of his acquiescence to the Nazi regime after being elected by the latter as the rector of Freiburg University and because of his anti-Semitism in his thinking, undeniable since the posthumous publication of the *Black Notebooks*. Peter Trawny provides a rather sympathetic reading of the latter. Trawny, *Freedom to Fail*.

110   Or, as Halberstam deftly puts it: "To live is to fail, to bungle, to disappoint, and ultimately to die." Halberstam, *The Queer Art of Failure*, 186–87.

111   And as Berlant says, which also brings us back to failure's problematization of any reparative move: "Dread raises uncomfortable questions about repair, the unclarity of what repair would fix, how it would feel as process and telos, and whether it would be possible, desirable, or worth risking." Berlant and Edelman, *Sex, or the Unbearable*, 39.

112   Here, I refer to an earlier note on the psychoanalytic term *jouissance*, and I should admit that I was simply scratching the surface of psychoanalysis there. Readers will find that I will do likewise with other psychoanalytic terms such as *mourning, melancholia, drift [dérive]*, and *narcissism* in the rest of this work. Indeed, I have no intention or ambition for this work to be a psychoanalytic understanding of failure. Neither do I seek to present psychoanalytic readings of the selected texts here. I believe furthermore that psychoanalysis is not the right theoretical interlocutor for the latter, given too that most of these texts, as mentioned earlier, are in fact suspicious of psychoanalysis. In a way, then, I am respecting their preferences to explicate failure and its accompanying genres in an idiom other than this theoretical language. My personal worry about relying on psychoanalysis here also has to do with it having the tendency to be a "strong theory," seeing rather reductively psychoanalytic tropes such as the family drama, sexual drives, or the unconscious at work everywhere. This is not to say, however, that psychoanalysis has nothing interesting to say about failure. To the contrary, one will find interesting psychoanalytic insights into failure in Edelman's works (both *No Future* and *Bad Education* as well as *Sex, or the Unbearable*, written with Berlant) and Schuster's *The Trouble with Pleasure* (especially the preface, which includes the section "The Failure Not to Be") or even Phillips's *On Giving Up*.

113   On a descriptive method that draws out relations, I am following more or less Love in "Close but Not Deep."

114   Harney and Moten, *All Incomplete*, 44, 68.

115   Since we have already referenced Agamben, and given that we have noted how genres in Berlant's sense are also of gestures or the gestural, as well as us announcing right at the beginning of this introduction that we are reckoning with a general nonutilitarian ends of a study of failure and its genres, let us highlight here Agamben's notes on gesture, which underscore a certain uselessness of gestures. According to him, "Nothing is more misleading for an understanding of gestures . . . than representing, on the one hand, a sphere of means as addressing a goal (for example, marching seen as a means of moving the body from point A to point B) and, on the other hand, a separate and superior sphere of gesture as

a movement that has its end in itself (for example, dance seen as an aesthetic dimension." Agamben, *Means without Ends*, 58. He goes on to say, "If dance is gesture, it is so, rather, because it is nothing more than the endurance and exhibition of the media character of corporal movements. *The gesture is the exhibition of a mediality: it is the process of making a means visible as such*" (58). The gestures or flailing genres that we are interested in in this present work likewise do not have "an end in itself" but are "of a pure and endless mediality" (59)—that is, manifesting or expressing how the body responds to the sense of failure, doing so especially when words fail to articulate or communicate that sense of failure. As Agamben will also say: "The gesture is . . . communication of a communicability. It has precisely nothing to say because what it shows is the being-in-language of human beings as pure mediality. . . . [The] gesture is essentially always a gesture of not being able to figure something out in language; it is always a *gag* in the proper meaning of the term" (59).

116   With respect to the critical relation between race, gender, and failure, this present work admittedly does not go as deeply into this issue as Love in *Feeling Backward*, Muñoz in *Cruising Utopia*, Halberstam in *The Queer Art of Failure*, Harney and Moten in *All Incomplete*, and Bey in *Cistem Failure*, for example, do. Any real engagement with this issue certainly demands a work on its own, to which I am definitely committed. I am particularly interested in the failure of certain Asians to be engaged in race discourse and activism in a timely manner, including their failure to form critical solidarity with other minority races. As said, though, this will have to be left for another occasion. Besides, for a critical understanding of those failures in racial terms, I also believe in the necessity of first explicating the affective structure of failure, the fact that some of us never leave our sense of failure, and some of the genres that are flailing in response to it, hence this present work before that commitment.

117   Here, I also note the epic quality of Cusk's trilogy. Arguably, that quality can also be found in Moshfegh's *My Year of Rest and Relaxation* with the narrative's year-long temporality. With the notion of epic, I want to bring us back again briefly to "epic fail." What is really missing or wanting in the latter's articulation is a thinking or even rethinking of epic and, keeping in mind Aristotelian poetics, pose the question of how the epic might be more fitting to contemporary failure as opposed to tragedy, not forgetting that the tragic is the preferred quality of "grand narratives" of twentieth-century failures of Beckett and other modernists.

CHAPTER 1 FLOPPING TO SLEEP

1. Looking ahead to the next chapter, we will also find in Cusk a reckoning with the overdetermination of failure. As Malete, friend of the narrator's friend Elena, says: "You could spend your whole life ... trying to trace events back to your own mistakes. People in legend thought that their misfortunes could be traced back to their failure to offer libations to certain gods." In today's more secular terms, one might be neurotic in trying to identify an original failure, but this is almost impossible. Doing so would only undoubtedly contribute to the accumulative effect of the sense of failure that we underscored in our Introduction. Cusk, *Outline*, 187.
2. Stefano Harney and Fred Moten have also taught us in *All Incomplete* that there is a critical relation between a break and a flow, one to which we must attend, especially if we were to launch a critique of neoliberal political economy's racist capitalism and its work ideology. We will indeed touch on these issues toward the end of this chapter.
3. Bradatan, *In Praise of Failure*, 9.
4. See, for example, Badiou, *Saint Paul*.
5. Kindly see Goh, *The Reject*.
6. Marin, *Rupture(s)*, 20. Translations from this text are mine.
7. Marin, *Rupture(s)*, 11.
8. See, of course, Petersen, *Can't Even*.
9. If genres are always flailing, as Berlant wants it, then perhaps flopping is the genre par excellence, if we follow the *Oxford English Dictionary*'s definitions of *flop* as "to swing or sway about heavily and loosely" or "to move clumsily"; it is moreover a genre that corresponds to failure if we think once again of it in terms of falling, since to flop is also, again, according to the OED, "to collapse" or "to move with a sudden bump or thud."
10. Before our contemporary corporate-speak of "self-care" and "mental well-being," Melissa Gregg had observed that earlier corporate training in "coping with stress" and "time management" had the effect of "imply[ing] that individuals who could not cope with growing job requirements were at personal fault." Gregg, *Work's Intimacy*, 5.
11. Malesic, *The End of Burnout*, 11.
12. The psychiatrist Pooja Lakshmin calls the latter "faux self-care." See Lakshmin, *Real Self-Care*.
13. Critics of work have also pointed how our naturalization of a work ethic—not to mention one that not only makes having a waged work a social norm but also one makes us work incessantly and chase after unrealistic ideals of hyperproductivity and overachievement—has only generated a sense of failure for many of us when we do not meet those goals. As Gavin Mueller notes, any deviation from such an ideology, which

might include joblessness or a refusal to work, will only be met with a discourse of failure: a "perceived failure to exhibit an appropriate kind and degree of ambition" or "judged to be failing the moral test of work." Mueller, *Breaking Things at Work*, 198, 199. Jonathan Malesic, meanwhile, critiques the burnout culture that work ideology actually breeds and celebrates. According to his observation, if one does not demonstrate or express burnout, one might be made to feel not doing as much as his or her fellow worker, which then "makes them feel like they have failed in life." Malesic, *The End of Burnout*, 2.

14 Incidentally, failure remains to be refused by certain players in this sport. When the Milwaukee Bucks, the 2021 championship team, did not make it to the 2023 Eastern conference semifinals, its star player Giannis Antetokounmpo was asked by a reporter during the postgame media session if the Bucks' season was thus a failure. His now-famous response was: "There's no failure in sports." According to him, all the defeats along the way to a championship are only "steps to success."

On another note, the relation between failure and sports has also been picked up by Halberstam, *The Queer Art of Failure*; and Setiya, *Life Is Hard*.

15 See especially Bataille, *La part maudite*.

16 I do not ignore the fact that my two examples involve women of color. There is no doubt the entanglements of gender and race in the problematic of failure, with the much-unspoken expectation that people of color, especially women, must do more than others in order to succeed, to not fail. I will touch on gender and failure later in this chapter and the next. I will also speak a little on the topic of race and failure later too; however, as said in a note in the introduction, I will leave a fuller discussion, which the topic deserves and definitely warrants, for another occasion.

17 Beckett, *All That Fall*, 5.

18 I am aware that Sharon Marcus gave a summer seminar on the theme of breakdown in relation to Moshfegh's text at the University of Pittsburgh Humanities Center in 2022. Till the time of the final revision of this present work, I still found no publication of this work, hence the absence of any reference to it here.

19 Moshfegh, *My Year of Rest and Relaxation*, 3.

20 Moshfegh, *My Year of Rest and Relaxation*, 36, 49.

21 Moshfegh, *My Year of Rest and Relaxation*, 154.

22 The narrator would also say of Reva: "Reva had, despite her hard work, simply failed to get what she wanted—no husband, no children, no fabulous career" (14).

23 Moshfegh, *My Year of Rest and Relaxation*, 4.

24 Moshfegh, *My Year of Rest and Relaxation*, 18, 21.

25 Moshfegh, *My Year of Rest and Relaxation*, 19.

26   Moshfegh, *My Year of Rest and Relaxation*, 21, 217.
27   Moshfegh, *My Year of Rest and Relaxation*, 253.
28   Moshfegh, *My Year of Rest and Relaxation*, 63.
29   As if to reinforce the sense of failure traversing her world and worldview, the narrator would also characterize her mother's death, which is a matter of organs shutting down, as "system failure" (151).
30   Moshfegh, *My Year of Rest and Relaxation*, 189.
31   This is also not to ignore the possibility that the narrator's sense of existential failure might be a remnant or belated (in Freud's, and after Freud, Laplanche's, sense) effect of her mother's harsh shaming of the narrator during her childhood, calling her a fashion embarrassment in New York City, an emotional weakling, fat, and insinuating that she is only capable of state-school essays (see Moshfegh, *My Year of Rest and Relaxation*, 67–69). And yet, I suspect that the narrator is very much over all that. As said, she is the envy of Reva in terms of looks and fashion, and she made it to Columbia. Something similar could be said about the narrator's self-representation in relation to Trevor too. In a self-denigrating way, she would ventriloquize what Trevor thought of her: "I was kids' stuff. I was nonsense. I wasn't worth the calories" (35). Yet she would be rational enough to check herself on that self-abjection. Soon, she would reflect on that and say, "I still couldn't accept that Trevor was a loser and a moron. I didn't want to believe that I could have degraded myself for someone who didn't deserve it. I was still stuck on that bit of vanity. But I was determined to sleep it away" (76).
32   Moshfegh, *My Year of Rest and Relaxation*, 17.
33   Moshfegh, *My Year of Rest and Relaxation*, 137.
34   Moshfegh, *My Year of Rest and Relaxation*, 217.
35   Moshfegh, *My Year of Rest and Relaxation*, 60.
36   Again, the narrator's dreams are very likely to lure psychoanalytic readings. As said, though, I want to sidestep such a reading of the novel here and consider other aspects of the novel that could have implications beyond the concerns of psychoanalysis.
37   Moshfegh, *My Year of Rest and Relaxation*, 189.
38   Moshfegh, *My Year of Rest and Relaxation*, 204.
39   Moshfegh, *My Year of Rest and Relaxation*, 137.
40   Moshfegh, *My Year of Rest and Relaxation*, 146, 162, 163.
41   Ngai, *Ugly Feelings*, 336.
42   Ngai, *Ugly Feelings*, 175, 179.
43   I am referring to Ngai's discussion of skin trope in relation to race politics and the writing of race in Nella Larson's *Quicksand* in her chapter on irritation. On another note, irritation as the registering of the jarring confluence between the internal and the external might recall Williams's understanding of the "structure of feeling." Here, we could add to our

consideration of failure as a "structure of feeling" as being traversed by the affect of irritation.

44   Moshfegh, *My Year of Rest and Relaxation*, 156.
45   Moshfegh, *My Year of Rest and Relaxation*, 252.
46   In contrast, for a more "productive" reading of sleep in Moshfegh's novel, see Strätz, "Revolt Through Passivity?" In her reading, "the trope of sleep bears a dual function in the construction of critique in the novel: firstly, it simultaneously serves as a metaphor for the exhaustion and fatigue induced by late modern life and becomes itself a potent cultural metaphor of biocapitalism and neoliberal politics . . . ; secondly, sleep is constructed as a form of resistance that effectively reveals the hidden, destructive nature of neoliberal ideology" (103). She goes on to say that sleep "not only helps the character to distance herself from work and to restore her energy but also becomes a performative act of revolt, a form of rebellion that turns passivity into an act of active resistance, disclosing not only the ultimate toll of her bullshit job, but also its absurdity" (108). For another political reading, within an Arendtian framework, of sleep in Moshfegh's novel, see also Dirschauer, "Sleep as Action?"
47   Moshfegh, *My Year of Rest and Relaxation*, 14, 35.
48   *Oxford English Dictionary*, "flop," accessed January 16, 2025, https://www.oed.com/search/dictionary/?scope=Entries&q=flop.
49   Moshfegh, *My Year of Rest and Relaxation*, 23, 26.
50   Moshfegh, *My Year of Rest and Relaxation*, 39, 42.
51   Moshfegh, *My Year of Rest and Relaxation*, 51.
52   Moshfegh, *My Year of Rest and Relaxation*, 79, 85, 87, 110.
53   See Crary, *24/7*; Moshfegh, *My Year of Rest and Relaxation*, 86.
54   Lacan, *Ou pire*, 217 (my translation).
55   Moshfegh, *My Year of Rest and Relaxation*, 193.
56   Moshfegh, *My Year of Rest and Relaxation*, 227.
57   Moshfegh, *My Year of Rest and Relaxation*, 197.
58   Of course, politics is invested in forms (of division) as well, as we know from Plato to Foucault and to Rancière. I do refer to Anna Kornbluh's work in the conclusion, in which she is interested in more positive social and political formations and forms. Political forms, however, are not the real interest of this book, and so I do not delve into them.
59   Moshfegh, *My Year of Rest and Relaxation*, 263.
60   Moshfegh, *My Year of Rest and Relaxation*, 263, 274, 276.
61   Moshfegh, *My Year of Rest and Relaxation*, 26, 51, 137.
62   Moshfegh, *My Year of Rest and Relaxation*, 261.
63   Moshfegh, *My Year of Rest and Relaxation*, 288.
64   Moshfegh, *My Year of Rest and Relaxation*, 64, 288.
65   Moshfegh, *My Year of Rest and Relaxation*, 263.
66   Moshfegh, *My Year of Rest and Relaxation*, 288.

67 Moshfegh, *My Year of Rest and Relaxation*, 287.
68 Moshfegh, *My Year of Rest and Relaxation*, 283.
69 Moshfegh, *My Year of Rest and Relaxation*, 283.
70 We do not ignore her racial stereotyping of Ping Xi when she remembers him: "I imagined his small, dark eyes staring at me and squinting.... He struck me as a reptilian, small-hearted being, someone placed on the planet to strike a chord with similar people, people who distracted themselves with money and conversation rather than sink their hands and teeth into the world around them" (281–82).
71 That it is fundamentally a racist world that is depicted in the novel is further reaffirmed when there is effectively no pushback against Dr. Tuttle's assurance to the narrator, who is of English, French, Swedish, and German blood, that the side effects of some of the prescribed meds, like hallucination, "happens mostly to Asians," and so "[she'll] be fine" (117). Another instance involves Reva, who has no qualms in quickly resorting to racial stereotyping or profiling by saying that economics as an academic subject is "the Asian nerd major" (13).
72 Moshfegh, *My Year of Rest and Relaxation*, 225.
73 Moshfegh, *My Year of Rest and Relaxation*, 5.
74 Moshfegh, *My Year of Rest and Relaxation*, 264.
75 Moshfegh, *My Year of Rest and Relaxation*, 263.
76 Moshfegh, *My Year of Rest and Relaxation*, 284.
77 Moshfegh, *My Year of Rest and Relaxation*, 196.
78 Moshfegh, *My Year of Rest and Relaxation*, 233.
79 Moshfegh, *My Year of Rest and Relaxation*, 227.
80 Benjamin, "The Work of Art in the Age of Its Technological Reproducibility," 260. The question of success and/or failure is no doubt central to the notion of testing. As Harney and Moten remind us in *All Incomplete*, testing is the regulatory mechanism of the knowledge economy, a means of disciplining and surveilling its subjects so that they will always be seeking to improve all the time. The question of success and/or failure is not foreign to Benjamin either. As Benjamin intimates here, the judgment of a film actress appearing in reproducible images as successful or a failure rests on the mercy of the audience who is empathetic only with the camera. But this is not how Benjamin himself thinks how success and failure are determined, even though the question of testing is still at stake. In the section "The Compass of Success" in "Ibizan Sequence" (1932), Benjamin argues that success is not the result of an individual's "willpower" (589). Instead, it depends on an intersection of internal and external forces, if not a dialectics between an individual's situating him- or herself in the world, either through action or inaction and the worldly forces that are acting on him or her. In this regard, success is a "caprice in the workings of the universe," and there are the universe's "favorites" (589). There

are signs for this, which rest in the "idiosyncrasy" (590) of the individual, which Benjamin proposes to be made manifest by the comic figure, who moves, if not fumbles along, the "compass of success" (590). This figure thus moves through throwing away convictions, either toward "normal success" or toward being a "genius of failure"; it can also move through testing every conviction, either toward being a "genius of success" or "normal failure" (590). This perhaps brings us back to the comic dimension of "epic fail" in our introduction, but I will leave aside any discussion of the comic figure since none of the characters in the texts discussed in this present work are such a figure. I do thank Adam Stern for bringing this little section of Benjamin's text to my attention.

81 Benjamin, "The Work of Art in the Age of Its Technological Reproducibility," 256.
82 Moshfegh, *My Year of Rest and Relaxation*, 289.
83 Moshfegh, *My Year of Rest and Relaxation*, 289.
84 Moshfegh, *My Year of Rest and Relaxation*, 289.
85 Interestingly, Benjamin argues that the cult of beauty can remain with works (re)produced by apparatuses of technological reproducibility Benjamin, "The Work of Art in the Age of Its Technological Reproducibility," 256.
86 See, of course, Sharpe, *In the Wake*. For Sharpe, this "wake work" involves attending to the memories of the history of slavery and to Black lives terrorized and subjugated under systemic racism and police brutality in the contemporary. It is, in short, a thinking that does the care work "of and for Black non/being in the world" (5).
87 Moshfegh, *My Year of Rest and Relaxation*, 204.
88 Moshfegh, *My Year of Rest and Relaxation*, 289. I simply note here that perhaps we could also frame the narrator's strange attraction to the image in terms of what Ngai calls "stuplimity" in *Ugly Feelings*. According to Ngai, "stuplimity" is "the aesthetic experience in which astonishment is paradoxically united with boredom" (271). And "boredom" here, which, for Ngai, "involves a deficiency of affect that is reflexively felt to be dysphoric—stultifying, tedious, irritating, fatiguing, or dulling" (269), does seem to describe well the narrator, especially before her sleep/hibernation project. This is also not to mention that the "stuplime path" also involves "confrontations with the systems encompassing them, formulating a resistant stance by going limp or falling down" (297), hence suggestive of failure as how we are understanding it.
89 Moshfegh, *My Year of Rest and Relaxation*, 289.
90 Moshfegh, *My Year of Rest and Relaxation*, 183.
91 Moshfegh, *My Year of Rest and Relaxation*, 262–63.
92 Moshfegh, *My Year of Rest and Relaxation*, 262.
93 Yao, *Disaffected*, 7.

94 Moshfegh, *My Year of Rest and Relaxation*, 12.
95 Moshfegh, *My Year of Rest and Relaxation*, 1.
96 See Nancy, *Tombe de sommeil* (*The Fall of Sleep*); Crary, 24/7.
97 See Hodson, "Rest Notes," 9–10.
98 Hodson, "Rest Notes," 12, 10.
99 Hodson, "Rest Notes," 12.
100 Hodson, "Rest Notes," 14, 24.
101 The literature on the critique of work is too vast to cover here. For what I have mentioned previously, I simply refer readers to Lafargue, *The Right to Be Lazy*; Weeks, *The Problem with Work*; Gregg, *Counterproductive*; Mueller, *Breaking Things at Work*; Frayne, *The Refusal of Work*; Malesic, *The End of Burnout*; and Lutz, *Doing Nothing*, among others.
102 Moshfegh, *My Year of Rest and Relaxation*, 206.
103 Harney and Moten, *All Incomplete*, 42.
104 Harney and Moten, *All Incomplete*, 39.
105 Harney and Moten, *All Incomplete*, 105, 40, 80.
106 Harney and Moten, *All Incomplete*, 44.
107 Harney and Moten, *All Incomplete*, 40.
108 Moshfegh, *My Year of Rest and Relaxation*, 193.
109 Vincent Bruyere has talked about "perishable fatigue." Here, perhaps one could also consider sustainable fatigue. Bruyere, *Perishability Fatigue*.
110 Moshfegh, *My Year of Rest and Relaxation*, 193 (my emphasis).
111 Moshfegh, *My Year of Rest and Relaxation*, 55.
112 Moshfegh, *My Year of Rest and Relaxation*, 264 (my emphasis).
113 Moshfegh, *My Year of Rest and Relaxation*, 11.
114 Jonathan Greenberg, however, argues that "losing track of time is the goal of both narrator and author in *My Year of Rest and Relaxation*." Greenberg, "Losing Track of Time," 189.
115 Moshfegh, *My Year of Rest and Relaxation*, 260.
116 Moshfegh, *My Year of Rest and Relaxation*, 258.
117 Moshfegh, *My Year of Rest and Relaxation*, 264.
118 Moshfegh, *My Year of Rest and Relaxation*, 265.
119 Instead of unproductive expenditure, it is more a case of possession of property in the narrator's case. Notions of possession and property, however, as Harney and Moten have taught us, are remnants of settler colonialism and the driving forces of racial capitalism.
120 Crary, "Powering Down," 28, 28–29.
121 See, of course, Sharma, *In the Meantime*.
122 Moshfegh, *My Year of Rest and Relaxation*, 58.
123 Moshfegh, *My Year of Rest and Relaxation*, 260.
124 Moshfegh, *My Year of Rest and Relaxation*, 57.
125 Eugenie Brinkema reminds us that emotional tears, for Sartre, not only mark a modulation of a body's relation to the world but can also affect the

world, potentially bringing about a qualitative change in the world. See Brinkema, *The Forms of the Affects*, 15. Tears, for Brinkema, signals an "interpretative imperative"; they "[form] a hermeneutic demand" (20). She would also argue that to read for structure in a tear, one must approach reading tears with an eye for "tears without bodies" (18). Given that Moshfegh's narrator is incapable of crying up till the end of the narrative, hence a body without tears rather, I suspect that Brinkema's hermeneutics runs up against a wall in the face of the narrator.

126   Harney and Moten, *All Incomplete*, 80. To be sure, the idea of a break or breaking down/apart in Harney and Moten is not as pessimistic, melancholic, and hopelessly despairing as how I have been articulating in this chapter. For Harney and Moten, where one falls and stays down and "stay[s] *there*," there is always another "plane" or "plain" (80) in which there can be room for what they call "study," which is a collective sharing of knowledge free from the institutional disciplining and surveillance as manifested through institutional forms of testing, scoring metrics, and demands for improvement. From the break, there is always the possibility of improvisation whereby something new, other, and different can arise (and such a notion of a regenerative break, I believe, can already be found in Moten's *In the Break*). In other words, and even though the question of failure traverses *All Incomplete*, Harney and Moten do not stay with failure and its negative affects as much as I would want it, in accordance with failure's duration or contretemps.

CHAPTER 2. DRIFTING IN A WORLD OF FAILURES

1   Moshfegh, *My Year of Rest and Relaxation*, 204.
2   This is according to Kate Briggs's translation of Barthes's *Comment vivre ensemble*. I will be quoting from the original French text here with my own translations. I also thank Marc Braydon Anthony for suggesting how Barthes's "idiorrhythmy" relates to Cusk's trilogy.
3   Barthes, *Comment vivre ensemble*, 38, 39.
4   Barthes, *Comment vivre ensemble*, 69.
5   Barthes, *Comment vivre ensemble*, 69, 38.
6   Barthes, *Comment vivre ensemble*, 39.
7   Barthes, *Comment vivre ensemble*, 39.
8   Barthes, *Comment vivre ensemble*, 177, 35, 37.
9   Barthes, *Comment vivre ensemble*, 40, 177.
10 Laplanche, "The So-Called 'Death Drive,'" 460. To be sure, too, such a drive must not be confused with that which is a narcissistic and aggressive projection of "self-affirmation" in terms of "living, active being" (468). This latter drive, Laplanche suggests, is associated with "salutary aggressivity" in "American culture," "a quality which could be a requisite factor

of successfulness" (468). No doubt, as chapter 4 will underscore, there can be a narcissistic contour to the genres that interest us, but this narcissism is really a dark one, and the drive in which we are invested is not one that is motivated by and/or oriented toward success. Instead, it is driven by a sense of failure and drifts toward failure. On Freud and the death drive, see, especially, Freud, "Beyond the Pleasure Principle."

On another note, we can find a hint of such a mode of drifting as discussed previously, albeit one of low speed, in Cusk's *Transit*, the second book of the *Outline* trilogy. Toward the end of *Transit*, the narrator Faye is driving "west out of London" (208) to visit her cousin Lawrence. She would follow "a series of narrow, circuitous roads that . . . wound lengthily through a dark countryside shrouded in thick fog. . . . At certain points the fog became so thick that it was blinding. The car felt its way along, sometimes nearly colliding with the steep verge when a corner loomed up unexpectedly. . . . It was entirely possible that I would crash at any moment. The feeling of danger was merged with an almost pleasurable sense of anticipation, as though some constraint or obstruction was about to be finally torn down, some boundary broken on the other side of which lay release" (211).

11   See Lacan, *Écrits*, 680.
12   Again, see Braunstein, "Desire and Jouissance in the Teachings of Lacan."
13   I am certainly not alone in thinking about the relation between Barthes's Neutral and Cusk's *Outline*. See Dimou-Grampa, "*Outline*'s Silence."
14   Williams, "Structures of Feeling," 129. And in contrast to such "explicit" social forms, the Neutral, according to Barthes, is of "the implicit," which is to say, "the thought that escapes power," a "zero degree" of thought. Barthes, *Le Neutre*, 52 (all translations from this text are mine). Barthes's lectures on "idiorrhythmy" and the Neutral include a critique of systematicity, if not the thinking with systems. For Barthes, "idiorrhythmy," the Neutral, and drifting are ways to undermine the latter. This is not the place to go into systems theories, but let us highlight just two works that entertain the thought of failure in relation to them. Dekker's *Drift into Failure* has argued that in the context of organizational thinking, where each organization would think itself as a quasi-closed or perfectible system while in fact always interconnected with other organizational and natural/environmental systems, "failure *is* always an option" (19). In other words, every decision made within an organization—and when considered in no linear cause-effect manner but in terms of the complexity of systems; that is, in its relation to the general capitalist backdrop of resource and market competition, laxed safety practices, the unpredictable changes in the environment to which the organization is not able to adapt in a timely fashion, "unruly technology" or unpredictably dysfunctional or noncooperative technological systems, and the "autoimmune" risk—to

use Derrida's rhetoric—of incorporating foreign elements within a system to supposedly protect it from them—can be the "invisible" (19) drift toward failure. To be sure, this drift into failure that is "something inevitable, something slow and unstoppable" (19) in Dekker is meant to be understood negatively and not as radical as I am presenting it here. Besides, Dekker's work drifts in a different direction from ours, as it aims for a "drifting into success" (185). Closer to our interest in literature, Franta's *Systems Failure* has argued that while Enlightenment philosophies might render the world "not only explicable but reducible to system," eighteenth-century novels show that "social forces," however, "are seemingly irreducible to system" (2, 3). In such novels, any "apparent order is perpetually disrupted and broken down" and "attempts to identify or impose systems are subject to the vagaries of chance and accident" (4). Furthermore, they can also "imagine a way of living with the inevitability of failure—or perhaps offer an image of life itself as a good-natured negotiation with failure" (9). While we are also underscoring the irreducibility of failure, the texts that interest us do not have that positive outlook in relation to failure.

15 Barthes, *Le Neutre*, 31.

16 Barthes, *Le Neutre*, 38. There is no letting-be under the paradigm, no letting-be of failure to be in its own terms, free from any binary capture that delimits it to always be in opposition to the terms of success.

17 Barthes, *Le Neutre*, 40. See 32–33 on the ethics beyond choice of the Neutral.

18 Barthes, *Le Neutre*, 31, 253. It is possible to translate *déjouer* as "unwork," which one would associate with Blanchot's *désœuvrer*. The latter is clearly in the backdrop of Barthes's lectures.

19 On the Neutral's resistance against becoming a concept or taking on a fixed meaning, see Barthes, *Le Neutre*, 36–37; on its refusal of philosophy, see 257. I am also referring to Deleuze and Guattari's *Qu'est-ce que la philosophie?* on the conflictual nature of a concept against others in laying claim to a field of meaning.

20 Barthes, *Le Neutre*, 36. Barthes will add that the descriptive nature of the Neutral needs no adjectives. Instead, the Neutral is of an "adjectival anesthetics" (*anesthésie adjectives*); it has no anxiety about being qualified or predicated upon any quality or characteristic (89). On Barthes's critique of adjectives, see Barthes, *Le Neutre*, 84–94. Our thinking of failure can be said likewise to be without adjectives. We are not seeking to think failure as either terrible or wonderful, disastrous or beautiful, etc. We even refuse putting an adverb to it. Unlike Derrida's riffing on Beckett's "fail well" in thinking about "fail better," we want to think failure that fails as it is. Just that.

21 Barthes, *Le Neutre*, 152, 155.

22 Barthes, *Le Neutre*, 169.
23 Barthes, *Le Neutre*, 169.
24 On the Neutral and affects, see Barthes, *Le Neutre*, 249.
25 Barthes, *Le Neutre*, 111. On the intensity of the Neutral, see 246.
26 Barthes, *Le Neutre*, 110.
27 Barthes, *Le Neutre*, 192.
28 Barthes, *Le Neutre*, 104–5.
29 Barthes, *Le Neutre*, 106.
30 Barthes, *Le Neutre*, 106.
31 Barthes, *Le Neutre*, 192.
32 Barthes, *Le Neutre*, 222.
33 Barthes, *Le Neutre*, 196. And if desire has to do much with the Imaginary in Lacan's terms, Barthes would say that the Neutral is "the repose of the imaginary" (*le repos de l'imaginaire*) (227), even though Barthes might not be thinking of Lacan's Imaginary here, despite Lacan being a reference for Barthes's thinking of the Neutral in general.
34 Barthes, *Le Neutre*, 197.
35 Barthes, *Le Neutre*, 34.
36 Barthes, *Le Neutre*, 34.
37 Barthes, *Le Neutre*, 69.
38 Barthes, *Le Neutre*, 67.
39 See Barthes, *Le Neutre*, 68.
40 Barthes, *Le Neutre*, 68.
41 Barthes, *Le Neutre*, 67. I am resisting translating *blanc* as white, keeping in mind Barthes's argument that the Neutral is "colorless" (*incolore*), or of "non-color" (82, 84). But Barthes will be precises to say that the Neutral is "not the absence of color," not "transparence" (84). If there is a color to the Neutral, it would be gray, a "subdued" (*feutré*) or "waned" (*éteint*) hue, not "marked" colors such as black and white, which are actually "on the same side" (84).
42 Barthes, *Le Neutre*, 67.
43 Barthes, *Le Neutre*, 68, 67.
44 Barthes, *Le Neutre*, 43.
45 Barthes, *Le Neutre*, 69. On the note of unproductivity, Barthes also argues that the Neutral's turn to the descriptive instead of the conceptual renders any discourse of the Neutral to be equally "unproductive"—that is, only of effects, if not affects, and "without results" or without any preoccupation with results (36).
46 Dekker, *Drift into Failure*, 32.
47 On the banality of the Neutral, see Barthes, *Le Neutre*, 119; on its impertinence to the rest of the world, 156.
48 Barthes, *Le Neutre*, 45.
49 Barthes, *Le Neutre*, 190.

50. Barthes, *Le Neutre*, 190.
51. Barthes, *Le Neutre*, 189.
52. Cusk, *Aftermath*, 119, 56.
53. Cusk, *Aftermath*, 42.
54. Cusk, *Aftermath*, 66, 70.
55. This is underscored in a 2014 interview with Cusk, conducted by Kate Kellaway, "*Aftermath* Was Creative Death."
56. Cusk, *Aftermath*, 68–9.
57. Cusk, *Aftermath*, 24.
58. Cusk, *Aftermath*, 82, 100.
59. Cusk, *Aftermath*, 100.
60. Cusk, *Aftermath*, 2.
61. Cusk, *Aftermath*, 5.
62. I am clearly referring to Berlant's *The Female Complaint*. Or else, to put it in Cusk's terms, *Aftermath*, as such, can be considered a "retributive text"—that is, one that calls out others' "ability to deny the truth about [themselves]" (*Transit*, 108), such as denying the truth of the family structure being a "prison" (*Aftermath*, 27) for women. The same could be said of the *Outline* trilogy, not just because it can be read as a response to readers who deny the truth about marriage and the modern family structure articulated in *Aftermath* but also because, as will be seen, it portrays characters who are largely in denial of their own failures.
63. Cusk, *Aftermath*, 23.
64. On these aspects as well as on the book in general, Camilla Long, in a 2012 review of *Aftermath* for the *Sunday Times*, has even called Cusk "a brittle little dominatrix and peerless narcissist who exploits her husband and her marriage with relish."
65. Cusk, *Aftermath*, 56.
66. Cusk, *Aftermath*, 20.
67. Cusk, *Aftermath*, 27.
68. Cusk, *Aftermath*, 58.
69. Cusk, *Aftermath*, 63.
70. Cusk, *Aftermath*, 27, 106.
71. Cusk, *Aftermath*, 65.
72. Ahmed, *Complaint!*, 1. We have mentioned earlier that Cusk's feminist complaint throws into disarray the "cruel optimism" of the sentimental "female complaint," which arguably incites the pushback against Cusk's work by some women. We can also understand such a pushback through Ahmed's articulation of complaints: "To complain is not only to be negative; it is to be stuck on being negative. To complain is how you would stop yourself from being happy, to stop others form being happy too, complaint as a killjoy genre" (1). As we have likewise said of failure, few

are willing to stick with the negative and/or the pessimistic, to stay with or in such an impasse.

73 Ahmed, *Complaint!*, 5. Or, as Ahmed would say later, "You are more likely to share a story of complaint if you have been stopped from sharing that story" (10). Ahmed would also add that all this "is exhausting, especially given that what you complain about is already exhausting" (5), and this notion of exhaustion surely recalls our discussion of fatigue with regard to Barthes's Neutral.

74 Cusk, *Aftermath*, 69.

75 Cusk, *Aftermath*, 73.

76 Meanwhile, *Transit*, the second book of the trilogy, is preoccupied with the question of the fear of changes and the possibility of freedom that might follow change; and *Kudos*, the third and final book, seems more concerned with art and the question of suffering for one's art.

77 Cusk, *Aftermath*, 91.

78 In *Kudos*, we find that Faye is married again, though.

79 *Outline*'s setting of Athens leads Pieter Vermeulen to contextualize the novel against the 2010 Greek austerity measures proposed as a countermeasure against its failing to pay off sovereign debt and to argue that the novel "ponder[s] the attractions of austere posture of affectlessness." Vermeulen, "Against Premature Articulation," 87. That posture, according to Vermeulen, is reflected in Cusk's "withholding of an empathetic voice" (87) in the novel—that is, Faye, "the quasi-invisible narrator does not become available for empathetic identification" (88). Through this "gendered aesthetics of self-curtailment," the novel "assert[s] [the] indifference to empathize experiences of suffering, even as [its] commitment to postponed articulation capitalizes on rather than denies the logic of austerity" (99).

80 Cusk, *Outline*, 19.

81 Cusk, *Outline*, 70.

82 Cusk, *Outline*, 201–2. Or, as Faye would say in *Kudos*, this would involve the "skill" of "skirting close enough to what appeared to be the truth without allowing what you actually felt about it to regain its power over you" (10).

83 It will not involve absolute silence, though. For, according to Barthes, "the Neutral would be defined, not by permanent silence—this would be systematic and dogmatic, and would become significant of an affirmation ("I am systematically silent")—but by the minimal cost of a speech operation tending to neutralize silence as a sign." Barthes, *Le Neutre*, 56. In Cusk's case, we must note that her thoughts on heteronormative marriage and the modern family life are not absolutely suppressed or repressed but are ventriloquized by the majority of characters in *Outline*. So, Faye's Greek

passenger-neighbor, her old friend Paniotis, her friend Elena's friend Malete, and Anne her fellow English writer teaching the same writing seminar as Faye in Athens and living in the same flat will deploy the violent languages of "war" (100, 166), "destruction" (100), and "disgust" (197) to talk about marriage. This is also not to mention that the Greek neighbor, Paniotis, and Anne are divorcees too, and in this regard, one could say that most characters in *Outline* function as Cusk's foil. This is not exceptional to *Outline*. In *Kudos*, there is Linda the first-time novelist who, not unlike Cusk, is averse to household chores, leaving such work to her husband, and who also does not look too kindly toward childbirth and motherhood (a perspective that Cusk put forward in *A Life's Work*). This present work does not have the space to consider Cusk's brand of feminism. To readers interested in pursuing that feminist aspect in Cusk's *Outline* trilogy, I would think it productive to consider Cixous's *Neutre* alongside Cusk's texts, especially her notion of a "narrator-without-Subject" (83), which might well describe Faye. We should not forget Halberstam's intriguing "shadow feminism" too here, which concerns "a feminism that fails to save others or to replicate itself, a feminism that finds purpose in its own failure." Halberstam, *The Queer Art of Failure*, 128.

On another note, we must not think that Faye's drifting is of a tranquil nature. It is no less troubled as Cusk's in *Aftermath*. In other words, Faye's drifting is rather aimless, refracted by a sense of lostness, if not hopelessness. As she recounts at the beginning of *Transit*, the second novel in the trilogy, an AI-generated astrologer says to her that it "could sense... that I had lost my way in life, that I sometimes struggled to find meaning in my present circumstances and to feel hope for what was to come." Cusk, *Transit*, 1.

84 See Cusk, *Kudos*, 182–83.
85 Cusk, *Outline*, 170–71.
86 Cusk, *Outline*, 130, 99.
87 This is seemingly in contrast to Faye who, in *Kudos*, remembers her interviewee from "more than ten years ago" (61). However, one could say that Faye remembers her only because of some shared similarities of their lives, of "certain details" of the interviewee's life with her husband (who incidentally works in the field of law as well) and two sons who "mirrored [Faye's]" (64). So, when she meets Ryan again in this book, who now has a "gaunt appearance and elderly demeanor" and "limping" with the aid of a walking stick (110), Ryan would say of Faye: "I could see you didn't recognize me for a second there" (113).
88 Cusk, *Outline*, 99–100. Paniotis also discerns that the "stages" are also what others would consider "progress." According to Valihora, such an "understanding of progress in strictly material terms, as acquisition, is another illusion, another version of the dream of freedom explored in vari-

ous guises throughout the trilogy: no matter how 'freedom' beckons here, whether as excitement, glamor, arrival, authenticity, upward mobility, or as a taste for ease, for unearned pleasure, it is a moral threat. Cusk's work positions such moral failure as the failure of sympathy, the sympathy that, along with and through the vicarious identifications promoted by the novel, and as an effect of its narrative structure, forges the felt connection to others on which the whole idea of the liberal community must rest." Valihora, "She Got Up and Went Away," 32.

89   Cusk, *Outline*, 162, 62.

90   As said, failed existences occupy the rest of the trilogy too. In *Transit*, there is Gerard, Faye's former partner, who failed to keep his new love's favorite dog on the leash. There is also Louis the writer who is afflicted with the sense of existential failure, who lives out "the inherently traumatic nature of living itself" (112). In *Kudos*, Betsy, the insomniac, depressive, neurotic, almost anorexic, and antisocial daughter of Faye's neighbor passenger, one who had a magnificent career and was thus able to retire at forty-five, is at one point referred to by her father as a "failed experiment" (16). There is also a failed architecture in *Kudos*: an underground concert hall that did not account for the acoustical interference of noises from the ground above.

91   Cusk, *Outline*, 140.

92   Cusk, *Kudos*, 98. Hermann also tells Faye that "kudos" can be "suggestive of something which might be falsely claimed by someone else." Perhaps the narrativizing of failure can also be said to take on this quality of "kudos," if we consider how a student such as Georgeou seeks to dominate such a discourse, as if his said failure is of greater pathos than others'. Otherwise, we might even say that it is the narrativizing of success, rather, that reeks of this aspect of "kudos," given that most of such narratives in the trilogy are actually undercut by some sense of failure. We will in fact see this soon in the diplomat in *Outline*.

93   Cusk, *Kudos*, 98.

94   Cusk, *Outline*, 218. As suggested in an earlier note, most of the characters in *Outline* seem to be foils of Cusk herself, and Penelope is no exception. Earlier, she would express a similar desire as Cusk for a Neutral drifting: "I would like . . . to see the world more innocently again, more impersonally, but I have no idea how to achieve this, other than by going somewhere completely unknown, where I have no identity and no associations" (157).

95   Cusk, *Outline*, 167.

96   Cusk, *Outline*, 38.

97   Cusk, *Outline*, 49.

98   As Valihora puts it, this world is "a world that does not listen, or connect." Valihora, "She Got Up and Went Away," 19.

99   Cusk, *Outline*, 20.
100 Cusk, *Outline*, 13.
101 Cusk, *Outline*, 66.
102 Cusk, *Outline*, 23.
103 Cusk, *Outline*, 174.
104 Cusk, *Outline*, 30.
105 Cusk, *Outline*, 30. And if the male species were to be able to so freely or unproblematically, without repercussion, thoughtlessly fault women in such stories of theirs, the same cannot be said when women tell their stories. This is according to Elena, Faye's "very beautiful" and "intelligent, exquisitely dressed" (179) friend, who "had visited the depths of disillusionment in the male character" that "feigned the need to possess her wholly when in fact what he wanted was to use her temporarily" (185). Elena thus seeks to reveal the "nasty side" to a man's character, refusing to have that "roaming unseen in the hinterland of the relationship" (190). Yet, as Elena realizes, her "need for [such a] provocation is something other people seem to find very difficult to understand" (191).

Away from heterosexual relationships but touching on the craft and business of writing, a similar bias against women can be found. In *Kudos*, we find Sophia, an attendee at a writers' festival participating "not on account of her credentials as a feminist writer but for her work as a translator" (132) of Luís's works. She would rave about the latter's focus on the ordinary, but she would add: "Though of course if he were a woman . . . he would be scorned for his honesty, or at the very least no one would care" (147). There is no doubt that we are made to think of Cusk's own plight here, in writing about her ordinary life not only in *Aftermath* but also in the *Outline* trilogy. To return to *Kudos*, there is also the female TV interviewer who is invested in the "problem of recognition for female writers and artists." As she says, "Few notable women were ever really recognized, or at least not until they had been judged to be no longer a public danger by having become old or ugly or dead" (189).

106 Cusk, *Outline*, 239.
107 Cusk, *Outline*, 239–40.
108 Cusk, *Outline*, 244.
109 Cusk, *Outline*, 245.
110 Cusk, *Outline*, 244.
111 Cusk, *Outline*, 92.
112 Cusk, *Outline*, 94.
113 Cusk, *Outline*, 94.
114 Cusk, *Outline*, 94.
115 Cusk, *Outline*, 119.
116 Cusk, *Outline*, 123.
117 Cusk, *Outline*, 123 (my italics).

118   Cusk, *Outline*, 160.
119   Cusk, *Outline*, 160, 15.
120   Cusk, *Outline*, 65.
121   Cusk, *Outline*, 41.
122   Cusk, *Kudos*, 118.
123   Cusk, *Kudos*, 118.
124   Cusk, *Kudos*, 98, 119.
125   Cusk, *Kudos*, 121.
126   Cusk, *Transit*, 118.
127   In fact, she is hardly treated better by fellow feminist writers. Sophia is clearly absolutely in awe of Luís's work while demonstrating little interest in Faye's, ignorant of the irony of her enunciation of "a saddening thought" regarding the failure of women, when they "get together," to "[advance] the cause of femininity." Cusk, *Kudos*, 132. Paola, Faye's editor in the country Faye visits in *Kudos*, even though, like Faye/Cusk, a solitary feminist, is guilty of giving preferential treatment to her male authors. She "lit up" and "leapt off her stool" (176) upon seeing one of the latter but does nothing of this sort with respect to Faye. And Faye's female TV interviewer, whom we have mentioned in an earlier note would also, like the male journalist/book reviewer, dominate the conversation, barely leaving little time and space to Faye. For Faye/Cusk, female/feminist solidarity is wanting. As Sophia, once again, would say: "Female truth—if such a thing can be said to exist," such as that of Cusk's true reflections on marriage and the modern family structure, "is so interior and involuted that a common version of it can never be agreed on" (131).
128   Cusk, *Kudos*, 232.

CHAPTER 3. EXSCRIBING A DARK CARE OF THE SELF OF FAILED EXISTENCE

Parts of chapter 3 appeared in "Exscription, or the Sense of Failure: Jean-Luc Nancy, Tecuciztecatl, and Édouard Levé," *MLN* 134, no. 5 (2019): 1080–97; and "Auto-thanato-theory: Dark Narcissistic Care for the Self in Sedgwick and Zambreno," *Arizona Quarterly* 76, no. 1 (2020): 197–213.

1   Foucault, "Technologies of the Self," 22.
2   Foucault, "Technologies of the Self," 22.
3   Puig de la Bellacasa, *Matters of Care*, 78. "Cut" is also one of her terms for the dimension of care. And like Derrida who had taught us how responsibility can also be an irresponsibility at the same time—for example, being responsible for one person can actually renounce responsibility toward the collective, and vice versa—Puig de la Bellacasa will also say, "We cannot possibly care for everything, not everything can count in the world" (78).
4   Malatino, *Side Affects*, 153.

5   For Malatino, who is invested in thinking about care for trans subjects helping others with transition-related medical issues—that is, those committed to "mutual aid in the service of social justice" and who might be suffering from "frustration, annoyance, and mistrust... directed at both medical professionals and one another"—this recognition is insufficient. Malatino, *Side Affects*, 153. Responses will be wanting to the questions that entail from such a recognition: "How do we deal with the terms of infrapolitical hostility that such situations inevitably produce? How do we mobilize the frustration that attends such work in order to effect change?" (153). These questions, which clearly touch on care at a larger collective or even institutional level, go beyond the concern and scope of this present work, however. (For some responses to those questions, I refer readers not only to the Care Collective, *The Care Manifesto*, which I will refer, but also to the volume Hamington and Flower, *Care Ethics in the Age of Precarity*.) If it is not already evident, I will be dealing with care at the strictly personal level, a certain care of the self.

6   Puig de la Bellacasa, *Matters of Care*, 85. Puig de la Bellacasa provides the other perspective, too, in saying that "care can also smother the subtleties of attention to the different needs of an 'other' required for careful relationality. It can be said then that it can also consume the cared for, leading to appropriating the recipients of 'our' care instead of relating to them" (85).

Or we can cite Malatino again, who articulates care fatigue in terms of burnout. Following the work of psychologist Christina Maslach, Malatino writes that "burnout happens when one allows themselves to care too much, which is a prelude to being, in effect, used up, depleted, and exhausted by servicing the needs of others. It is not, on Maslach's account, overwork that is the problem; rather, it is the affective responses and defense reactions that workers cultivate in order to survive overwork: emotional exhaustion, depersonalization, and *a sense of failure*, inadequacy, and reduced personal accomplishment." Malatino, *Side Affects*, 138 (my italics). Malatino goes on: "It's a labor-specific variant of Hell as other people, a rendering of folks in need on account of structural precarity as energy succubi, emotional vampires out to take all they can from a too-trusting, too-caring, too-empathetic worker" (139).

7   Care Collective, *The Care Manifesto*, 3. I note here that many of the essays in the volume *Care Ethics in the Age of Precarity* make similar observations to those previously on how thinking and practices of care have been threatened and diminished by the political economy of neoliberalism.

8   Care Collective, *The Care Manifesto*, 9–10.

9   Care Collective, *The Care Manifesto*, 3.

10 Puig de la Bellacasa, *Matters of Care*, 9. I note that Puig de la Bellacasa here draws a lot from Tronto, *Moral Boundaries*.
11 Care Collective, *The Care Manifesto*, 4.
12 Care Collective, *The Care Manifesto*, 4.
13 Care Collective, *The Care Manifesto*, 4.
14 Puig de la Bellacasa, *Matters of Care*, 11, 12.
15 Puig de la Bellacasa goes beyond the Care Collective's horizon because she wants to extend thinking about care to "beings other than human, in 'more than human' worlds," to "think of ethical 'obligations' in human-decentered cosmologies." Puig de la Bellacasa, *Matters of Care*, 13.
16 Puig de la Bellacasa, *Matters of Care*, 90–91.
17 Hamington and Flower, *Care Ethics in the Age of Precarity*, 6.
18 On the bracketing of feeling in French thought, see Terada, *Feeling in Theory*. On the placing of the other at an abstract distance, see, for example, LaCapra, *History in Transit*.

On another note, as Wendy Anne Lee has pointed out, eighteenth- and nineteenth-century literature can also be infused by what she calls "insensibles"; for example, Melville's Bartleby, which is to say, literary characters whose traits include "unfeeling combined with inaction," whose "essential absence of emotion" paradoxically motivates in us readers a "narrative tenacity with which we try to reconstruct it." Lee, *Failures of Feeling*, 1, 7.
19 Puig de la Bellacasa, *Matters of Care*, 13.
20 I recall the earlier note where I have stated that Puig de la Bellacasa's primary objective in *Matters of Care* is to include nonhuman beings and objects within the domain of thinking about care and/or acting with care.
21 Foucault, "Technologies of the Self," 27.
22 Foucault, "Technologies of the Self," 28.
23 Foucault's reading of this letter was first introduced in one of the *Hermeneutics of the Subject* lectures then reiterated in the "Technologies of the Self" seminar at the University of Vermont.
24 Puig de la Bellacasa, *Matters of Care*, 11, 12.
25 Puig de la Bellacasa, *Matters of Care*, 70.
26 Puig de la Bellacasa, *Matters of Care*, 90.
27 I mean this in the Derridean sense, whereby a supplement can be violent in terms of overshadowing, or even replacing, the main or primary material. See of course Derrida, *De la grammatologie*.
28 If the kind of writing that embraces a care of the self is inclined toward the recording of everyday routines and ordinary thoughts, as Foucault highlights in his *Hermeneutics of the Subject* lectures, he will not fail to remind us that ordinary thoughts also include meditations on death.
29 Freud, "On Narcissism," 73.
30 Freud, "On Narcissism," 76.

31   Freud, "On Narcissism," 88.
32   Freud, "On Narcissism," 88.
33   Freud, "On Narcissism," 73–74.
34   Freud, "On Narcissism," 76.
35   Freud, "On Narcissism," 94, 100. Bersani in *The Culture of Redemption* also has a critically nuanced reading of Freud's essay there, and he would suggest that Freud's formulations of the ego, primary narcissism or ego-libido, and the ego ideal in this essay would later be reiterated by Freud as ego, id, and the superego. Putting aside the libidinal economy of failed existences, which lies beyond the scope of this present work, we could no doubt articulate our high-performing culture of productivity and success as a superego imposing upon our ego, by which our id, which would rather see to our own breakdowns and wallow in debility or "inoperativity," would be repressed.
36   Freud, "On Narcissism," 96.
37   Freud, "On Narcissism," 90.
38   Freud, "On Narcissism," 98.
39   Ovid, *Metamorphosis*, l.510.
40   Ovid, *Metamorphosis*, l.449.
41   Ovid, *Metamorphosis*, l.536, l.588.
42   Ovid, Metamorphosis, l.564–67.
43   Ovid, *Metamorphosis*, l.577, l.610.
44   Ovid, *Metamorphosis*, l.633.
45   Ovid, *Metamorphosis*, l.522–53.
46   Ovid, *Metamorphosis*, l.582,
47   Ovid, *Metamorphosis*, l.612, l.615.
48   Foucault, *L'Herméneutique du sujet*, 272 (my translation).
49   Foucault, *L'Herméneutique du sujet*, 273.
50   Foucault, *L'Herméneutique du sujet*, 273, 271.
51   This is arguably a more radical, if not literal, take on narcissistic "self-shattering" than Bersani would have it. According to Bersani's reading of Freud on narcissism, Bersani makes the claim that Freud has already suggested in *Three Essays on the Theory of Sexuality* (1905) that "the human subject is originally *shattered into* sexuality"—that is, "sexual excitement" must be understood "as both a turning away from others and a dying to the self." Bersani, *The Culture of Redemption*, 36, 45. Bersani continues: "The concept of narcissism can be thought of as an extension of that definition. It is as if the inherently solipsistic nature of sexuality—and its correlative indifference to object and to organ specificity—allowed for a development of autoeroticism in which the source of pleasure and, consequently, the object of desire became the very experience of *ébranlement* or self-shattering" (37). He elaborates further on: "Primary narcissism allows the infantile ego to be masochistically shattered with-

out being destroyed. It is perhaps the infant's best erotic defense against the eroticizing bombardments of his environment. Narcissism replays the shattering stimulations of that environment in the paradoxical form of a *structuralizing self-shattering*.... primary narcissism is that ego's (nonethical) appreciation of its capacity to be sexually shattered" (40–41).

52 Morton, *Dark Ecology*, 147.
53 See, of course, Sedgwick's "Paranoid Reading, Reparative Reading." The quote on "deep pessimism" is on 138.
54 Sedgwick, *A Dialogue on Love*, 6. Subsequent quotations from this text will be indicated by page numbers in parenthesis in the main text.
55 Sedgwick, *A Dialogue on Love*, 123.
56 Sedgwick, *A Dialogue on Love*, 167.
57 Sedgwick, *A Dialogue on Love*, 125.
58 Sedgwick, *A Dialogue on Love*, 108.
59 Sedgwick, *A Dialogue on Love*, 101.
60 Sedgwick, *A Dialogue on Love*, 116.
61 Sedgwick, *A Dialogue on Love*, 6.
62 Sedgwick, *A Dialogue on Love*, 17.
63 Sedgwick, *A Dialogue on Love*, 15.
64 Sedgwick, *A Dialogue on Love*, 111.
65 Sedgwick, *A Dialogue on Love*, 184. I note here that the original quotation of Shannon's notes appears in capital letters.
66 Sedgwick, *A Dialogue on Love*, 197.
67 Sedgwick, *A Dialogue on Love*, 291.
68 Sedgwick, *A Dialogue on Love*, 96.
69 Sedgwick, *A Dialogue on Love*, 62.
70 Sedgwick, *A Dialogue on Love*, 69.
71 Sedgwick, *A Dialogue on Love*, 69.
72 See the chapter "Of Voluntary Death" in part 1 of Nietzsche, *Thus Spoke Zarathustra*, which begins with the proclamation that "many die too late and some die too early," hence the dictum to "die at the right time" (97). The dictum also springs from Zarathustra's observation that "for many a man, life is a failure" (Manchem missräth das Leben), and so, dying at the right time would be to "let him see to it that his death is all the more a success" (97–98). There is clearly an overarching success narrative in relation to failure in Nietzsche, which we are resisting in our present work.
73 Sedgwick, *A Dialogue on Love*, 18.
74 Sedgwick, *A Dialogue on Love*, 219.
75 Neither can it pave the way toward a perfectibility of the self or the constitution of a true subject according to Foucault in *The Hermeneutics of the Subject*. Instead, the discourse on a dark narcissistic care of the self

reveals what I have elsewhere called the *reject* in oneself, which I hear reverberate in Sedgwick's self-declaration of "I, the refusal / of a refusal" (150).

76   Sedgwick, *A Dialogue on Love*, 197.

77   I have recognized that *A Dialogue on Love* is not Sedgwick's typical theoretical writing. Nevertheless, I do believe it still can constitute an "auto-thanato-theory," by which I am also saying—and no doubt I can be charged with a "paranoid reading" here—that there is an underlying or irreducible element in *A Dialogue on Love* that problematizes Sedgwick's theoretical aim of a "reparative reading."

78   Nancy, *Corpus*, 14, 20. All translations from this text are mine. On another note, it is necessary to say more about writing in Nancy. Writing must not be restricted to its representational function. As in Derrida, writing must also be understood as the "archi-originary" trace or inscription that is nonsecondary and noninstrumental to voice; it is *not* a mimetic medium coming after voice. For Nancy, writing also goes beyond all signifying operations: "'Writing' indicates that which *distance itself from signification*, and for that reason, *exscribes itself* [*s'excrit*]. Exscription occurs in the play of a non-signifying spacing: that which detaches, in a way always anew, words form their meanings, and which abandons them to their extension" (63). Meanwhile, one is surely also mindful of Derrida's oft-cited phrase, "Il n'y pas de hors-texte," in *De la grammatologie*, where there is a clear refusal of any "hors-texte," in contrast to Nancy's argument above. The difference between Derrida and Nancy on the question of "hors-texte," not to mention that "hors-texte" is also at stake in Blanchot's *Le pas au-delà* (1973), is beyond the scope and concern of this present book, however.

79   Nancy, "L'exscrit," 62. All translations from this text are mine.

80   Nancy, *Corpus*, 52.

81   Nancy, *Corpus*, 20, 31, 44, 52, 92.

82   I certainly do not forget that Nancy has written about his own body in pain after his heart transplant in *L'intrus*. There is even a moment of dark ek-sistence there when Nancy almost nonchalantly remarks, following an observation of one of his sons, that he takes on the countenance of a zombie in a horror film. Nevertheless, I still find that Nancy does not go far with this sense of ek-sistence. In a follow-up piece to *L'intrus*, titled "Dialogue Under the Ribs," he would say that it is more interesting to restart life.

   I do not forget either that Scarry, prior to Nancy, has already written extensively about the body in pain in the eponymous *Body in Pain*.

83   Nancy, *Corpus*, 66.

84   I am referring to Woolf's work *On Being Ill*. I will make more mention of this work in another note in the following chapter.

85 Nancy, *Corpus*, 103. And again, Scarry has noted that while pain is definite, certain, and unequivocal for the sufferer, it might raise doubt in the other who is listening about this pain. As she puts it, "To have great pain is to have certainty; to hear that another person has pain is to have doubt." Scarry, *Body in Pain*, 7. And in a vocabulary close to Nancy's here and ours on "shared unshareability," she will also say that "pain comes unsharably into our midst as at once that which cannot be denied and that which cannot be confirmed" (4).

86 Nancy, "L'excrit," 60.

87 Nancy, *Corpus*, 76.

88 Nancy, *Corpus*, 83, 88. Perhaps we can also articulate the question of touch here in terms of that which we have been associating with failure as well: affect. As said earlier, affect is a matter of pressure and this infinitesimal pressing of bodies, even though it largely goes unnoticed, surely creates some sort of pressure between bodies. After all, as Nancy would also say, a body "weighs," and as such, "it presses against other bodies, just as other bodies do against it" (82).

89 On tact, see Nancy, *Corpus*, 85.

90 See Hamacher, "Other Pains." While Hamacher, in his "deconstructive" mode of thinking, refuses to make cries of pain "primal" to language, Scarry says, "Physical pain does not simply resist language but actively destroys it, bringing about an immediate reversion to a state anterior to language, to the sounds and cries a human being makes before language is learned." Scarry, *Body in Pain*, 4.

91 Nancy, *Corpus*, 20.

92 Nancy, *Corpus*, 49.

93 Nancy, *Corpus*, 44.

94 Nancy, *Corpus*, 72. Or, in the words of Scarry: "Whatever pain achieves, it achieves in part through its unshareability, and it ensures this unshareability through its resistance to language." Scarry, *Body in Pain*, 4.

95 I believe that playing down the more personal, psychic, or existential pain occurs also in the "Peine. Souffrance. Malheur" chapter in Nancy, *Le sens du monde*. There, pain and suffering refer to more general phenomena such as famine, evil, sickness, and so on, caused by some injustice somewhere in the world. To be sure, Nancy demands that thought be committed to combat these evils or injustices, but he is keener to instruct us not to see in them a deficit in the meaning of existence in the world, a deficit, according to him again, that afflicts us with an epistemological pain.

96 When such a reading is granted, it sometimes leads to what I see as an uncritical understanding of the text, as the novelist Zadie Smith has done in seeing in *Suicide* an "adolescent aesthetic" (*Harper's Magazine*, May 2011). Critchley, in his *Notes on Suicide*, gives it a more sympathetic read-

	ing, considering it some form of suicide note worthy of philosophical inquiry.
97	Levé, *Autoportrait*, 50. Translations from this text are mine.
98	I note here that "exscription," according to Nancy, is also of the order of fragments. As he writes in *Corpus*: "In fact, the fragmentation of writing, from where it takes place where it takes place (be it always and everywhere, or else through the exigency of 'genre'), responds to a repeated instance of the body in—toward [*contre*]—writing" (21).
99	Levé, *Suicide*, 108. Translations from this text are mine.
100	While the friend in *Suicide* has a wife who loves him, which clearly does not change his decision to commit suicide, the narrator in *Autoportrait* says, "I love myself less than I have been loved. It surprises me that others love me." Levé, *Autoportrait*, 12. Earlier, he would also say, "I don't love myself. I do not dislike myself" (7). As I see it, all this only reaffirms my earlier point, following Woolf, that all the love in the world can never really talk the loved one out of wanting *out* of existence.
101	Levé, *Suicide*, 77.
102	Levé, *Suicide*, 91, 90, 83.
103	Levé, *Suicide*, 108. Also, I am taking up Nancy's recommendation in *Corpus* on the way of reading exscription in terms of developing a corpus not of interpreted bodies, bodies that have been subjected to close reading, but one of bodies that are in fact already "announced, recorded, and repeated" (52) in writing, all but waiting for us to acknowledge them, list them. On another note, I also add that other than *Autoportrait* and *Suicide*, Levé's other written text *Œuvres* also constitutes some sort of exscription. This text is a list of *descriptions* of photographic works that the author conceptualizes but never materialized, a list of bodies observed either in a posed or natural state. According to Nancy, the body as photography is also a form of exscription: "A body, firstly, exposes itself as its photography." Nancy, *Corpus*, 43.
104	Alvarez, *The Savage God*, 57.

CHAPTER 4. THE MELODRAMA OF FAILURE'S SHARED UNSHAREABILITY, SUICIDAL IDEATION INCLUDED

	A version of chapter 4 appeared as "Shared Unshareability, Suicidality, and the Melodrama of Living on after Failure in Yiyun Li," *Modern Fiction Studies* 69, no. 3 (2023): 539–62.
1	Cusk, *Outline*, 245.
2	Cusk, *Outline*, 246.
3	I have already noted in the introduction how this phrase echoes Scarry's work on pain. I add here that we have in fact seen a similar phrase in the previous chapter: the "unshareable sharing" (*impartageable part-*

age) of a body paradoxically rejoicing in pain according to Nancy. As I see it, my *shared unshareability* is quite the inverse of Nancy's formulation, and so the French translation of mine would be as follows: *partage impartageable*.

4   In her work *On Being Ill*, Woolf has written: "About sympathy . . .—we can do without it. That illusion of a world so shaped that it echoes every groan, of human beings so tied together by common needs and fears that a twitch at one wrist jerks another, where however strange your experience other people have had it too, where however far you travel in your own mind someone has been there before you—is all an illusion. We do not know our own souls, let alone the souls of others. Human beings do not go hand in hand the whole stretch of the way. There is a virgin forest in each; a snowfield where even the print of birds' feet is unknown. Here we go alone, and like it better so. Always to have sympathy, always to be accompanied, always to be understood would be intolerable" (11–12).

5   Halberstam, *The Queer Art of Failure*, 3. Arguably, Halberstam's claim approximates itself dangerously toward some kind of identity politics for failure, not too different from Beckett's appropriation of failure as a badge of artistic genius.

6   Graham, *Failing Gloriously*, 126. Let me just remind readers that I have also noted Cvetkovich's work on the communitarian dimension and collective pedagogy involved in the elucidating, the aesthetic narrativization or representation, the sharing, and the archiving of a negative affect. See, of course, Cvetkovich, *Depression*.

7   To return to Sedgwick's *A Dialogue on Love*, insofar as there is that *"me"* who withdraws from the world, including the therapist Shannon, the promise of any form of community is at best precarious, barely sustainable. One could say the same about love in this text. Love, as Sedgwick tries to conceptualize through her relationship with Shannon, is "a matter of suddenly, globally, 'knowing' that another person represents your only access to some vitally / transmissible truth / or radiantly heightened / mode of perception" (168). She also claims that such a love does not bear "sexual connotations" (168), but the text will reveal that Sedgwick cannot resist entertaining possible sexual relations with Shannon, hence threatening to undermine the love she is attempting to establish.

8   Ngai, *Ugly Feelings*, 2.

9   Critchley, in his *Notes on Suicide*, has also observed that hardly anyone wants to partake in the discourse of suicide. The latter tends to be overtaken by moralistic or religious arguments that only repeat how selfish or irresponsible it is to either leave loved ones behind or take away something (i.e., life, which is seemingly not one's own but given by a higher, divine entity). See also Daniel Zender, "A Debate over 'Rational Suicide,'" *New York Times*, August 31, 2018.

10. Li, *Dear Friend*, 12; Cusk, "The Case of Yiyun Li."
11. Li, *Dear Friend*, 18.
12. Li, *Dear Friend*, 51.
13. Li, *Dear Friend*, 54.
14. Li, *Dear Friend*, 15.
15. Li, *Dear Friend*, 113.
16. Li, *Dear Friend*, 51. Derrida, though, has already posed the following questions: "Who said that we *had* to live? . . Must we live, really? Can 'living,' 'live,' be taken as an imperative, an order, a necessity? Where do you get this axiomatic, valuationary certainty that we (or *you*) must live? Who says that living is worth all the trouble? That it's better to live than to die? That, since we've started, we have to keep on living? In other words living on?" Derrida, "Living On," 79.
17. Berlant, *The Female Complaint*, 6.
18. Berlant, *The Female Complaint*, 21.
19. Berlant, *The Female Complaint*, x, viii, xi.
20. Li, *Dear Friend*, 52.
21. Li would also say in *Dear Friend* that "melodrama is never political" (65), which is also to say that melodrama has no grand ambition or aspiration to make any critical intervention in larger social, cultural, and/or economic institutions disseminating ideologies of success that might have exacerbated any personal "structure of feeling" of failure.
22. Li, *Dear Friend*, 52.
23. Li, *Dear Friend*, 52.
24. Nietzsche, *Thus Spoke Zarathustra*, 97.
25. Berlant, *The Female Complaint*, 2.
26. Li, *Dear Friend*, 54.
27. Li, *Dear Friend*, 51.
28. Li, *Dear Friend*, 18.
29. Li, *Dear Friend*, 6.
30. Li, *Dear Friend*, 54.
31. Li, *Dear Friend*, 151.
32. One must also not forget melodrama's resistance to silence, which is to say, like "structure of feeling," it seeks its articulation in order to attend to a feeling that likewise cannot be ignored or left unaddressed. This is perhaps how one could understand what Li means in the following: "Silence is not melodrama, or at least it is not presenting itself to be." Li, *Dear Friend*, 67.
33. Li, *Dear Friend*, 159.
34. Li, *Dear Friend*, 140.
35. Li, *Dear Friend*, 114.
36. Li, *Dear Friend*, 114.
37. Li, *Dear Friend*, 46.

38   Li, *Dear Friend*, 172.
39   Li, *Dear Friend*, 200.
40   Li, *Dear Friend*, 172.
41   Li, *Dear Friend*, 46.
42   Li, *Dear Friend*, 134.
43   Li, *Dear Friend*, 81.
44   I am referring to Li's gesturing toward the shared unshareability of loneliness/emptiness: "A moment of recognition between two people only highlights the inadequacy of language. What can be spoken does not sustain; what cannot be spoken undermine." Li, *Dear Friend*, 151. In other words, what is considered acceptable, according to social norms, to be shared between people does not actually strengthen or reinforce the relation between them; what is left unspoken, unspeakable, unshareable thus only threatens to undo or tear apart that relation.
45   See Li's interview with Rosemarie Ho, "For Yiyun Li, All Writing Is Autobiographical," in *The Nation*, October 21, 2019.
46   With terms like *work of mourning* and *phantasmatic*, I am admittedly deploying the language of psychoanalysis, which one could also find in Derrida's writings that follow Freud and Nicholas Abraham and Mária Török. In texts like *Politics of Friendship*, *Memoirs for Paul de Man*, *Circumfession*, and *The Work of Mourning*, Derrida takes into account the processes of interiorization and incorporation of the dead other in oneself while mourning, accompanied by the phantasm of sustaining the memory, image, or even life of that other beyond his or her death. No doubt, one could read all these in *Where Reasons End*, but, as said, I am not invested in a psychoanalytic reading of Li's writings here, nor of any of the texts in question in this present work. I am more interested in foregrounding the affective force or implications of witnessing failure's shared unshareability in another.
47   Indeed, the term *sentimental* is mobilized more in this novel than melodrama. See especially Li, *Where Reasons End*, 76. Nonetheless, as mentioned earlier, it is not unrelated to melodrama.
48   Cusk, "The Case of Yiyun Li."
49   Perhaps it would be interesting to consider here Merback's thesis on how necessary it was for the genius and perfectionist artist Albrecht Dürer to work on *Melancholia* in order to move forward. See Merback, *Perfection's Therapy*.
50   Li, *Where Reasons End*, 119.
51   In one instance in the novel, Nikolai also says to his mother, "I can forgive everyone ... for being imperfect," to which, his mother responds, "But not yourself." Li, *Where Reasons End*, 78.
52   Li, *Where Reasons End*, 122.
53   Li, *Where Reasons End*, 143.

54   Li, *Where Reasons End*, 146.
55   Li, *Where Reasons End*, 40.
56   Li, *Where Reasons End*, 34.
57   Li, *Where Reasons End*, 145.
58   Li, *Where Reasons End*, 125.
59   Li, *Dear Friend*, 143.
60   Li, *Where Reasons End*, 144, 145.
61   The mother never did share, justly or reasonably so, her depressive mood. Recalling a spring trip at a seaside town when Nikolai was alive, she says: "We looked happy.... In the street, people smiled at our linked arms and choreographed steps, yet I was far from what they imagined. It was the year of my disintegration, and I could find few delusions to live for." Li, *Where Reasons End*, 63.
62   Li, *Where Reasons End*, 56. According to Nikolai, for people who want or know how to feel, it is not writing but reading to which they turn.
63   Li, *Where Reasons End*, 56.
64   Li, *Where Reasons End*, 56.
65   Li, *Where Reasons End*, 167.
66   Li, *Where Reasons End*, 167.
67   Li, *Where Reasons End*, 85.
68   Li, *Must I Go*, 124.
69   Li, *Must I Go*, 124.
70   Li, *Must I Go*, 164.
71   Li, *Must I Go*, 286.
72   Li, *Must I Go*, 181–82.
73   Li, *Must I Go*, 182.
74   Li, *Must I Go*, 233.
75   According to Berlant, sentimentality and melodrama are predicated, rather, on "emotional knowledge" or "the critical intelligence of affect, emotion, and good intentions." Berlant, *The Female Complaint*, viii, 2.
76   Li, *Must I Go*, 233.
77   Li, *Must I Go*, 257, 327.
78   Li, *Must I Go*, 117.
79   Li, *Must I Go*, 207.
80   Li, *Must I Go*, 23.
81   Li, *Must I Go*, 229.
82   Li, *Must I Go*, 234.
83   Li, *Must I Go*, 238.
84   Li, *Must I Go*, 38. Perhaps one should recognize that Lilia's supposed inability to feel, or her apparent coldness toward those around her, is melodrama no less. Like the attitude of "hardness" she adopts toward life, that coldness or inability to feel is born out of Lucy's death: "Better to be cruel

than to be receiving cruelty. That was the lesson Lucy taught everyone by killing herself." Li, *Must I Go*, 92.
85 Li, *Must I Go*, 229.
86 Li, *Must I Go*, 335.
87 Li, *Must I Go*, 217.
88 Li, *Must I Go*, 217.
89 Li, *Must I Go*, 228.
90 Li, *Must I Go*, 347.
91 Li, *Must I Go*, 347.
92 Li, *Must I Go*, 347.
93 Li, *Must I Go*, 161.
94 Li, *Must I Go*, 309.
95 Li, *Must I Go*, 210.
96 Li, *Must I Go*, 348.
97 There is certainly no lack of the discourse on failure surrounding Lucy's death. Lilia is keenly aware that others might think how she could "fail so terribly" (*Must I Go*, 228) in allowing such a thing to happen to Lucy; Gilbert, Lilia's first husband and who took on the role of Lucy's father, would feel guilty of having "failed to give Lucy the love she needed" (325); and Lilia herself would question her failure, "a mother's failure," in not being a "circuit breaker" (165) when she did not address Lilia's self-harm scars or her apparent acting-out as she cried out, wanting to kill herself.
98 Li, *Dear Friend*, 143.
99 Li, *Dear Friend*, 144.
100 Berlant, *Cruel Optimism*, 10.
101 Berlant, *Cruel Optimism*, 10, 11, 10.
102 Berlant, *Cruel Optimism*, 10, 11.
103 Berlant, *Cruel Optimism*, 10.
104 Derrida, "Living On," 77.
105 Derrida, "Living On," 135.
106 See, of course, Derrida's *La vie la mort* (Life Death) seminars.
107 Derrida, "Living On," 138.
108 Cusk, *Aftermath*, 5.
109 Cusk, *Aftermath*, 5.
110 Cusk, *Aftermath*, 5. It is tempting to think of the *Outline* trilogy as such a creative—and no doubt a dark one, given the reticence of its narrator and how she is very much in the background or shadows of the narrative most of the time—aftermath after *Aftermath*. Nevertheless, *Kudos* does suggest that it can actually be *not* easy to reach such an aftermath. Paola, Faye's editor there, wants to bring Faye to view a church that was "ravaged one night by a terrible fire" but was never restored and "allowed to continue in its true state" (211, 212). As Paola describes it, "Inside it is

completely black," "as if the trauma of the fire had turned it into a natural form" (212). And some of the new installed lights "had the strange effect of making you see more in the empty space than you would have seen had it been filled with a statue [which was the case before the fire]" (213). The church as it stands now, in other words, is nothing short of aftermath. Yet, we will read that when Paola and Faye got to the church, they only find it locked. The "detour," if not drifting, to the church, then, came to signify for Paola a "failed purpose" (215).

CONCLUSION

Parts of the conclusion appeared in "Auto-thanato-theory: Dark Narcissistic Care for the Self in Sedgwick and Zambreno," *Arizona Quarterly* 76, no. 1 (2020): 197–213.

1. Otherwise, as we have also said in the introduction, if failure is constitutive of the sense of existence, if not *the* incontrovertible sense of existence, then, as long as there is sense in the world, then there is always failure. In this respect, too, failure elides closure.
2. Zambreno, *Appendix Project*, 54.
3. Zambreno, *Appendix Project*, 54.
4. Zambreno, *Appendix Project*, 65.
5. Zambreno *Appendix Project*, 120.
6. Zambreno, *Appendix Project*, 13.
7. Zambreno, *Appendix Project*, 30.
8. Zambreno, *Appendix Project*, 39.
9. Zambreno, *Appendix Project*, 33, 143.
10. Zambreno, *Appendix Project*, 47.
11. Zambreno, *Appendix Project*, 19.
12. Zambreno, *Appendix Project*, 131.
13. Zambreno, *Appendix Project*, 77, 131.
14. Zambreno, *Book of Mutter*, 102.
15. Zambreno, *To Write as if Already Dead*, 65.
16. Zambreno, *To Write as if Already Dead*, 85.
17. Zambreno says as much when writing about Loden in *Screen Tests*. First, she admits that she is not sure if Loden "thought of her film career as a failure." Nevertheless, she goes on to say, "I'm drawn—always—to failures.... Yes, Barbara Loden was, in a way, in terms of concepts of career and the canon, a failure" (274). And as much as in *Appendix Project* and *To Write as if Already Dead*, Zambreno's own sense of failure is rampant here. She would speak of "the sense of badness and dumbness and failure I carry around with me as a woman, as a woman writer" and "a sort of voluptuousness...about permanently occupying this realm of failure" to not land either a permanent or even part-time job at a university (268, 243).

18 Zambreno, *To Write as if Already Dead*, 66, 65.
19 Zambreno, *To Write as if Already Dead*, 85, 79.
20 Zambreno, *To Write as if Already Dead*, 34.
21 Zambreno, *To Write as if Already Dead*, 91.
22 There is a very brief reference to Foucault's care of the self, which Zambreno calls "selfcare" (33).
23 Not only the leitmotif of death betrays the desire for negative ek-sistence but so too the desire to stay with one's negative affects. We have already seen this in Sedgwick's attachment to the spectral "*me*" that does not want to dissociate itself with depression and/or negative ek-sistence and in Li's seeing her sense of "nothingness" that only made sense in her existence. We find this in Zambreno as well. In *Screen Tests*, where she talks about her depression, she would write: "Even though I am trying so hard, to be free of distractions and noise, of a cycle of anxiety and negative thinking, I am not sure I want to be a completely balanced, enlightened person" (271).
24 Zambreno, *To Write as if Already Dead*, 140–41.
25 Zambreno, *To Write as if Already Dead*, 85.
26 Zambreno, *To Write as if Already Dead*, 67.
27 Zambreno, *To Write as if Already Dead*, 10. My emphasis.
28 See Zambreno, *To Write as if Already Dead*, 17.
29 Zambreno, *To Write as if Already Dead*, 144.
30 Zambreno, *To Write as if Already Dead*, 144.
31 I note here that a knowing but unstated reference to Derrida's work appeared too in Moshfegh, *My Year of Rest and Relaxation*. In one of the narrator's waking states after three nights of "Infermiterol blackout," she does some word-association exercise, and when she comes to "Plato," one of the words that came to her mind was "*carte postale*." Moshfegh, *My Year of Rest and Relaxation*, 270.
32 Derrida, *La carte postale*, 33 (my translation).
33 Derrida, *La carte postale*, 35.
34 Derrida, *La carte postale*, 39.
35 Derrida, *La carte postale*, 35.
36 Derrida, *La carte postale*, 21.
37 Jones, *Failure and the American Writer*, 38, 49. In Jones's reading of Henry James's *The American Scene*, he would also note how "crises of forms and failures of discourse provide the rigorous language in which failure takes shape as an expansive, complex, and fundamental category of experience" (154).
38 See Derrida, *Chaque fois unique, la fin du monde* (*The Work of Mourning*). "To fail *well*" (144) is Pascale-Anne Brault and Michael Naas's translation of "il … faudra bien *échouer, bien* échouer," which, if were to save Derrida from any charge of a progress or success narrative, can also be

translated as "one must *indeed* fail." And yet, one does not fail to highlight that where this phrase is found, the sentence starts, in fact, with "in order to succeed" (*pour réussir*). Even the preceding sentence would end with "it would have to fail in order to succeed" (il ... faudra bien échouer pour réussir). See Derrida, *Chaque fois unique, la fin du monde*, 179.

39   I have elsewhere suggested that the mode of thinking associated more or less with "deconstruction," otherwise known in Anglo-American academia to be "high theory," has been rather resistant to, if not resilient against, failure. Despite the incessant proclamations of the "death of theory" across the decades since the 1980s, which had also outlined certain failures of "high theory," the latter has nevertheless stood its ground in US institutions (perhaps until the more recent fascination with affect theory and the more social conscious investments in race issues and decolonization) and continue to do so in several European universities. Otherwise, I do not need to remind readers of Agamben's embarrassing anxious effort to keep his theory of "bare life" alive in contemporary times by raising it again during the COVID-19 pandemic while saying that the virus is nothing more than the common flu. Of course, Agamben does not belong to the "deconstructive" camp, as evident through his disagreements with Derrida, but his thinking and writings have been labeled "high theory" no less. In any case, and to use Derrida's term, "high theory" lives on—a *survivre*—over and beyond the death sentences dealt to it. For more of this (other than the Agamben affair), see Goh, "Epic Fail." Otherwise, on the relation between failure and the language of "deconstruction," see Ziarek, *The Rhetoric of Failure*.

40   See Tomkins, *Affect, Imagery, Consciousness*, 460.

41   Perhaps one might think of the "botched text" here, which Jones has noted to interest Melville. Jones, *Failure and the American Writer*, 41.

42   Brinkema, *The Forms of the Affects*, xvi.

43   Kornbluh, *The Order of Forms*, 4, xi.

44   Kornbluh, *The Order of Forms*, 4.

45   Kornbluh, *The Order of Forms*, 2.

46   I am clearly alluding to Levine's work on the "affordances" of forms. See especially the introduction to Levine, *Forms*.

47   I no doubt have Agamben's thinking of "form-of-life" in mind here (see the eponymous chapter in his *Means without Ends*), which is to say, an organic form that responds or corresponds to every moment and mode of existing and which does not separate mere living—or bare/naked life, in Agamben's vocabulary—from the more fixed form of useful, political life as encapsulated by the category of the citizen. To put it in relation to our work, I would want to think of a "form-of-life" that accommodates genres that are flailing in response to the sense of failure, hence assuming a formless form, and one that accepts, again in response to the sense of fail-

ure, its very own dissolution or deformation. And to return to what has been professed in our introduction that our elucidation and explication of *failure as failure* and failed existence serve no political usage, this arguably resonates with Agamben's claim that there can in fact be indeed *no* political utility in forms of lives that seem so. As he says at the outset of *The Use of Bodies*, where he returns to the question of "form-of-life": "It is as if each of us obscurely felt that precisely the opacity of our clandestine life held within it a genuinely political element, as such shareable par excellence—and yet, if one attempts to share it, it stubbornly eludes capture and leaves behind it only a ridiculous and incommunicable remainder" (xxi). Agamben might even suggest that here lies happiness: "The happy life ... appears as a life that does not possess its form as a part or a quality but *is* this form, has completely passed into it" (219). But we take distance from Agamben in being reserved in attributing the notion of happiness to a life that assumes the deforming or even deformed form of failed existence, that completely passes into it, that does not set it apart from the normative form of "normal," useful existence.

48   Levine, *Forms*, 7.

49   I note here that Cusk can be quite suspicious of form too. She would say that "form is important in stories." Cusk, *Aftermath*, 3. However, the stories of marriage, modern family life, and motherhood have clearly left her disenchanted. It is not surprising, then, that further on in *Aftermath*, she would expound on her thoughts on form as follows: "Form is both safety and imprisonment, both protector and dissembler: form, in the end, conceals truth, just as the body conceals the cancer that will destroy it. Form is rigid, inviolable, devastatingly correct; that is its vulnerability. Form can be broken" (55). One could argue that this reveals how Cusk suggests how the novel form deployed in the critique of marriage and modern family life, as practiced in the *Outline* trilogy, might bear less veracity than the more memoir-like *Aftermath*, which, however, finds less kind reception from readers.

The suspicion of form can be found in *Outline* too. We cite the case of Anne again. According to her, "The polarization of man and woman was a structure, a form" (Cusk, *Outline*, 236), and we do not need to remind ourselves that Cusks is opposed to such a form of gender polarization. But to go back to Anne's case. It suggests that the reliance on such a form is only detrimental to the woman, to feminist sensibility, even incidentally exposing Anne to violence. In Anne's recounting, "she had only felt [that form] once it was gone, and it almost seemed as though the collapse of that structure, that equipoise, was responsible for the extremity that followed it" (236), which concerns the assault on Anne by a stranger. But losing that form also leads to Anne realizing that she has lost her old self before she met her husband. Anne comes to the reckoning that through her marriage, she had become a secondary existence: "She had become, through him, someone else. In a sense he had created her, and when she phoned him that day of the incident [i.e., the assault], she was, she supposed, referring herself back to him as his creation. Her links to the life before him had been completely severed—that person no longer existed, and so when the incident occurred it had been two kinds of crisis, one of which was a crisis of identity. She didn't know, in other words, quite who it happened to.... She was like someone who had forgotten their native language" (237). Through the form of marriage, Anne has become a created form; she could no longer be the creative being capable of aesthetic works.

50 Kornbluh, *The Order of Forms*, 3.
51 See Garrido, *La formation des formes*.
52 Levine, *Forms*, 3. I note here that I am reading Levine radically, because things that break down, or "fissures and interstices, vagueness and indeterminacy, boundary-crossing and dissolution" (9) are *not* forms according to her.
53 Brinkema, *Life-Destroying Diagrams*, 151, 157.
54 Bradatan, *In Praise of Failure*, 6.
55 One does not forget the possibility of "essayism," as Brian Dillon calls it, which, in his terms, is a gathering of writings that registers how writing and thinking intersect at the same time, the failures and vulnerabilities of the writer, and the writer's sense of depression and melancholia, all of which also involve some sort of *postscripting*, as I have called it, since it inscribes the writer's sense of being already dead while writing. This form of "essayism" is found no doubt in Zambreno's *Screen Tests* and Li's *Dear Friend*. In the vein of essayism, perhaps one could imagine a collection of writings that are close to streams of consciousness, except the book will not write itself as some form of continuous flow. On the contrary, if there should be something like a flow, it takes place within the suspended state of failure, in the state of failure that puts in suspension the continuity of normal, functional, routine, and productive or efficient life as we know it. Or else, it is to write in a way more or less truthful to the rhythm of the sense of failure—that is, where the moments of feeling down, the moments when the affects of shame, anxiety, nervous folly and laughter, guilt, depression, etcetera take over, are juxtaposed in no regular, stable, coherent, or orderly way with moments of feeling able to look at things calmly and approach them in a quasi-rational manner.
56 Brinkema, *Life-Destroying Diagrams*, 153.

BIBLIOGRAPHY

Agamben, Giorgio. *Means Without Ends: Notes on Politics.* Translated by Vincenzo Binetti and Cesare Casarino. Minneapolis: University of Minnesota Press, 2000.
Agamben, Giorgio. *Potentialities: Collected Essays in Philosophy.* Edited and translated by Daniel Heller-Roazen. Stanford, CA: Stanford University Press, 1999.
Agamben, Giorgio. *The Use of Bodies.* Translated by Adam Kotsko. Stanford, CA: Stanford University Press, 2016.
Ahmed, Sara. "Affective Economies." *Social Text* 22, no. 2 (2004): 117–39.
Ahmed, Sara. *Complaint!* Durham, NC: Duke University Press, 2021.
Ahmed, Sara. *What's the Use? On the Uses of Us.* Durham, NC: Duke University Press, 2019.
Alvarez, A. *The Savage God: A Study of Suicide.* London: Weidenfeld and Nicolson, 1970.
Antebi, Nicole, Colin Dickey, and Robby Herbst, eds. *Failure! Experiments in Aesthetic and Social Practices.* Los Angeles: Journal of Aesthetics and Protest Press, 2007.
Appadurai, Arjun, and Neta Alexander. *Failure.* Cambridge: Polity, 2019.
Badiou, Alain. *Saint Paul: The Foundation of Universalism.* Translated by Ray Brassier. Stanford, CA: Stanford University Press, 2003.
Ball, Jesse. *A Cure for Suicide: A Novel.* New York: Vintage, 2015.
Barthes, Roland. *Comment vivre ensemble: Cours et séminaires au Collège de France (1976–1977).* Paris: Éditions du Seuil, 2002. Translated by Kate Briggs as *How to Live Together: Novelistic Simulations of Some Everyday Spaces.* New York: Columbia University Press, 2012.
Barthes, Roland. *Le Neutre: Cours au Collège de France (1977–1978).* Paris: Éditions du Seuil, 2002. Translated by Rosalind E. Krauss and Denis Hollier as *The Neutral: Lecture Course at the Collège de France (1977–1978).* New York: Columbia University Press, 2005.
Bataille, Georges. *La part maudite, précédé de la notion de dépense.* Introduction by Jean Piel. Paris: Minuit, 1967.
Baudelaire, Charles. *De l'essence du rire et généralement du comique dans les arts plastiques.* Paris: René Kieffer, 1925.
Beckett, Samuel. *All That Fall and Other Plays for Radio and Screen.* London: Faber and Faber, 2009.

Beckett, Samuel. *Company/Ill Seen Ill Said/Worstward Ho/Stirrings Still*. London: Faber and Faber, 2009.

Beckett, Samuel. *L'innommable*. Paris: Minuit, 1953. Translated by Samuel Beckett as *The Unnamable*. New York: Grove, 1958.

Beckett, Samuel. *Proust and Three Dialogues with Georges Duthuit*. London: John Calder, 1965.

Benjamin, Walter. "Ibizan Sequence." 1932. Translated by Rodney Livingstone. In *Selected Writings*, vol. 2, part 2, *1931–1934*, edited by Michael W. Jennings, Howard Eiland, and Gary Smith, 587–94. Cambridge, MA: Belknap Press of Harvard University Press, 1999.

Benjamin, Walter. "The Work of Art in the Age of Its Technological Reproducibility." 3rd ed. 1939. Translated by Harry Zohn and Edmund Jephcott. In *Selected Writings*, vol. 4, *1938–1940*, edited by Howard Eiland and Michael W. Jennings, 251–83. Cambridge, MA: Belknap Press of Harvard University Press, 2003.

Bering, Jesse. *Suicidal: Why We Kill Ourselves*. Chicago: University of Chicago Press, 2018.

Berlant, Lauren. *Cruel Optimism*. Durham, NC: Duke University Press, 2011.

Berlant, Lauren. *The Female Complaint: The Unfinished Business of Sentimentality in American Culture*. Durham, NC: Duke University Press, 2008.

Berlant, Lauren. "Genre Flailing." *Capacious: Journal for Emerging Affect Inquiry* 1, no. 2 (2018): 156–62. https://capaciousjournal.com/article/genre-flailing/.

Berlant, Lauren. *On the Inconvenience of Other People*. Durham, NC: Duke University Press, 2022.

Berlant, Lauren, and Lee Edelman. *Sex, or the Unbearable*. Durham, NC: Duke University Press, 2013.

Bersani, Leo. *The Culture of Redemption*. Cambridge, MA: Harvard University Press, 1990.

Bey, Marquis. *Cistem Failure: Essays on Blackness and Cisgender*. Durham, NC: Duke University Press, 2022.

Blanchot, Maurice. *La part du feu*. Paris: Éditions Gallimard, 1949.

Blanchot, Maurice. *Le pas au-delà*. Paris: Éditions Gallimard, 1973.

Blanchot, Maurice. *L'écriture du désastre*. Paris: Éditions Gallimard, 1980.

Blanchot, Maurice. *L'instant de ma mort*. Paris: Éditions Gallimard, 2002.

Bradatan, Costica. *In Praise of Failure: Four Lessons in Humility*. Cambridge, MA: Harvard University Press, 2023.

Braunstein, Néstor A. "Desire and Jouissance in the Teachings of Lacan." Translated by Tamara Francés. In *The Cambridge Companion to Lacan*, edited by Jean-Michel Rabaté, 102–15. Cambridge: Cambridge University Press, 2003.

Brennan, Teresa. *The Transmission of Affect*. Ithaca, NY: Cornell University Press, 2004.

Brinkema, Eugenie. *Life-Destroying Diagrams*. Durham, NC: Duke University Press, 2022.

Brinkema, Eugenie. *The Forms of the Affects*. Durham, NC: Duke University Press, 2014.
Bruyere, Vincent. *Perishability Fatigue: Forays into Environmental Loss and Decay*. New York: Columbia University, Press, 2018.
Butler, Judith. *Notes Toward a Performative Theory of Assembly*. Cambridge, MA: Harvard University Press, 2015.
Camus, Albert. *Le mythe de Sisyphe* (*The Myth of Sisyphus*). Paris: Éditions Gallimard, 1942.
Cardona, Karen Borg. *Global Failure and World Literature: Reading the Contemporary Quest Novel*. Berlin: De Gruyter, 2023.
Care Collective. *The Care Manifesto: The Politics of Interdependence*. London: Verso. 2020.
Carr, Allison D. "Failure Is Not an Option." In *Bad Ideas About Writing*, edited by Cheryl E. Ball and Drew M. Loewe, 76–81. Morgantown, WV: Digital Publishing Institute, 2017.
Carr, Allison D. "In Support of Failure." *Composition Forum* 27 (Spring 2013). https://compositionforum.com/issue/27/failure.php.
Carr, Allison D., and Laura R. Micciche, eds. *Failure Pedagogies: Learning and Unlearning What It Means to Fail*. New York: Peter Lang, 2020.
Cixous, Hélène. *Neutre*. Paris: Éditions Grasset, 1972.
Crary, Jonathan. "Powering Down." *October* 176 (2021): 27–29.
Crary, Jonathan. *24/7: Late Capitalism and the Ends of Sleep*. London: Verso, 2014.
Critchley, Simon. *Notes on Suicide*. London: Fitzcarraldo, 2016.
Cusk, Rachel. *Aftermath*. London: Faber and Faber, 2019.
Cusk, Rachel. "*Aftermath* Was Creative Death. I Was Heading into Total Silence." Interview with Kate Kellaway. *Guardian*, August 24, 2014.
Cusk, Rachel. "The Case of Yiyun Li." *New York Review of Books*. July 18, 2019. https://www.nybooks.com/articles/2019/07/18/case-of-yiyun-li/.
Cusk, Rachel. *Coventry: Essays*. London: Faber and Faber, 2019.
Cusk, Rachel. *Kudos: A Novel*. New York: Picador, 2019.
Cusk, Rachel. *A Life's Work: On Becoming a Mother*. New York: Picador, 2001.
Cusk, Rachel. *Outline: A Novel*. New York: Picador, 2016.
Cusk, Rachel. *Transit: A Novel*. New York: Picador, 2017.
Cusset, Catherine. *L'autre qu'on adorait*. Paris: Folio, 2018.
Cvetkovich, Ann. *Depression: A Public Feeling*. Durham, NC: Duke University Press, 2012.
Dekker, Sidney. *Drift into Failure: From Hunting Broken Components to Understanding Complex Systems*. Surrey: Ashgate, 2011.
Deleuze, Gilles. "How Do We Recognize Structuralism?" In *Desert Islands and Other Texts 1953–1974*, edited by David Lapoujade and translated by Michael Taomina, 170–92. New York: Semiotext(e), 2004.
Deleuze, Gilles. *The Logic of Sense*. Translated by Mark Lester and Charles Stivale and edited by Constantin V. Boundas. New York: Columbia University Press, 1990.

Deleuze, Gilles, and Félix Guattari. *Qu'est-ce que la philosophie?* Paris: Minuit, 1991.
Derrida, Jacques. "Living On," translated by James Hulbert. In *Deconstruction and Criticism*, 75–176. New York: Continuum, 1979.
Derrida, Jacques. *Apories*. Paris: Éditions Galilée, 1996. Translated by Thomas Dutoit as *Aporias*. Stanford, CA: Stanford University Press, 1993.
Derrida, Jacques. *Chaque fois unique, la fin du monde*. Paris: Éditions Galilée, 2003. Translated as *The Work of Mourning*, edited and translated by Pascale-Anne Brault and Michael Naas. Chicago: University of Chicago Press, 2001.
Derrida, Jacques. *De la grammatologie*. Paris: Minuit, 1967.
Derrida, Jacques. *La carte postale: De Socrate à Freud et au-delà*. Paris: Editions Flammarion, 1980.
Derrida, Jacques. *La vie la mort: Séminaire (1975–1976)*. Paris: Éditions Seuil, 2019.
Derrida, Jacques. *L'écriture et la différence*. Paris: Éditions du Seuil, 1967.
Dillon, Brian. *Essayism*. London: Fitzcarraldo, 2017.
Dimou-Grampa, Aspasia. "*Outline*'s Silence." Unpublished undergraduate dissertation, Malmö University, 2020. http://diva-portal.org/smash/get/diva2:1482153/FULLTEXT01.pdf.
Dirschauer, Marlene. "Sleep as Action? World Alienation, Distance, and Loneliness in Ottessa Moshfegh's *My Year of Rest and Relaxation*." *AmLit* 2, no. 1 (2022): 42–61.
Edelman, Lee. *Bad Education: Why Queer Theory Teaches Us Nothing*. Durham, NC: Duke University Press, 2022.
Edelman, Lee. *No Future: Queer Theory and the Death Drive*. Durham, NC: Duke University Press, 2004.
Feltham, Colin. *Failure: The Art of Living*. Durham, NC: Acumen, 2012.
Feltham, Oliver. *Anatomy of Failure: Philosophy and Political Action*. London: Bloomsbury, 2013.
Firestein, Stuart. *Failure: Why Science Is So Successful*. Oxford: Oxford University Press, 2016.
Foucault, Michel. *L'Herméneutique du sujet: Cours au Collège de France, 1981–1982*. Paris: Seuil, 2001. Translated by Graham Burchell as *The Hermeneutics of the Subject*, edited by Frédéric Gros. New York: Picador, 2005.
Foucault, Michel. "Technologies of the Self." In *Technologies of the Self: A Seminar with Michel Foucault*, edited by Luther H. Martin, Huck Gutman, and Patrick H. Hutton, 16–49. Amherst: University of Massachusetts Press, 1988.
Flatley, Jonathan. *Affective Mapping: Melancholia and the Politics of Modernism*. Cambridge, MA: Harvard University Press, 2008.
Franta, Andrew. *Systems Failure: The Uses of Disorder in English Literature*. Baltimore, MD: Johns Hopkins University Press, 2019.
Frayne, David. *The Refusal of Work: The Theory and Practice of Resistance to Work*. London: Zed Books, 2015.

Freud, Sigmund. "Beyond the Pleasure Principle." In *The Standard Edition of the Complete Psychological Works*, vol. 18, 7–64. Translated by James Strachey. London: Hogarth, 1955.

Freud, Sigmund. "Mourning and Melancholia." In *The Standard Edition of the Complete Psychological Works*, vol. 14, 243–58. Translated by James Strachey. London: Vantage, 2001.

Freud, Sigmund. "On Narcissism: An Introduction." In *The Standard Edition of the Complete Psychological Works*, vol. 14, 73–102. Translated by James Strachey. London: Vantage, 2001.

Garrido, Juan-Manuel. *La formation des formes*. Paris: Éditions Galilée, 2008.

Goh, Irving. "Epic Fail." In *What's Wrong with Antitheory?*, edited with an introduction by Jeffrey R. Di Leo, 60–72. London: Bloomsbury Academic, 2020.

Goh, Irving. *The Reject: Community, Politics, and Religion After the Subject*. New York: Fordham University Press, 2014.

Graham, Shawn. *Failing Gloriously and Other Essays*. Grand Forks: Digital Press at the University of North Dakota, 2019.

Greenberg, Jonathan. "Losing Track of Time." *Daedalus* 150, no. 1 (2021): 188–203.

Gregg, Melissa. *Counterproductive: Time Management in the Knowledge Economy*. Durham, NC: Duke University Press, 2018.

Gregg, Melissa. *Work's Intimacy*. Cambridge: Polity, 2011.

Halberstam, Judith. *The Queer Art of Failure*. Durham, NC: Duke University Press, 2011.

Hamacher, Werner. "Other Pains." Translated by Ian Alexander Moore. *Philosophy Today* 61, no. 4 (2017): 963–89.

Hamacher, Werner. *Pleroma—Reading in Hegel*. Translated by Nicholas Walker and Simon Jarvis. Stanford, CA: Stanford University Press, 1998.

Hamington, Maurice, and Michael Flower, eds. *Care Ethics in the Age of Precarity*. Minneapolis: University of Minnesota Press, 2021.

Harney, Stefano, and Fred Moten. *All Incomplete*. London: Minor Compositions, 2021.

Hodson, Josie Roland. "Rest Notes: On Black Sleep Aesthetics." *October* 176 (2021): 7–24.

Hong, Cathy Park. *Minor Feelings: A Reckoning on Race and the Asian Condition*. London: Profile Books, 2020.

Hong, Renyi. *Passionate Work: Endurance After the Good Life*. Durham, NC: Duke University Press, 2022.

Jones, Gavin. *Failure and the American Writer: A Literary History*. Cambridge: Cambridge University Press, 2014.

Kendi, Ibram X. *How to Be an Antiracist*. New York: One World, 2019.

Khúc, Mimi. *dear elia: Letters from the Asian America Abyss*. Durham, NC: Duke University Press, 2024.

Klein, Melanie. "A Contribution to the Psychogenesis of Manic-Depressive States." In *The Selected Melanie Klein*, edited by Juliet Mitchell, 115–45. New York: Free Press, 1986.

Klein, Melanie. "Mourning and Its Relation to Manic-Depressive States." In *The Selected Melanie Klein*, edited by Juliet Mitchell, 146–74. New York: Free Press, 1986.

Kornbluh, Anna. *The Order of Forms: Realism, Formalism, and Social Space*. Chicago: University of Chicago Press, 2019.

Lacan, Jacques. *Écrits: The First Complete Edition in English*. Translated by Bruce Fink. New York and London: W. W. Norton, 2002.

Lacan, Jacques. *Écrits II*. Paris: Éditions du Seuil, 1966.

Lacan, Jacques. *L'éthique de la psychanalyse: Le séminaire, livre VII*. Paris: Éditions du Seuil, 1996.

Lacan, Jacques. *Ou pire: Le séminaire, livre XIX*. Paris: Éditions du Seuil, 2011.

LaCapra, Dominick. *History in Transit: Experience, Identity, Critical Theory*. Ithaca, NY: Cornell University Press, 2004.

Lafargue, Paul. *Le droit à la paresse*. Paris: François Maspero, 1965. Translated by Alex Andriesse as *The Right to Be Lazy and Other Writings*, with an introduction by Lucy Sante. New York: New York Review Books, 2022.

Lakshmin, Pooja. *Real Self-Care: A Transformative Program for Redefining Wellness*. New York: Penguin, 2023.

Laplanche, Jean. "The So-Called 'Death Drive': A Sexual Drive." *British Journal of Psychotherapy* 20, no. 4 (2004): 455–71.

Lee, Wendy Anne. *Failures of Feeling: Insensibility and the Novel*. Stanford, CA: Stanford University Press, 2019.

Levé, Édouard. *Autoportrait*. Paris: P.O.L, 2013.

Levé, Édouard. *Œuvres*. Paris: P.O.L, 2015.

Levé, Édouard. *Suicide*. Paris: P.O.L, 2008.

Levine, Caroline. *Forms: Whole, Rhythm, Hierarchy, Network*. Princeton, NJ: Princeton University Press, 2015.

Li, Yiyun. *Dear Friend, from My Life I Write to You in Your Life*. New York: Random House, 2017.

Li, Yiyun. *Must I Go*. London: Hamish Hamilton, 2020.

Li, Yiyun. *Where Reasons End*. New York: Random House, 2019.

Long, Camille. Review of *Aftermath*, by Rachel Cusk. *Sunday Times*, March 4, 2012.

Love, Heather. "Close but Not Deep: Literary Ethics and the Descriptive Turn." *New Literary History* 41 (2010): 371–91.

Love, Heather. *Feeling Backward: Loss and the Politics of Queer History*. Cambridge, MA: Harvard University Press, 2009.

Lukianoff, Greg, and Jonathan Haidt. *The Coddling of the American Mind: How Good Intentions and Bad Ideas Are Setting Up a Generation for Failure*. New York: Penguin, 2018.

Lutz, Tom. *Doing Nothing: A History of Loafers, Loungers, Slackers, and Bums in America*. New York: Farrar, Strauss and Giroux, 2006.

Magnet, Shoshana. *When Biometrics Fail: Gender, Race, and the Technology of Identity*. Durham, NC: Duke University Press, 2011.

Malatino, Hil. *Side Affects: On Being Trans and Feeling Bad*. Minneapolis: University of Minnesota Press, 2022.
Malatino, Hil. *Trans Care*. Minneapolis: University of Minnesota Press, 2020.
Malesic, Jonathan. *The End of Burnout*. Berkeley: University of California Press, 2022.
Marche, Stephen. *On Writing and Failure*. Windsor, ON: Biblioasis, 2023.
Marin, Claire. *Rupture(s)*. Paris: Éditions de l'Observatoire, 2019.
Massumi, Brian. *Politics of Affect*. Cambridge: Polity, 2015.
Melville, Herman. *Pierre: or, The Ambiguities*. Evanston, IL: Northwestern University Press, 1995.
Merback, Mitchell B. *Perfection's Therapy: An Essay on Albrecht Dürer's Melancholia I*. New York: Zone Books, 2017.
Mika, Adriana, Mikolaj Pawlak, Anna Horolets, and Paweł Kubicki, eds. *Routledge International Handbook of Failure*. London: Routledge, 2023.
Morton, Timothy. *Dark Ecology: For a Logic of Future Coexistence*. New York: Columbia University Press, 2016.
Moshfegh, Ottessa. *My Year of Rest and Relaxation*. New York: Penguin, 2018.
Moten, Fred. *In the Break: The Aesthetics of the Black Radical Tradition*. Minneapolis: University of Minnesota Press, 2003.
Mueller, Gavin. *Breaking Things at Work*. London: Verso, 2021.
Muñoz, José Esteban. *Cruising Utopia: The Then and There of Queer Futurity*. New York: New York University Press, 2009.
Nancy, Jean-Luc. *Corpus*. Paris: Éditions Métailié, 2006.
Nancy, Jean-Luc. *Derrida, suppléments*. Paris: Éditions Galilée, 2019.
Nancy, Jean-Luc. *La communauté désœuvrée*. Paris: Éditions Christian Bourgois, 1990.
Nancy, Jean-Luc. *Le sens du monde*. Paris: Éditions Galilée, 1993.
Nancy, Jean-Luc. "L'excrit." In *Une pensée finie*, 55–64. Paris: Galilée, 1991.
Nancy, Jean-Luc. *Tombe de sommeil*. Paris: Éditions Galilée, 2007. Translated by Charlotte Mandell as *The Fall of Sleep*. New York: Fordham University Press, 2009.
Nancy, Jean-Luc, and Adèle van Reeth. *La jouissance*. Paris: Éditions Plon, 2014.
Ngai, Sianne. *Ugly Feelings*. Cambridge, MA: Harvard University Press, 2007.
Nietzsche, Friedrich. *Thus Spoke Zarathustra*. Translated and with an introduction by R. J. Hollingdale. London: Penguin, 1961.
Ochoa, John A. *The Uses of Failure in Mexican Literature and Identity*. Austin: University of Texas Press, 2004.
Ovid. *Metamorphoses*. Translated and edited by Charles Martin. New York: W. W. Norton, 2004.
Petersen, Anne Helen. *Can't Even: How Millennials Became the Burnout Generation*. London: Chatto and Windus, 2021.
Phillips, Adam. *On Giving Up*. New York: Farrar, Straus and Giroux, 2024.
Potts, Jason, and Daniel Stout, eds. *Theory Aside*. Durham, NC: Duke University Press, 2014.

Puig de la Bellacasa, María. *Matters of Care: Speculative Ethics in More than Human Worlds*. Minneapolis: University of Minnesota Press, 2017.

Sandage, Scott A. *Born Losers: A History of Failure in America*. Cambridge, MA: Harvard University Press, 2005.

Sartre, Jean-Paul. *Baudelaire*. Paris: Éditions Gallimard, 1948.

Sartre, Jean-Paul. *Saint Genet: Comédien et martyr*. Paris: Éditions Gallimard, 2011.

Scarry, Elaine. *The Body in Pain: The Making and Unmaking of the World*. New York: Oxford University Press, 1985.

Schuster, Aaron. *The Trouble with Pleasure: Deleuze and Psychoanalysis*. Cambridge, MA: MIT Press, 2016.

Sedgwick, Eve Kosofsky. *A Dialogue on Love*. Boston: Beacon Press, 1999.

Sedgwick, Eve Kosofsky. "Paranoid Reading and Reparative Reading, or, You're So Paranoid, You Probably Think This Essay Is About You." In *Touching Feeling: Affect, Pedagogy, Performativity*, 123–51. Durham, NC: Duke University Press, 2003.

Setiya, Kieran. *Life Is Hard: How Philosophy Can Help Us Find Our Way*. New York: Riverhead Books, 2022.

Sharma, Sarah. *In the Meantime: Temporality and Cultural Politics*. Durham, NC: Duke University Press, 2014.

Sharpe, Christina. *In the Wake: On Blackness and Being*. Durham, NC: Duke University Press, 2016.

Stewart, Kathleen. *Ordinary Affects*. Durham, NC: Duke University Press, 2007.

Strätz, Juliane. "Revolt Through Passivity? Getting High and Staying in with Ottessa Moshfegh's *My Year of Rest and Relaxation*." In *Work: The Labors of Language, Culture, and History in North America*, edited by J. Jesse Ramínez and Sixta Quassdorf, 99–120. Tübingen: Narr Francke Attempto, 2021.

Terada, Rei. *Feeling in Theory: Emotion After the "Death of the Subject."* Cambridge, MA: Cambridge University Press, 2003.

Thacker, Eugene. *Infinite Resignation*. London: Repeater Books, 2018.

Tomkins, Silvan. *Affect Imagery Consciousness: The Complete Edition*. New York: Springer, 2008.

Trawny, Peter. *Freedom to Fail: Heidegger's Anarchy*. Translated by Ian Alexander Moore and Christopher Turner. Cambridge: Polity Press, 2015.

Tronto, Joan C. *Moral Boundaries: A Political Argument for an Ethic of Care*. New York: Routledge, 1993.

Valihora, Karen. "She Got Up and Went Away: Rachel Cusk on Making an Exit." *ESC: English Studies in Canada* 45, no. 1–2 (March/June 2019): 19–35.

Vattimo, Gianni. *Weak Thought*. Translated by Peter Carravetta. Albany: State University of New York Press, 2012.

Vermeulen, Pieter. "Against Premature Articulation: Empathy, Gender, and Austerity in Rachel Cusk and Katie Kitamura." *Cultural Critique* 111 (Spring 2021): 81–103.

Weeks, Kathi. *The Problem with Work: Feminism, Marxism, Antiwork Politics, and Postwork Imaginaries.* Durham, NC: Duke University Press, 2011.
Williams, Raymond. "Structures of Feeling." In *Marxism and Literature*, 128–35. New York: Oxford University Press, 1977.
Woolf, Virginia. *On Being Ill.* Introduction by Hermione Lee. Ashfield, MA: Paris Press, 2002.
Yao, Xine. *Disaffected: The Cultural Politics of Unfeeling in Nineteenth-Century America.* Durham, NC: Duke University Press, 2021.
Zambreno, Kate. *Appendix Project.* South Pasadena, CA: Semiotext(e), 2019.
Zambreno, Kate. *Book of Mutter.* South Pasadena, CA: Semiotext(e), 2017.
Zambreno, Kate. *Drifts: A Novel.* New York: Riverhead Books, 2020.
Zambreno, Kate. *Screen Tests: Stories and Other Writing.* New York: Harper, 2019.
Zambreno, Kate. *To Write as if Already Dead.* New York: Columbia University Press, 2021.
Ziarek, Ewa Płonowska. *The Rhetoric of Failure: Deconstruction of Skepticism, Reinvention of Modernism.* Albany: State University of New York Press, 1996.

INDEX

addendum, failure as, 130–31
aestheticization, in Moshfegh's writing, 55
affect theory: Barthes's Neutral concept and, 69–70; development of, 10–14, 23–24, 148n19, 149n30; emergence of, 138–40; epic fail and, 9–10; failure and, 2, 4–5, 141–43, 145n2; feminist and queer theory and, 140; touch and, 183n88
Aftermath (Cusk), 3, 73–77, 173n82, 189n110, 193n49
Agamben, Giorgio: bare life theory of, 192n39; on destituent potential, 141; on failure, 16, 159n115; form-of-life theory of, 192n47; on impasse, 25, 151n49; on impotentiality, 71; work in writings of, 59
Ahmed, Sara, 10, 13, 16, 74–75, 150n34, 172n72, 173n73
AIDS epidemic, failure and, 134
All Incomplete (Harney and Moten), 58, 161n2, 165n80, 168n126
All That Fall (Beckett), 43–44
altruism, 87
Alvarez, Al, 105
The American Scene (James), 191n37
aneconomical ethics (Derrida), 87, 89–90, 177n3
Antetokounmpo, Giannis, 162n14
Appendix Project (Zambreno), 3, 36, 132–38, 190n17
The Argonauts (Nelson), 91, 93
attunement to failure, 29–31; Heidegger's *Gestimmtsein* and, 128
Aufhebung (uplifting), failure and, 23
autofiction: exscription and, 99; failure narratives as, 31, 36, 137; Li's novels as, 116–19
Autoportrait (Levé), 3, 34–35, 91, 104–5, 137, 184n100
auto-thanato-theory, 99, 182n77

Bad Education (Edelman), 16–17, 151n52
bad education, failure as, 16–17, 151n52
Badiou, Alain, 40
Barthes, Roland, 22; *idiorrythmie* concept of, 65–67, 79; Neutral concept of, 64–65, 67–73, 81, 127, 169n14, 170n16, 170n19, 171n41; Zambreno on, 132
Bartleby (Melville), 179n18
basketball, flopping, 42–43, 162n14
Bataille, Georges, 154n81
Baudelaire, Charles, 157n102
Beckett, Samuel, 6, 8, 18, 23, 42–44, 138, 147n11, 147n13, 147n15, 156n92, 185n5
Benjamin, Walter, 53–54, 165n80, 166n85
Berlant, Lauren: communitarianism of, 141; on crisis ordinariness, 125–26; cruel optimism of, 99; Cusk's work and influence of, 172n62; on failure, 9, 27–28, 140, 148n16, 156n95, 158n104, 159n111; infrastructuralism of, 25–26, 156n94; Li's novels and influence of, 109; on melodrama, 111–12, 118–19, 188n75
Bersani, Leo, 180n35, 180n51
Biles, Simone, 43

Black sleep, Hodson's concept of, 57
blame, failure and, 41
Blanchot, Maurice, 16, 25, 151n49, 157n102, 182n78
body: Nancy's exscription and, 100–103, 182n82, 183n88, 184n103; suicide and, 104–5
Book of Mutter (Zambreno), 132–33
boomeranging, work culture and, 59
Bradatan, Costica, 2, 14–15, 40, 69, 142, 150n43, 153n65, 158n107
Braunstein, Néstor, 154n81
Brennan, Teresa, 10
Brinkema, Eugenie, 141–43, 147n13, 167n125
Bruyere, Vincent, 167n109
burnout, care fatigue as, 178n6
Butler, Judith, on failure, 148n20

Cabin in the Woods (film), 147n13
Camus, Albert, 101, 126, 158n107
Care Collective, 88–89, 178n5, 179n15
care ethics, self-care *vs.*, 86–92
Care Ethics in the Age of Precarity, 89, 178n7
care fatigue, 87–88, 178n6
Carr, Allison D., 16, 150n46, 153n65
Chernobyl disaster, 8
China, flopping as resistance in, 58
Cixous, Hélène, 87, 174n83
class, in Moshfegh's narrative, 52–53, 57–62
close reading, 103–5
communitarianism, failure and, 16, 156n93, 185n6
conceptualization, Barthes's Neutral and, 69
contemporary life, failure in, 2–4, 145n3
Corpus (Nancy), 99–102, 184n98
COVID-19 pandemic, 145n3, 192n39; care ethics and, 88–89; Great Resignation movement and, 58
Crary, Jonathan, 49, 57, 60
credit system, failure and role of, 153n75

crisis ordinariness, living with failure and, 125–28
Crisp, Quentin, 108
Critchley, Simon, 158n107, 183n96, 195n9
cruel optimism: in Cusk's *Aftermath*, 74–75; failure and, 28; impasse and, 31; in Sedgwick's work, 98–99
Cruel Optimism (Berlant), 26–28, 158n104
cultural theory, failure and, 152n63
The Culture of Redemption (Bersani), 180n35, 180n51
Cusk, Rachel: *Aftermath* by, 73–77; Barthes's Neutral in novels of, 68, 127; care fatigue in work of, 88; Derrida's lifedeath and work of, 127; drifting in work of, 64, 68, 131; exscription in work of, 106–7; failure narrative in work of, 3, 12, 20–21, 31, 33–34, 160n117, 161n1; on form, 141, 193n49; Li's work and, 110, 116
Cusset, Catherine, 22
Cvetkovich, Ann, 138, 141, 185n6

Dalke, Anne, 19–20
Daoism, Barthes and, 71
dark narcissism, self-care as, 92–96, 181n75
Dear Friend, from My Life I Write to You (Li), 3, 35–36, 108–15, 117–18, 120, 127, 137, 186n21; essayism in, 194n55
death drive, 67, 168n10
deconstruction, failure writing and, 138–39, 192n39
Dekker, Sidney, 72–73, 169n14
Deleuze, Gilles, 21, 28, 101, 156n98, 157n102, 170n19
Delphic oracle, 86
depressive position of failure, 24–25, 158n107
Derrida, Jacques: on altruism, 87; on aneconomic ethics, 87, 89–90, 177n3; Barthes's Neutral and work of, 169n14, 170n20; on decon-

struction, 138; on end of the book, 140–41; on failing well, 191n38; on Hegel, 130; on high theory, 192n39; on impasse as aporia, 26–27; life-death concept of, 126–28, 186n16; Nancy and, 182n78; postal principle of, 136–37; psychoanalysis in work of, 187n46; on self-care, 179n27

désœuvrement, 16, 25, 32, 40, 151n49, 170n18

Dewey, John, 90

A Dialogue on Love (Sedgwick): auto-thanato-theory in, 182n77; community in, 185n7; crisis ordinariness and, 126; drifting and failure in, 34–35; ek-sistence and, 96–99, 130–31; impasse and depression in, 25; as memoir, 137; narcissism in, 132; self-care in, 91, 135; suicide and, 101–2, 105

Dillon, Brian, 194n55

double failure, Nancy's exscription and, 100–103

drifting (*dérive*): Barthes's *idiorrythmie* concept and, 65–67; Barthes's Neutral concept and, 67–73; in Cusk's *Aftermath*, 73–75; in Cusk's *Outline* trilogy, 76–82; failure and, 33–34, 63–67, 82–84; Lacan's sense of, 67, 70–71

Drift into Failure (Dekker), 169n14

Drifts (Zambreno), 3, 137

drives: desire and, 71; Lacan on, 71

Duras, Marguerite, 135

Dürer, Albrecht, 187n49

Edelman, Lee, 16–17, 24, 151n52, 155n86, 156n92, 156n98

ek-sistence, Nancy's concept of, 86, 95–96; bodily pain and, 182n82; exscription and, 99–103; Levé's *Suicide* and, 105, 131; in Sedgwick's *A Dialogue on Love*, 96–99, 131; in Zambreno's writing, 132–38, 191n23

emergent formations, structures of feeling and, 11–12

endless work, flopping and sleeping and, 50–57

entrepreneurship of failure, 153n65

epic fail: contemporary examples of, 6–8, 145n3; jouissance and, 24; in literature and film, 8–10, 147n13, 148n16; thought paralysis and, 28

essayism, writing and, 194n55

existence: as coexistence, 85–86; exscription and, 99–100; failure and, 1–2, 153n78, 190n1

existence, failure and structure of, 20–22

exscription, Nancy's concept of, 34–35; in Cusk's *Outline* trilogy, 106–7; failure and, 129–30; fragmentation and, 184n98; in Levé's *Suicide*, 99–100, 103–5; sensing and, 99–100; writing and, 182n78

external law, selflessness and, 86

Failing Gloriously (Graham), 108

failure: crisis ordinariness and, 125–28; definitions of, 14–24; drifting and, 33–34, 63–67; existence and, 1–2; forms of, 42–44, 138–43; in Li's writing, 110–15, 189n97; in marriage, 73–77; melodrama in Li's work and, 110–15; Nancy's exscription and, 101–3; original failure of Adam and Eve, 7; renunciation of, 14–15; repetition of, 8; responses to, 129–38; structures of feeling and, 11–13; twentieth-century examples of, 6, 145n3; twenty-first-century examples of, 2, 6, 145n3; in Zambreno's *Appendix Project*, 132–38

Failure and the American Writer (Jones), 17–18, 147n11, 147n15, 148n17

failure as failure: basic concepts of, 2, 4–5; definitions and, 22–24; impasse of, 16

"Failure Is Not an Option" (Carr), 150n46

failure of care, theories of, 85–92
failure studies: deconstruction and, 139–40; evolution of, 3–4; grit and resilience in, 18; literature and, 17; optimism in, 19–20; shared unshareability and, 107–8; success and, 15; thought paralysis and, 30–31
falling, failing as, 23–24
falling man image, in Moshfegh's narrative, 44, 55
family life, Cusk on failure in, 73–77, 172n62
fatigue, Barthes on, 71–72
feeling, failure of reason and, 118–19
Feltham, Colin, 153n75
The Female Complaint (Berlant), 119
feminism, failure perspectives in, 74–77
feminist complaint, in Cusk's *Aftermath*, 73–77, 172n72
Firestein, Stuart, 15
Flatley, Jonathan, 10, 148n19
Flaubert, Gustave, 140–41, 157n102
flopping: in basketball, 42–43, 162n14; defined, 161n9; endless work and, 50–57; failure and, 32–33, 41–44; Great Resignation and, 58; in Moshfegh's *My Year of Rest and Relaxation*, 47–50, 57–62; as pretense, 42–43; self-care and, 88–89; sleeping linked to, 48–49; suicidal body and, 101–2; work culture and, 57–62
flowing, drifting vs., 64–65
Floyd, George, murder, 145n3
form, failure and role of, 42–44, 138–43
form-of-life theory, 192n47
Foucault, Michel: on parrhesia, 98–99; "plunging view" of, 70, 93–96; on self-care, 34, 90–91, 95–96, 114, 179n23, 179n28, 181n75, 191n23; on selflessness, 86–87; Zambreno's work and, 132
France Telecom suicides, 58

Franta, Andrew, 169n14
Freud, Sigmund, 71, 87; on death drive, 168n10; on drifting, 67; on failure, 163n31; on narcissism, 92–93, 180n35, 180n51
Fukushima disaster, 8

Garrido, Juan-Manuel, 152
gender: failure and, 80–82, 160n116; in Moshfegh's narrative, 52–53, 57–62, 162n16
gesture, Agamben's discussion of, 159n115
Glissant, Édouard, 54
Graham, Shawn, 108
Great Resignation movement, 58
Gregg, Melissa, 161n10
grit, failure and, 18
Guattari, Félix, 170n19
Guibert, Hervé, 134, 136

Halberstam, Jack, 15–16, 29–30, 107–8, 141, 157n102, 158n106, 173n83, 185n5
Hamacher, Werner, 102–3, 154n80, 183n90
Harney, Stefano, 19, 31, 58, 61, 64, 152n62, 161n2, 167n126
hate crimes, care ethics and, 87
Hegel, G. W. F., 130
Heidegger, Martin, 29–30, 86, 128, 158n109
Hellenistic period, self-care in, 90–91
The Hermeneutics of the Subject lectures (Foucault), 86, 98–99, 132, 179n23, 179n28, 181n75
high theory, 192n39
Hinton, Elizabeth, 145n3
Hodson, Josie Roland, 57
Hong, Renyi, 145n2
humility: in Cusk's *Outline*, 78; failure and lesson of, 69
humor, epic fail and, 148n16

"Ibizan Sequence" (Benjamin), 165n80
identity politics, selflessness vs., 87

idiorrhythmy, Barthes's concept of, 65–67, 169n14
imaginary, Barthes and Lacan on, 171n33
impasse: as aporia, Derrida's discussion of, 26–27; depression and, 24–25, 158n107; failure as, 16, 24–31, 138–39, 155n85, 155n90, 156n95; writing and, 115
Infinite Resignation (Thacker), 143
infrastructuralism of Berlant, 26, 156n94
inoperativity, failure and, 16, 25, 32, 151n49

James, Henry, 191n37
Jones, Gavin, 17–18, 22, 137, 147n11, 147n15, 148n17, 153n71, 155n91, 191n37
jouissance, failure as, 24, 154n81, 159n112

Kafka, Franz, 135
karoshi (death from overwork), 58
Khúc, Mimi, 155n91
Klein, Melanie, 24–25, 51, 96
Kornbluh, Anna, 141, 164n58
Kudos (Cusk), 33, 77, 83–84, 173nn82–83, 176n105, 177n127, 189n110

Lacan, Jacques, 67, 70–71, 154n81, 155n90, 171n33
Lafargue, Paul, 58
Laplanche, Jean, 67, 168n10
Larson, Nella, 163n43
Lee, Wendy Ann, 179n18
Le sens du monde (Nancy), 99, 183n95
Levé, Édouard, 3, 12, 31, 34–35, 91, 103–5, 184n100, 184n103; crisis ordinariness in work of, 126; shared unshareability of failure in work of, 141
Levinas, Emmanuel, 87
Levine, Caroline, 141, 192n46, 194n52

Li, Yiyun: autofictional genre and writing of, 137; crisis ordinariness in work of, 126–28; essayism in writing of, 194n55; on existence and nothingness, 191n23; on failure, 3, 24, 31, 35–36; failure in writing of, 110–15, 189n97; melodrama in work of, 108–15, 120–25, 131, 186n21; shared unshareability of failure in work of, 108–10, 141, 187n44
lifedeath: Derrida's concept of, 126–28, 186n16; postscripting and, 131–38
Life-Destroying Diagrams (Brinkema), 142
L'intrus (Nancy), 182n82
literature on failure, 3–4, 147n11; early examples of, 179n18; epic fail in, 8–10; examples of, 17–18
Loden, Barbara, 134, 190n17
Long, Camilla, 172n64
loss, failure and, 156n98

macro failures, 2–4
Malatino, Hil, 87, 178nn5–6
Malesic, Jonathan, 41, 161n13
Marche, Stephen, 156n94
Marcus, Sharon, 162n18
Marcus Aurelius, 90–91
Marin, Claire, 40, 151n47
marriage, Cusk on failure in, 73–77, 172n62
Maslach, Christina, 178n6
Massumi, Brian, 148n19
Matters of Care (Puig de la Bellacasa), 178n6, 179n20
melodrama: failure and, 32, 35–36; in Li's novels, 108–15, 120–25, 186n21; resistance to silence in, 186n32
Melville, Herman, 17–18, 137, 153n71, 153n77, 179n18, 192n41
memoir, failure narratives as, 137
Merback, Mitchell B., 187n49
mess, failure and, 157n102
Morton, Timothy, 98

Moshfegh, Ottessa: crisis ordinariness in work of, 126; Derrida in work of, 191n31; drifting in work of, 63; on failure, 3, 12, 31–33, 44–47, 137, 160n117; flopping narrative of, 57–62
Moten, Fred, 19, 31, 58, 61, 64, 152n62, 161n2, 167n126
Mueller, Gavin, 161n13
Museum of Failure (Sweden), 6, 147n12
Must I Go (Li), 3, 35–36, 108, 110, 119–25, 128, 137
Myth of Sisyphus (Camus), 158n107
My Year of Rest and Relaxation (Moshfegh): crisis ordinariness in, 126; Derrida and, 191n31; drifting in, 63; failure narrative in, 3, 32–33, 44–47, 137, 160n117; flopping in, 47–50, 57–62, 131; self-care in, 88–89

Nancy, Jean-Luc, 16, 25, 151n49; being-listening (*être-à-l'écoute*) concept of, 128; care ethics and work of, 85–86; exscription concept of, 34–35, 92, 99–103, 184n98; on pain, 102–3, 182n82, 183n95, 184n3; on sleep, 56–57; on writing, 182n78
narcissism: Bersani on, 180n51; death drive and, 168n10; ek-sistence and, 103; Freud on, 92–93, 180n35, 180n51; Sedgwick's discussion of, 96–99; self-care and, 92–96
"On Narcissism: An Introduction" (Freud), 92–93
Narcissus (Ovid), 93–94, 103
Narcissus, myth of, 93–95
National Basketball Association (NBA), 42–43
negative affects, of failure, 23–24
negativity, failure as, 24–25, 28, 155n86, 155n90
Nelson, Maggie, 91
neoliberal capitalism: care crisis and, 88–90; failure and, 18–19; in Moshfegh's narrative, 55–57; sleep and, 60–62; work ideology and, 161n1
Neutral: Barthes's concept of, 67–73, 169n14, 170n16, 170n20, 171n41; in Cusk's *Aftermath*, 76–77; in Cusk's *Outline* trilogy, 77–82; silence and, 173n83
Neutre (Cixous), 173n83
Ngai, Sianne, 10, 23, 47, 109, 163n43, 166n88
Nietzsche, Friedrich, 98, 112, 181n72
nothing, failure and, 16–17, 151n52

Ochoa, John, 153n77
Œuvres (Levé), 184n103
On Being Ill (Woolf), 182n84, 185n4
On the Inconvenience of Other People (Berlant), 24
original failure, Adam and Eve as, 7
Osaka, Naomi, 43
Outline (Cusk novel), 33, 76–84, 173n79, 175n94, 176n105, 193n49
Outline trilogy (Cusk), 3; crisis ordinariness in, 126; drifting in, 64, 68, 131; failure narrative in, 20–21, 33–34, 75–82, 106–7, 137, 173n83, 189n110; form in, 193n49; marriage and family in, 172n62; noise of the world in, 85–86
"outside-text" (*hors-texte*), Nancy's exscription and, 100–103, 182n78
Ovid, 93–94, 103

pain: failure and, 156n93; Nancy's exscription and role of, 102–3, 182n82, 183n95; Scarry on, 182n82, 183n85, 183n90, 183n94; self-care and, 96–97; shared unshareability of failure and, 184n3
paranoid position of failure, 25
paranoid reading, Sedgwick's discussion of, 102–3, 138–39, 182n77
parrhesia, 98
pathos, failure and, 69–70
perfectionism, failure and, 20–21, 116–19
personal, failure linked to, 10–12, 146n8

perspective, on failure, 20–21
Petersen, Anne Helen, 40
The Phenomenology of Spirit (Hegel), 130
Pierre (Melville), 18, 137, 153n71
Ping Xi, 33
Plato, 86, 90
pleroma, failure as, 24, 154n80
posthumous sharing, 119
postscripting: essayism and, 194n55; failure and, 32, 36–37, 130–32, 137–38; in Zambreno's writing, 132–38
power, rhythm and, 65–66
Preciado, Paul B., 91
progress, failure and, 174n88
psychoanalysis, failure and, 159n112, 187n46
Puig de la Bellacasa, María, 87–92, 177n3, 178n6, 179n20
punctum of failure, 117

queer narcissism, 92–93
queer theory, failure in, 107–8
The Queer Art of Failure (Halberstam), 107–8
Qu'est-ce que la philosophie? (Deleuze and Guattari), 170n19
quit lit phenomenon, 145n3

racism: Black sleep, Hodson's concept of, 57; failure and, 145n3, 155n91, 160n116, 163n43; in Moshfegh's narrative, 52–53, 57–62, 162n16, 165nn70–71
reasoning, failure of, 118–19
regime of failure, 153n64
reparative reading: Sedgwick's concept of, 96–99, 130, 139; shared unshareability of failure and, 107–8
resilience, failure and, 18, 152n62
rhythm, Barthes *rhuthmos* and, 72, 79
Ricoeur, Paul, 96
rupture, failure and, 40

Sandage, Scott, 153n75
Sartre, Jean-Paul, 157n102
Scarry, Elaine, 156n93, 182n82, 183n85, 183n90, 183n94
Screen Tests (Zambreno), 36, 134, 137, 190n17, 191n23; essayism in, 194n55
Sedgwick, Eve Kosofsky, 24–25; affect theory of failure and, 138–39; on community, 185n7; on love, 185n7; on self-care, 34–35, 91, 96–99, 131, 181n75, 191n23
self-care: as dark narcissism, 91–96; endless work and, 161n10; failure and, 32, 34–35, 41; neoliberal economics and, 88–90; reservations concerning, 86–87; Sedgwick's discussion of, 96–99; writing and, 114; in Zambreno's work, 135–38
self-harm, in Li's *Must I Go*, 120–25
self-knowledge, narcissism and, 94
selflessness, failure and, 86–93
September 11, 2001, attacks: as epic fail, 6–8, 145n3; flopping and, 44; in Moshfegh's narrative, 44, 51–52
shadow feminism, Halberstam's concept of, 173n83
shared unshareability of failure, 26, 31–37, 106–10, 156n93; crisis ordinariness and, 125–26; in Li's *Dear Friend*, 108–10, 127, 187n44; in Li's *Must I Go*, 120–25, 127–28; in Li's *Where Reasons End*, 115–19, 127–28; melodrama and, 113–15; pain and, 183n85, 184n3; posthumous sharing and, 119; self-awareness and, 119–20
Sharma, Sarah, 60
Sharpe, Christina, 55, 166n86
silence: Barthes's Neutral and, 173n83; failure and, 105–6; melodrama's resistance to, 186n32
slavery, endless work and, 166n86
sleeping: Barthes on, 72–73; endless work and, 50–57, 59–62; fatigue and, 72; flopping as, 47–50; in Moshfegh's *My Year of Rest*, 47–50, 131, 164n46
Smith, Zadie, 183n96

social, structure of feeling and, 11–13
Socrates, 86, 90
sports, failure and, 42–43, 162n14
Stewart, Kathleen, 90
Stoner (Williams), 147n11
structuralism, failure in context of, 21, 28, 145n3, 157n102
structures of feeling: failure and, 11–14, 36–37, 149n29, 149n31, 154n79, 163n43, 186n21; melodrama and, 186n32; suicidal ideation and, 110–15
stuplimity, Ngai's concept of, 166n88
success/failure complex, 15, 19–20, 23–24, 147n10
suicide: Critchley on, 195n9; ek-sistence and, 101–3; failure and, 158n107; in Li's *Dear Friend*, 110–15; in Li's *Must I Go*, 120–25; in Li's *Where Reasons End*, 115–19; narcissism and, 94–96; in Zambreno's work, 132–33
Suicide (Levé), 3, 34–35, 91, 103–5, 183n96, 184n100; ek-sistence in, 131; as memoir, 137; self-care in, 135
Suzuki, Alex, 135
sympathy, Woolf's rejection of, 185n4
Systems Failure (Franta), 169n14
Szasz, Thomas, 158n107

"Technologies of the Self" seminar (1982), 86
technology, failure and, 18–19, 153n65
testing, failure and, 165n80
Testo Junkie (Preciado), 91, 93
Thacker, Eugene, 28–29, 143
thought paralysis, failure and, 27–31, 157n101
Three Essays on the Theory of Sexuality (Freud), 180n51
Thus Spoke Zarathustra (Nietzsche), 181n72
time, failure and, 117–18
Tiresias, 94
Tomkins, Silvan, 139
To the Friend Who Did Not Save My Life (Guibert), 134

touch, Nancy's philosophy of, 102–3, 183n88
To Write as if Already Dead (Zambreno), 3, 36, 133–37, 190n17
Transit (Cusk), 33, 84, 168n10, 173n76, 173n83, 174n87, 175n90, 175n92

Une pensée finie (Nancy), 99
The Unnamable (Beckett), 42
unproductivity: Barthes on, 171n45; flopping as, 43
The Use of Bodies (Agamben), 192n47
utopian sleep, Barthes's concept of, 72–73

Valihora, Karen, 174n88
Van Velde, Bram, 147n15
Van Wey, Shannon, 96–97
Vattimo, Gianni, 157n101
Vermeulen, Pieter, 173n79
violence, care ethics and, 86–90
Virno, Paolo, 23

Where Reasons End (Li), 3, 35–36, 108–9, 115–19, 121, 127, 137
Williams, John, 147n11
Williams, Raymond: on Barthes, 68; on structures of feeling, 11–14, 21, 23, 110, 149n29, 149n31
Woolf, Virginia, 182n84, 185n4
work culture: failure and, 42; flopping and sleeping and, 50–57; naturalization of, 161n13; race, gender, and class and, 57–62; sabotage of, 58–62
"Worstward Ho!" (Beckett), 22
writing: crisis ordinariness in, 126; essayism in, 194n55; failure in, 140–43; Nancy's discussion of, 182n78; suicidal ideation and, 114–15, 118–19, 123–25; Zambreno on, 133–38

Zambreno, Kate, 3, 12, 31, 36–37, 131–38, 190n17; essayism in writing of, 194n55

www.ingramcontent.com/pod-product-compliance
Lightning Source LLC
Chambersburg PA
CBHW020236170426
43202CB00008B/108